How To Bu
BIG-INCH FORD SMALL BLOCKS

GEORGE REID

CarTech®

Edited By: Travis Thompson

ISBN-13 978-1-884089-83-1
ISBN-10 1-884089-83-6

Printed in China

CarTech®
39966 Grand Avenue
North Branch, MN 55056
Telephone (651) 277-1200 • (800) 551-4754 • Fax: (651) 277-1203
www.cartechbooks.com

OVERSEAS DISTRIBUTION BY:

Brooklands Books Ltd.
P.O. Box 146, Cobham, Surrey, KT11 1LG, England
Telephone 01932 865051 • Fax 01932 868803
www.brooklands-books.com

Brooklands Books Aus.
3/37-39 Green Street, Banksmeadow, NSW 2019, Australia
Telephone 2 9695 7055 • Fax 2 9695 7355

Front Cover: ***This is the 414-horsepower Coast High Performance/Trans am Racing 408ci stroker. With 450 ft-lbs of torque on tap, this is a budget stroker that is easy to afford and live with.***

Back Cover, Upper Left: ***The heart of any small-block Ford is a strong stroker crank. In this photograph, a Scat 331 crank is being installed prior to having its end play checked. Be careful when checking those clearances, especially when building a stroker.***

Back Cover, Upper Right: ***If too much traction is your problem, nothing can add to your low-end grunt like stroking your small block for some extra cubic inches. The huge torque and relatively light weight of big-inch small blocks makes them perfect for increasing your weight transfer.***

Back Cover, Lower: ***You can add a few extra cubes to your big-inch mill with a larger bore. But remember, too much of a good thing may not be the right answer. Increasing the bore makes the cylinder walls thinner and increases the compression ratio, neither of which is necessarily beneficial to the lifespan of your engine.***

Table of Contents

Introduction and Acknowledgements

When CarTech® asked me to tackle this book project, it seemed like an easy undertaking, but it did not turn out that way. What made this book particularly challenging was the abundance of stroker engine kits and projects out there for the taking. I found there were almost too many to choose from. The selection is impressive today compared to what it was even 20 years ago. Two decades ago, few of us had ever heard of a stroker kit, especially for Fords.

In the 1950s, we had the Ford flathead and overhead-valve Y-block. The FE series big block didn't come along until 1958. The small-block Ford came along in 1962. Ford enthusiasts had to live with what was available from Ford and the current aftermarket. And that wasn't saying much, since the aftermarket was only in its infancy. Then, as now, Chevy got the nod more often than Ford, especially when the Bow Tie's legendary small block first appeared in 1955. Flatheads and Y-blocks got passed up by Chevy power. However, that situation is changing with the continuing growth of the high-performance Ford movement. Chevrolet is actually taking a back seat to Ford more and more these days thanks to the 5.0L Mustang. The late-model, FOX-body Mustang has been called the 1955-57 Chevrolet of the new age. And no wonder, the Mustang is affordable and fast.

When I reflect on a lifetime of high-performance Ford projects, both personally and professionally, I clearly remember a time when we had to use our imaginations when it came to displacement increases. We had to improvise and get close to a reputable machinist that we could trust, who knew how to work cylinder heads and offset grind a good crankshaft. Today, I understand perfectly just how good things are for the Ford buff who wants to go racing. It is better than it has ever been.

Through the years, we have watched Ford V-8 power evolve from the early flatheads, to Y-blocks, to big blocks, to lightweight small blocks, and finally to the fuel-injected pushrod iron we enjoy today. Forty to fifty years ago, we would have never thought these levels of power in a small-block V-8 possible.

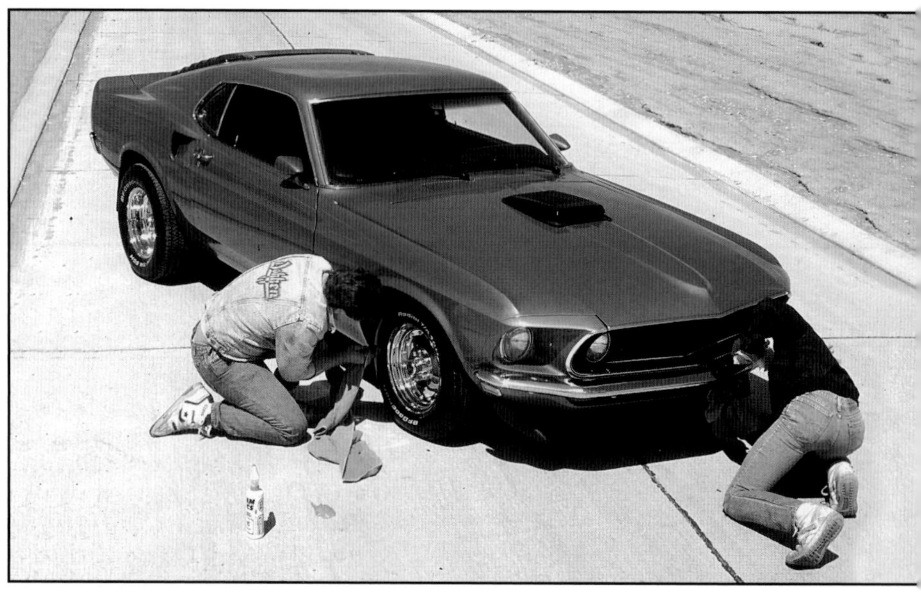

Big-inch stroker Ford small-blocks make it possible to have big block power in a light weight Mustang. This allows you to keep your Mustang's good handling, while having abundant displacement (and power!) available.

Today, we celebrate what this book is all about – pumping displacement into your small-block Ford V-8. The beauty of the stroker is the displacement of a big block without the weight penalty. You can get as get as much as 355ci out of a 289/302ci small block. And just imagine getting 429ci from a 351W. Displacement continues to go even higher at press time with the availability of new aftermarket aluminum blocks. With these roomy blocks, you can pump 360+ cubic inches into the 302 and 460ci into the 351W. When you couple this additional displacement with the bonus of improved cylinder heads and fuel injection, it means having your cake and eating it too.

The only concern I have about this book's contents is the ever-changing stroker kit marketplace. What is current at press time, may not be available when you read this book, or in the reprints to follow. We have done our very best to be as accurate as possible in the execution of this book. And most of the information inside will remain constant for years to come. If you have any questions regarding the content of this book, or you are a manufacturer with new information to share about your product line, we invite your letters and e-mails.

Thank you for adding this book to your Ford reference library.

Acknowledgements

A publication of this caliber could not have happened without the help of a lot of people in the industry. When this assignment arrived over the internet from CarTech editor, Steve Hendrickson, thoughts turned to a quartet of trusted friends – John Da Luz, Julio Mayen, Mark Jeffrey, and Jim Smart. It has been through Jim Smart that I've been able know the other three at all. Jim Smart is the Senior Editor for two very respected magazine titles in the industry, *Mustang & Fords* and *Mustang Monthly*. Jim has come to my rescue many times with needed photos, contacts, and information from his many efforts through the years. I can't thank him enough.

Likely the greatest enlightenment I've had in my career has come from John Da Luz of JMC Motorsports in San Diego, California. John brings to this book a great wealth of experience from more than 25 years as an engine builder and tuner. John has taught me many aspects of engine building that I had not considered before I met him. John, thank you for all of your help.

While John provided the knowledge and experience, Julio Mayen, of JME Enterprises, also in San Diego, has provided the platforms on which to build, some of which have already appeared in the magazines mentioned earlier. Julio has provided me with many of the engine projects and contacts that have gone into this book. Julio, thank you for your undying efforts.

Down-to-earth, savvy engine-builder and Ford/Shelby buff, Mark Jeffrey of Trans Am Racing, in Gardena, California, also provided us with engine-building platforms and expertise. A good many of his customer's engines have served this book quite well through the eyes and lenses of Jim Smart, who shot many of these images as a special favor to me. Mark, our thanks for always coming to the rescue.

I also want to thank George Ullrich of Speed-O-Motive, as well as everyone at Coast High Performance, Edelbrock, Comp Cams, Holley Performance Products, Demon Carburetors, Airflow Research, Performance Automotive Warehouse, Mustangs Plus, Performance Distributors, Pertronix, Crane Cams, and Mustangs Etc. for their help in the execution of this book. I could not have written this book without your help.

George Reid
March 2003

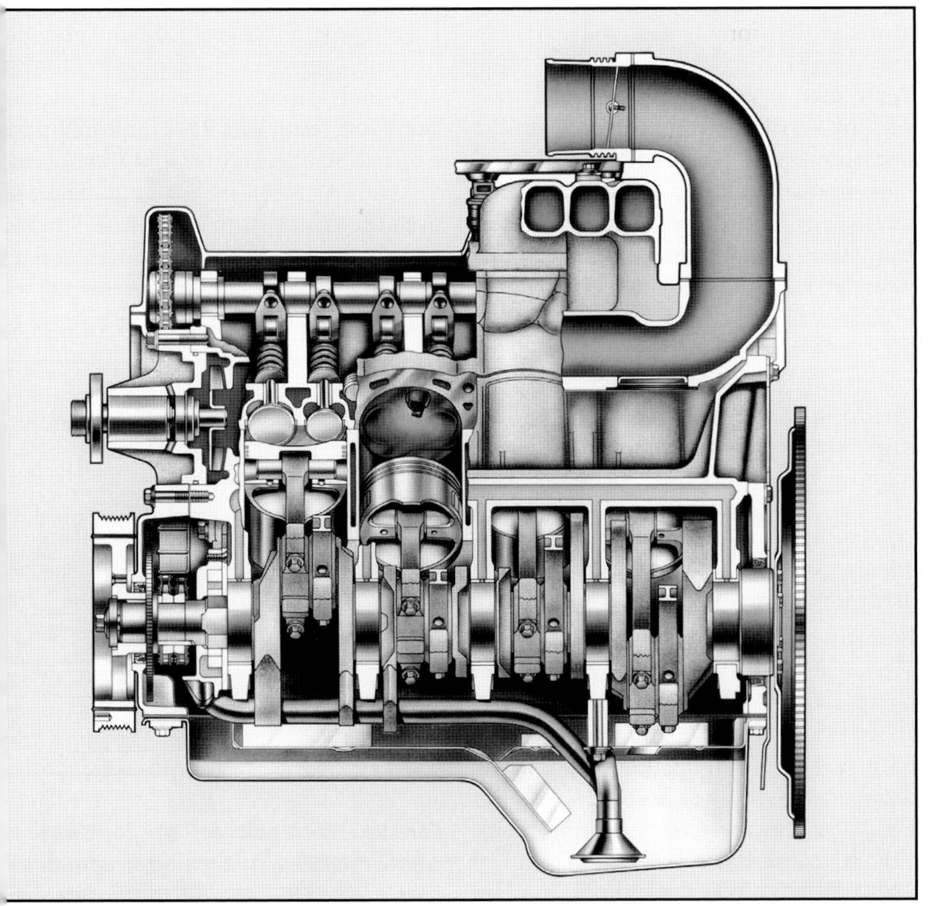

The heart and soul of stroker power is the fuel-injected 5.0L small block V8. On the outside, it looks like a 5.0L EFI small-block. Inside, you can enjoy up to 355 cubic inches of displacement.

Chapter 1

Ford Small Block V-8 Basics

When Ford Motor Company introduced the 90-degree Fairlane V-8 in 1962, not many of us understood the great potential of this engine. In its original form as a 221ci V-8, it had a 3.50-inch cylinder bore with a 2.87-inch stroke. That same year, Ford also offered an optional 260ci small block with a 3.80-inch bore and the same 2.87-inch stroke. Both of these engines had the same 2.87-inch stroke 1M cast-iron crankshaft and C3AE, 5.153-inch long (center-to-center) connecting rod forgings. Both engines were fitted with Autolite 2100 two-barrel carburetors and single-point distributors with vacuum spark advance.

In 1963, Ford pumped up the bore size to 4.00-inches to create the 289ci small block. The 289-2V V-8 was a hardy engine, long on power potential and reliability. Fitted with the same 1M cast crank as the 221 and 260, the 289 also had the same C3OE rods. Also in 1963, Ford introduced the 289 High Performance V-8, a more powerful version of this engine that produced 271 horsepower. It featured a mechanical high-performance camshaft, Autolite dual-point distributor, Autolite 4100 four-barrel carburetion, and special cylinder heads. What made this engine unique was its aggressive camshaft and dual-point distributor, designed to enable this engine to reach 6,000 rpms. Hi-Po-specific cylinder heads also provided better valvetrain stability at high revs.

This is the 260-2V small-block V-8 in stock form. Introduced in 1962, the small Fairlane V-8 became a legendary performer.

The 221, 260, and 289ci engines lived side-by-side during 1963. For 1964, the 221 was dropped, leaving the 260-2V, 289-2V, 289-4V, and 289 High Performance engines in production. In 1964, the 289-4V engine was a low-compression V-8, just like the 289-2V. It ran on regular fuel and was available only in the Mustang. For 1965, Ford dropped the 160-horse 260-2V, leaving the 289-2V as the standard small-block V-8. Also for 1965, Ford increased the 289-4V's compression ratio with flat-top pistons, boosting the horsepower rating from 210 to 225. The 289 High Performance V-8 remained the same through 1967.

For 1968, Ford stroked the small-block 0.13-inch, raising the displacement to 302ci to compete with Chevrolet's 307ci small block. The 302 had the 289's 4-inch bore with a longer 3.00-inch stroke. The longer stroke came as a result of a 2M crankshaft with a 3-inch stroke, shorter C8OE connecting rods at 5.088-inches long. The 302 used the same piston as the 289. The 302 also had a revised block with longer cylinder skirts (.015-inch longer) to improve piston stability at the bottom of

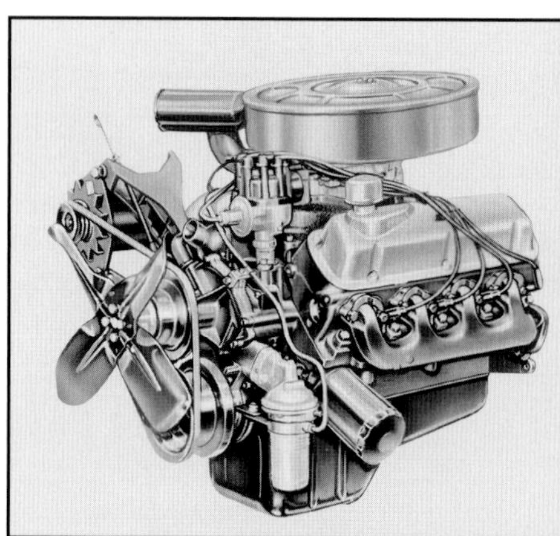

For 1963, Ford enlarged the 260's bore to create the 289ci, a very mainstream small-block V-8. This engine ultimately propelled racer and car builder, Carroll Shelby, to three SCCA B/Production championships, spanking Chevrolet's Corvettes along the way.

Also introduced in 1963 was the 289 High Performance V-8. It sported Autolite 4100 four-barrel carburetion, an aggressive mechanical lifter camshaft, special cylinder heads, a larger harmonic balancer, thicker main bearing caps, a hand-picked cast crankshaft, and cast iron headers. The result was 271 horsepower at 6,000 rpm.

the bore. This block was actually introduced in mid-1967. Quite a few 1967 289ci engines were produced using the C8OE 302 block casting. This means the 302 block can easily be used with 289 internals. We suggest avoiding the use of 302 internals in a 289 block, however.

The 302ci small block has continually evolved since its introduction in 1968. Beginning in 1985, Ford redesigned the 302 block to accommodate hydraulic roller tappets. Meatier connecting rods and a high-nodular iron crankshaft have been the key to solid reliability. Cylinder heads continue to suffer from modest port sizing, which is why aftermarket heads tend to be preferable to factory iron.

For 1969, Ford raised the 289/302 deck 1.275-inch to conceive the 351ci small-block. The 351ci V-8 had the 289/302's 4-inch bore with a 3.50-inch stroke. This was accomplished with the taller deck block, of course, with a 3M crankshaft (3.50-inch stroke) and 5.956-inch (center-to-center) connecting rods.

For 1970, Ford introduced another type of 351ci small-block V-8, called the 335-series engine, with a different block casting and crankshaft, larger cylinder heads, and a dry intake manifold. The objective of this engine was to produce more torque and horsepower via its large-port cylinder heads. It was a heavier engine than the 289/302-based small blocks. Enthusiasts came to know the 335-series 351ci V-8 as the small block that acted like a big block. It made boatloads of torque and became popular with drag racers. It was in production just four short years – 1970-1974.

When Ford introduced 351ci in two different engine families for 1970, this created an identity problem. To quickly identify the two engines displacing 351ci, Ford called the 289/302-based 351ci engine the 351 Windsor (351W), named for its engine foundry and manufacturing plant in Windsor, Ontario, Canada across the Detroit River from Detroit, Michigan. The 335-series engine would be named the 351 Cleveland (351C), also named for its foundry and plant in Northeastern Ohio. Although we call the 289/302 "Windsor" small blocks, they were also cast and manufactured in the Cleveland Engine Plant. "Windsor" is a designation Ford applied to the 351ci engine only, never the 221/260/289/302.

In 1972, Ford revised the 335-series engine family to conceive the 400ci Midland (also known as the "Modified" in some circles) V-8. The 400 Midland (400M) was a raised deck 335-series engine with a four-inch bore and four-inch stroke. It was conceived to replace the FE-series 360 and 390ci big blocks, although these engines remained in production until 1976. The 400M also had a 385-series Ford big-block bellhousing bolt pattern, unlike the 351C's small-block pattern.

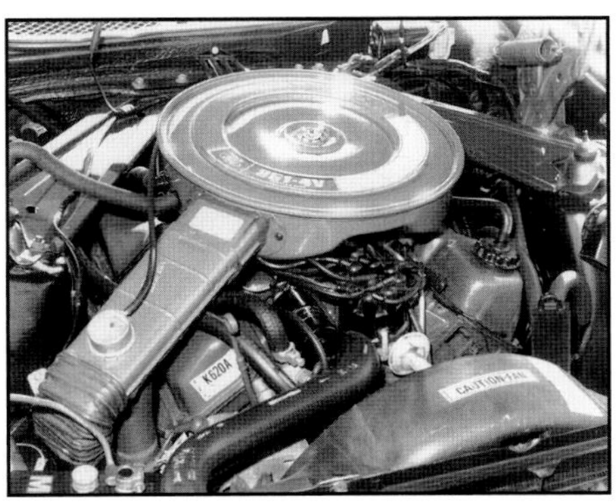

In 1970, Ford introduced a V-8 displacing 351ci with a 4-inch bore and 3.50-inch stroke called the 351 Cleveland or 351C. This engine has large-port heads with a dry intake manifold. In 1972, the 351C was stroked to achieve 400ci using a raised deck. Ford called this engine the 400M. The 400M had a 4.00-inch bore with a 4.00-inch stroke. In 1975, Ford destroked the 400M to 3.50-inches to get 351ci, known as the 351M. Both the 351M and 400M have a big-block bellhousing bolt pattern. Neither engine is a recommended build.

For 1968, Ford introduced the 302ci small-block based on the 90-degree Fairlane V-8. Externally, the 302 can't be distinguished from the 289 that it replaced. This is a 1978 302-2V V-8. Note the aluminum air cleaner, first used in 1978.

In 1975, Ford dropped the 335-series 351C engine and destroked the 400 to 351ci to simplify production and reduce costs. The 351M is not a suggested engine project platform because it is decidedly heavy, with not much brawn. Don't get the 351M confused with the 351C, which is clearly the better 351 to build.

The 351C, 351M, and 400M all use the same cylinder heads. The 351C-2V head is the same casting used on the 351M and 400M. For street use, this is a good cylinder head because compression is conservative, as is port size. Conservative port sizing is what makes the 351C-2V head more desirable for street use where we need good low-end torque. The 351C-4V head has huge ports designed for high-RPM use. But these heads make little sense for street use, since their low-end torque is poor. The best 351C head was cast in Australia, with the 351C-2V intake and exhaust ports, yet with the closed wedge chamber common to the U.S. 351C-4V head. These heads are available in the United States from a couple of sources, but they don't come cheap.

Chapter 2

Making Stroker Power!

Just what is a stroker anyway? A stroker is an engine with increased or decreased stroke. By increasing an stroke (the distance the piston travels in the cylinder bore), we gain displacement. By the same token, when we decrease an engine's stroke, we reduce the distance the piston travels in the bore. This changes when and how the engine makes power. Short-stroke engines like high RPM, where they make the most torque. Our focus here is more about increasing stroke in order to achieve greater amounts of torque and horsepower.

Stroking an engine does more than just increase displacement. It increases torque by giving the engine more of an internal mechanical advantage. When we increase stroke, we increase the engine's crankshaft arm or lever, which makes the most of a combustion cycle. The longer the stroke, the greater the torque or twist.

Stroke comes from the length of the crankshaft's rod journal arm. Then, we double that length to come up with the engine's stroke. We double the length of the crankshaft's arm because we get that arm in two directions- top dead center (TDC), then bottom dead center (BDC). This is a simple 2:1 ratio. Take the crankshaft arm, measured from the crankshaft centerline, and double the measurement. If the arm is 1.5-inches, you have a 3-inch stroke.

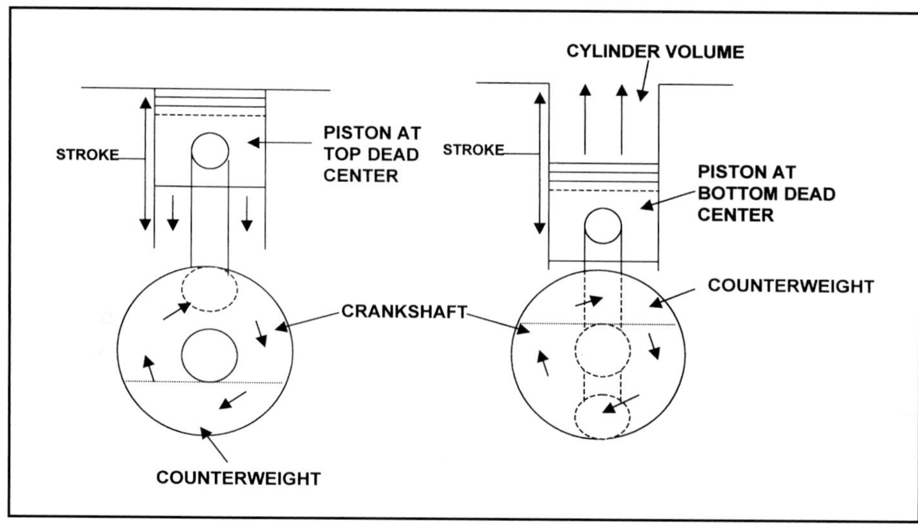

Stroke comes from the distance from the crankshaft centerline to the center of the journal. We take this distance and double it to come up with stroke. If we have 1.5-inches between the crankshaft and rod journal centerlines, we have 3-inches of stroke.

Factory stock small and middle-block (Cleveland/Midland) Fords have four basic strokes. The 221, 260, and 289ci engines have a 2.87-inch stroke. The 302 and Boss 302 have a 3.00-inch stroke. The raised deck 351W engine has a 3.50-inch stroke, as do the 351C and 351M middle-blocks. The 400M has a 4.00-inch stroke.

Stroker engines generate more power in two ways. First, the greater mechanical advantage of a longer crankshaft arm generates more torque. Secondly, we are also filling the cylinder with a greater volume of air and fuel, which gives us more power all by itself. We get torque from increased stroke and cylinder swept volume. Torque is the truest measure of an engine's power output.

When we consider the crankshaft's arm – the distance from the crankshaft centerline to the center of the rod journal – this is where torque is born. Torque is an engine's grunt factor. Grunt is that physical pressure at your backside when the accelerator is pressed. So what is torque exactly? Think of the crankshaft's arm as a lever, like you were taught in high school physics class. Torque equals

he greater the distance between the rankshaft and rod journal centerlines, he greater the stroke. To increase stroke, e increase this distance. This is done sing a crankshaft with a greater throw, or elding and offset grinding the rod jour-al on an existing crankshaft. You can chieve significant stroke increases by off-et grinding an existing crankshaft.

he downward force of the stroke times he length of the lever or arm. If we look a 5.0L engine's 240 ft-lbs of peak torque, this means each cylinder bore is produc-ng 480 pounds of pressure on each pow-er stroke. We increase torque when we ncrease the length of the arm, which we accomplish by increasing the stroke.

We know a stock 5.0L engine's arm is 1.5-inches. This means the 5.0L engine has a 3.00-inch stroke. If we add 1/4-inch to the arm, this increases the arm to 1.750-inches. Double the 1.750-inches and you have 3.50-inches, which combines with the standard 4.00-inch bore to make 351ci. This gives us 40 additional foot-pounds of torque. Overbore the cylinders .030-inch and you have 355ci. Push the bore to 4.060-inches and you're courting 360ci. You are also making more torque.

Strokers are engines with greater amounts of stroke than we find from the factory. For example, this is a 302ci engine with 3.00-inches of stroke. When we offset grind the crankshaft, creating a greater distance between the crankshaft and rod journal centerlines, we can increase the stroke to 3.25-inches, which gives us 320+ cubic inches, depending on bore size.

If we opt for a custom crankshaft with even greater stroke, we can achieve 3.50-inches of stroke, which balloons our 302 into 355ci.

Despite the advantages of a stroker, there are disadvantages as well, especially if you're bent on pumping the most displacement possible into a 302 or 351ci engine. When we stroke a 302 or 351 to its limits, we lose piston skirt, which hurts stability. We also push the piston pin into the piston ring land area, which weakens piston design. It also puts the pin close to the piston dome, which exerts too much heat on the pin and boss. These are disadvantages that shorten engine life.

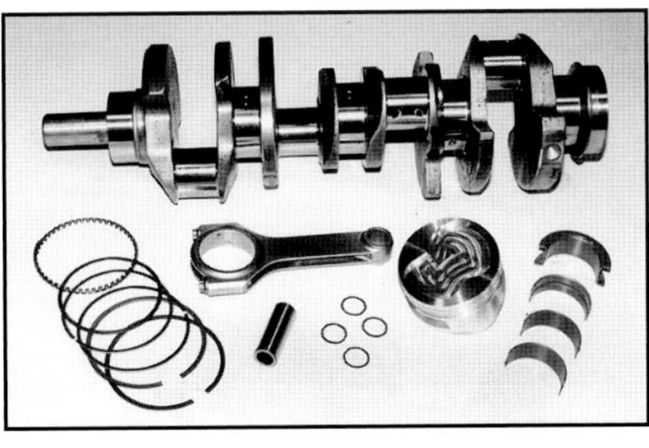

Stroker kits are packages that enable us to increase stroke without a lot of complex research. Someone else has done the thinking for us.

Another factor with stroking is rod length. When we haul that piston deep into the cylinder bore, we are also bringing it closer to the crankshaft counterweights, which creates conflict. This means we need a longer connecting rod to get the piston down there without interference with the counterweights. Sometimes, we can find off-the-shelf connecting rods to complete our stroker. And other times, we are forced to custom make connecting rods that will work. More expensive stroker kits have custom parts, like rods and pistons. More affordable kits have off-the-shelf parts that have made the kit possible without expensive tooling costs.

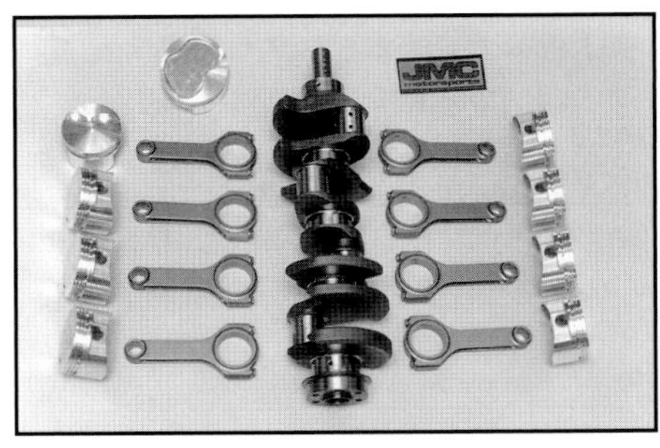

This is the Eagle 331ci stroker kit from JMC Motorsports in San Diego, California. It is very high end, with a forged steel crankshaft, H-beam rods, and forged pistons. This kit employs a custom crank, rods, and pistons that are ready to go.

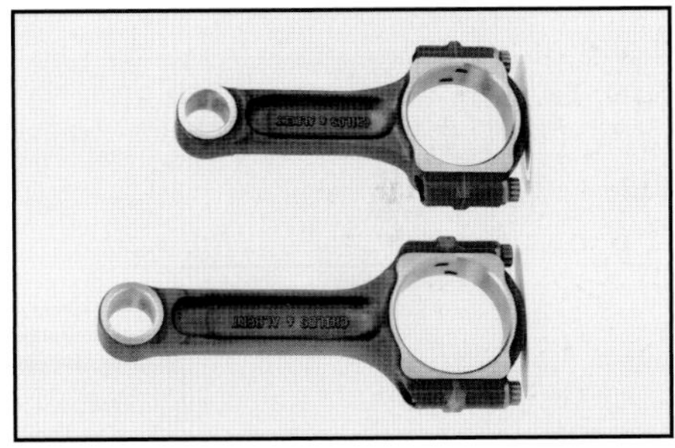

Rod length matters just as much as stroke. A longer connecting rod allows the piston to dwell longer at the bottom and top of the cylinder bore, which allows for a greater fuel/air charge.

Whenever we have to custom make connecting rods, this drives the cost of a stroker kit up. The same is true for custom pistons. Stroker kits often mandate custom pistons to keep things friendly at the top of the bore. A 347 or 355ci stroker, for example, has custom pistons with pin bosses pushed way up into the ring lands. This also drives the cost up and shortens engine life for reasons explained earlier.

Understanding Bore, Stroke, & Compression Ratio

Whenever we increase the stroke length, we are squeezing more volume into the same combustion chamber. This means we need to concern ourselves with an increase in compression. With that increase in stroke and compression comes an increase in cylinder volume. In that volume comes an increase in air and fuel, which gives us more power.

Compression ratio is a subject that is often misunderstood. One popular misconception is that pistons, alone, determine compression ratio. But this isn't true. Compression ratio comes from not only piston dome features, but also from stroke, bore, and combustion chamber size. Compression comes from piston travel from bottom dead center to top dead center with both valves closed. We are simply squeezing the cylinder volume (displacement) into the combustion chamber. This is called compression ratio. Compression ratio is cylinder volume at top dead center versus cylinder volume with the piston at bottom dead center. If cylinder volume with the piston at bottom dead center is 10 times more than it is with the piston at top dead center, then we have a compression ratio of 10.0:1, or simply 10 to 1. It is the proverbial ten pounds of fertilizer in a one-pound bag, not that we would be inclined to show you an example.

Five basic facts affect compression ratio. Cylinder swept volume, piston dome shape, head gasket thickness, clearance volume, and combustion chamber size. Swept volume is how much air or volume the piston displaces during its journey to the top of the bore. If we enlarge the swept volume by boring the cylinder oversize or increasing stroke, we increase compression ratio.

We may also increase or decrease compression ratio by changing the piston dome. If we dish the top of the piston, we lose compression. This is common with stock pistons that are often dished to reduce compression. A good example is a the 289-2V and 4V engines from 1965-67. The 289-2V cast piston is dished to keep the compression around 9.0:1. The 289-4V engine has a flat-top piston to increase compression to 10.0:1. The same is true for the 289 High Performance V-8. Later model 5.0L High Output engines sport compression ratios of 10.0:1 with flat top pistons and valve reliefs.

To raise compression ratio, we can dome the piston, with a surface shaped like the combustion chamber. This reduces clearance volume at the top of the bore. When we reduce clearance volume we increase compression ratio.

Compression ratio may also be increased by reducing combustion chamber size. For example, older 289/302/351W heads have smaller chambers, which means plenty of compression with a stroker kit. While this has its power benefits, it also can cause engine damage and destruction. A 347ci stroker kit with a 289's 57cc chambers can yield too much compression, and with catastrophic results. For one thing, a 289 head wouldn't be an intelligent choice for a 347ci stroker. Port size would greatly limit the engine's potential. This leads us to a better aftermarket cylinder head for the 347. And don't discount the 351W head for your 347ci stroker either. It makes for a stealthy factory cylinder head for the 347.

Whenever you step up to an aftermarket head, keep combustion chamber size in mind. Most aftermarket heads have chamber sizes around 64cc. If you desire greater compression, you can make adjustments with proper piston selection.

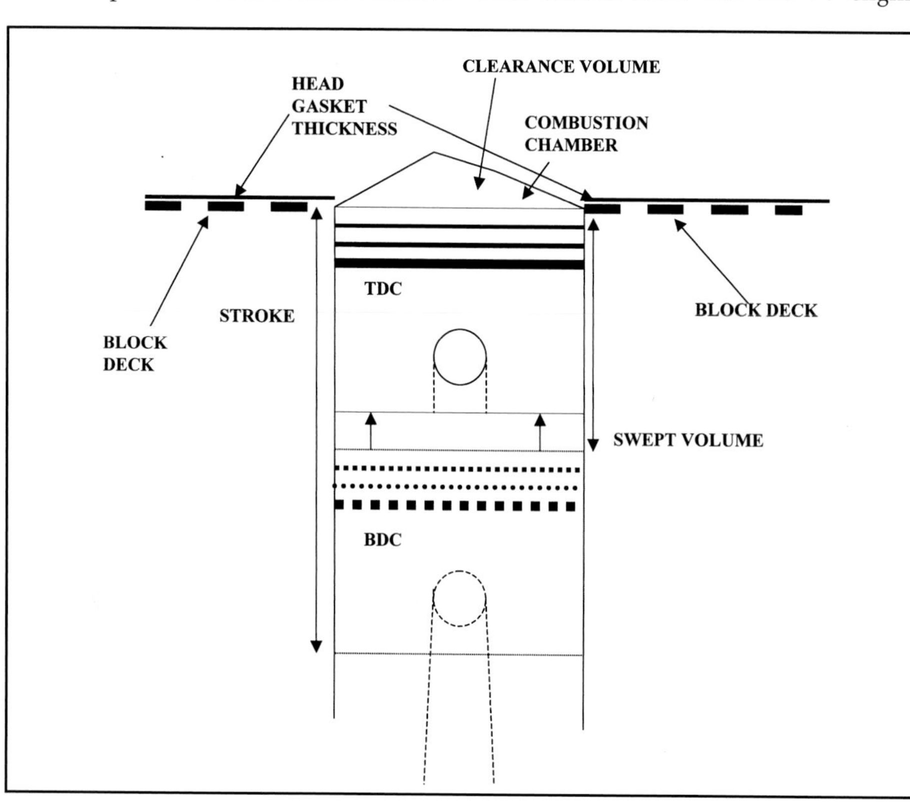

This is a basic cylinder bore arrangement, with the piston at both bottom dead center (BDC) and top dead center (TDC).

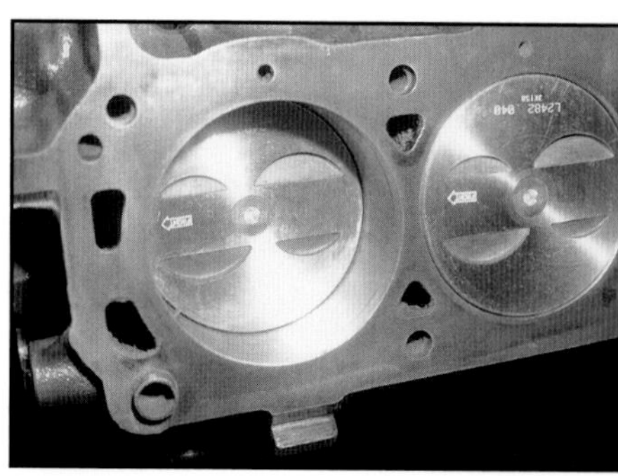

The area above the piston is considered swept volume. Swept volume is the area the piston consumes on the up stroke. When the piston reaches top dead center, the area above the piston is considered clearance volume.

Cylinder volume is figured using a simple formula. Using a standard 351W or 351C bore and stroke (4.00 x 3.50 inches), work the following numbers.

Displacement

Bore	Stroke	Displacement
3.500"	2.87"	220.90ci (221ci)
3.800"	2.87"	260.39ci (260ci)
4.000"	2.87"	288.52ci (289ci)
4.030"	2.87"	292.86ci (293ci)
4.040"	2.87"	294.32ci (294ci)
4.060"	2.87"	297.24ci (297ci)
4.000"	3.00"	301.59ci (302ci)
4.030"	3.00"	306.13ci (306ci)
4.040"	3.00"	307.65ci (308ci)
4.060"	3.00"	310.70ci (311ci)
4.000"	3.20"	321.69ci (322ci)
4.030"	3.20"	326.54ci (327ci)
4.040"	3.20"	328.16ci (328ci)
4.060"	3.20"	331.42ci (331ci)
4.000"	3.25"	326.72ci (327ci)
4.030"	3.25"	331.64ci (332ci)
4.040"	3.25"	333.29ci (333ci)
4.060"	3.25"	336.60ci (337ci)
4.000"	3.40"	341.80ci (342ci)
4.030"	3.40"	346.95ci (347ci)
4.040"	3.40"	348.67ci (349ci)
4.060"	3.40"	352.13ci (352ci)
4.000"	3.50"	351.85ci (352ci)
4.030"	3.50"	357.15ci (357ci)
4.040"	3.50"	358.93ci (359ci)
4.060"	3.50"	362.49ci (362ci)
4.000"	3.75"	376.99ci (377ci)
4.030"	3.75"	382.66ci (383ci)
4.040"	3.75"	384.56ci (385ci)
4.060"	3.75"	388.38ci (388ci)
4.000"	3.80"	382.01ci (382ci)
4.030"	3.80"	387.76ci (388ci)
4.040"	3.80"	389.69ci (390ci)
4.060"	3.80"	393.56ci (394ci)
4.000"	4.00"	402.12ci (402ci)
4.030"	4.00"	408.17ci (408ci)
4.040"	4.00"	410.20ci (410ci)
4.060"	4.00"	414.27ci (414ci)
4.000"	4.20"	422.23ci (422ci)
4.030"	4.20"	428.58ci (429ci)
4.040"	4.20"	430.71ci (431ci)
4.060"	4.20"	434.99ci (435ci)

Cylinder Volume =
0.7853982 x Bore x Bore x Stroke

When we apply this formula, we come up with 43.982ci per cylinder. Multiply this number by eight and you have 351ci. Truth is, you have 351.858, which is closer to 352ci. If we bore the 351 to 4.030-inches, we then have 44.644ci per cylinder, which comes out to 357ci. See the accompanying table for easy answers.

If we take a standard 4.000-inch bore and overbore it by .030-inch to 4.030-inch, compression will increase by a fraction of a compression ratio point. If we have compression ratio of 10.0:1, compression will increase by less than a point with a .030-inch overbore. We compute the compression increase (or decrease) by figuring the clearance volume, which is the area left above the piston when it reaches top dead center. It is important to understand that the piston doesn't always reach top dead center flush with the block deck. In most applications, the piston comes within 0.005 to 0.020-inch below the deck surface. It looks more flush with the block deck than it actually is. This is called piston deck height. Piston deck height affects compression because it determines clearance volume at the top. If we have a lot of clearance volume, we have less compression. The greater the piston deck height, the lower the compression ratio.

The following is a formula for figuring clearance volume.

Clearance Volume =
0.7853982 x Bore x Bore x Deck Height

Again, let's look at our 351ci small-block with a 4.000-inch bore and 3.50-inch stroke. Let's say our 351 has a piston deck height of 0.015-inch below the block deck. When we use our formula of 0.7853982 x 4.000" x 4.000" x 0.015", we get 0.188ci, or just a fraction of the cylinder's 43.98ci. If the deck height increased any amount, compression would drop. If deck height decreased any amount, compression would increase.

After figuring how to compute displacement in each cylinder and how to figure in the effect of piston deck height on compression, it's time to figure in the piston's role in all of this. Remember that if we dish the piston, we lose compression. If we dome the piston, we increase compression. Most piston manufacturers will give you the specifications on a pis-

The piston's design is a huge factor in both compression and clearance volume at top dead center. Here's a dished piston. We have to figure in clearance volume on both the dish and the valve reliefs. A dished piston increases clearance volume, which decreases compression ratio.

A domed piston decreases clearance volume at the top of the bore, which increases compression ratio.

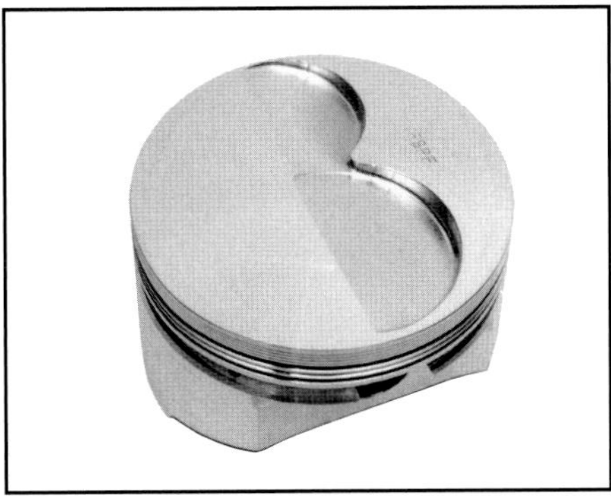

This is a flat-top piston with valve reliefs. Valve reliefs are necessary, but they increase clearance volume, which lowers compression.

This is a 347ci stroker piston and rod. Note the raised dome (which reduces clearance volume) and the valve reliefs (which increase clearance volume).

ton. If it is dished, the manufacturer will tell you how much. Likewise for a domed piston. This is performed in cubic-centimeters (cc's). How many cc's are in the dish? How many cc's of volume are in the dome?

If you are baffled by cubic-centimeters versus cubic inches, you're not alone. A lot of us are confused by metric versus SAE. Follow this formula and end your confusion.

Cubic Inches = cc's x 0.0610237

Back to our 351ci engine. Lets say our 351 has dished pistons with 4.00cc dishes. Using our formula, we multiply 4cc times 0.0610237, which equals 0.244ci. This lowers compression ratio because we have more clearance volume above the piston. If we dome the piston by the same amount, we increase compression accordingly.

The next factor in compression ratio is cylinder head gasket volume, which contributes to clearance volume above the piston. The thickness of the head gasket affects compression ratio. The thicker the head gasket, the greater the clearance volume. This lowers compression. The thinner the head gasket, the lower the clearance volume, which increases compression. To figure the head gasket volume (displacement), use the following formula.

Cylinder Head Gasket Volume/Thickness = 0.7853982 x Gasket Bore x Gasket Bore x Compressed Thickness

Again our 351ci engine with a 4.000-inch bore. We have a cylinder head gasket that is 0.040-inch thick. We take 0.7853982 x 4.000" x 4.000" x 0.040" to arrive at 0.502ci of clearance volume.

With all of these issues out of the way, it's time to focus on combustion chamber volume. Combustion chamber volume is the actual size of the chamber in cubic-centimeters (cc's). Think of the combustion chamber as the ultimate clearance volume. Chamber sizes for small-block Fords (289/302/351W) range from 53cc to 64cc. For the

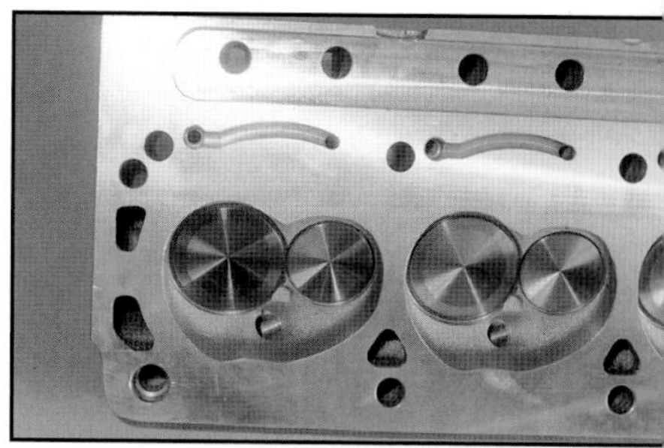

Combustion chamber size figures into clearance volume at top dead center. These are 64cc chambers in an aftermarket cylinder head.

351C/351M/400M, chamber sizes run much larger. The 351C-4V head has small wedge chambers. The 351C-2V, 351M and 400M head has larger open chambers.

Combustion chamber volume is figured with a graduate scale using fluid. We meter fluid into the chamber and figure how much fluid is used. We get this figure in cubic-centimeters. Our sample cylinder head has 64cc chambers. Here's how we turn cubic-centimeters into cubic inches.

Combustion Chamber cc's x 0.0610237 = Combustion Chamber ci's

Based on our formula above at 64cc, we have 3.90ci of volume in the chamber alone. Now, we have all of the information needed to compute compression

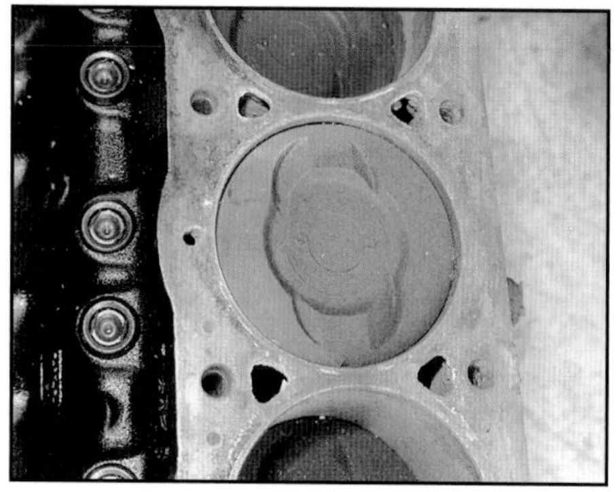

This is a 289-2V engine short block. Note the dished low-compression pistons, which give this engine a compression ratio of 9.0:1. Were this a 289-4V or 289 High Performance V-8, it would be fitted with flat-top pistons to bump the compression one full point.

Here's a 351C with a dished piston to control compression. Note the odd-duck valve reliefs for the canted-valve Cleveland heads. Ford called these poly-angle valves. These features figure in to clearance volume at the top of the bore.

Head gasket thickness counts in clearance volume. The thicker the head gasket, the greater the clearance volume. This reduces compression. The thinner the head gasket, the lower the clearance volume, and the higher the compression.

ratio in our 351ci engine. Add up all of the numbers for bore and stroke, piston deck height, head gasket thickness, and combustion chamber size. Use the following formula.

$$\frac{\text{Cylinder Vol.} + \text{Clearance Vol.} + \text{Piston Vol.} + \text{Chamber Vol.} + \text{Gasket Vol.}}{\text{Clearance Vol.} + \text{Piston Vol.} + \text{Head Gasket Vol.} + \text{Chamber Vol.}} = \text{Compression Ratio}$$

Our 351ci engine, with its 4.00-inch bores and 3.50-inch stroke, 0.020-inch deck height, 0.040-inch head gasket thickness, 64cc chamber heads, and 4.00cc dished pistons winds up like this.

$$\frac{43.982\text{ci} + 0.188\text{ci} + 0.244\text{ci} + 3.90\text{ci} + 0.502\text{ci}}{.188\text{ci} + 0.244\text{ci} + 0.502\text{ci} + 3.90\text{ci}} = 10.10{:}1$$

When we work this formula, we are taking cylinder volume, clearance volume, piston volume, chamber volume and gasket volume, and adding them together to arrive at 48.816ci. Then we add up clearance volume, piston volume, head gasket volume and chamber volume to get 4.834ci. Then, we take 48.816ci and divide it by 4.834ci to arrive at 10.098, which, rounded off to the nearest tenth, is 10.10:1.

Huge open chambers in a 351C-2V head account for a lot of clearance volume.

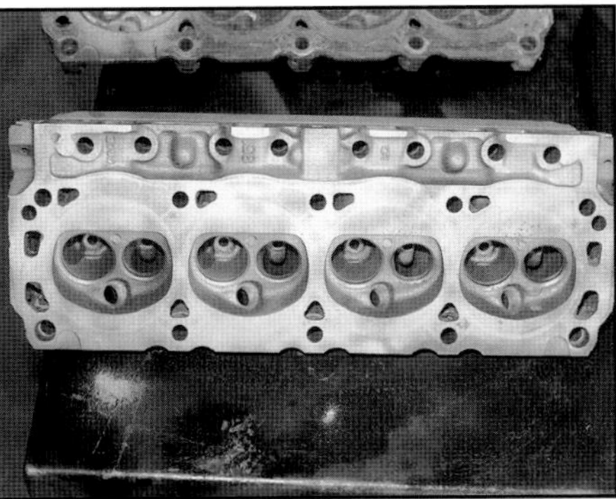

This is a 1969 351W cylinder head with smaller chambers, which makes it perfect for the 289/302 if you are seeking a factory head.

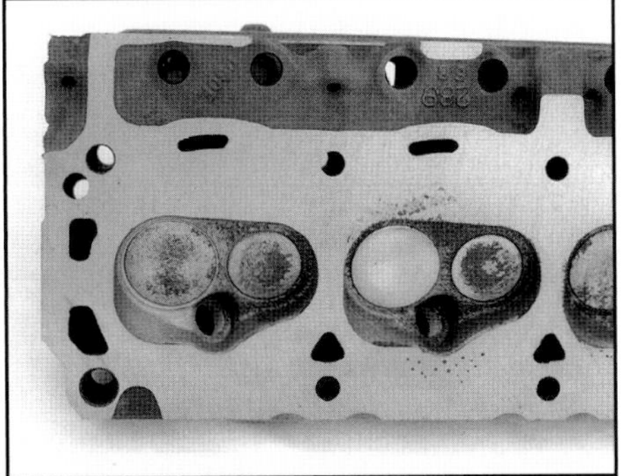

Early 289/302 heads have small 53-57cc chambers, which mean less clearance area and higher compression ratios.

Here are two examples of 351W cylinder heads. On the right is an early 351W head with a different wedge chamber than we see with the 289/302 head. The 351W head chamber changes later on in the 1980s with a larger wedge chamber (left). The larger chamber does two things. It reduces compression by increasing clearance volume. And it changes the way the fuel and air ignite and travel across the chamber.

Another factor to consider with clearance volume is cylinder head gasket crush when the heads are torqued. As the gasket crushes between the head and block, we are reducing clearance volume, which does raise compression. This should be figured into your calculations.

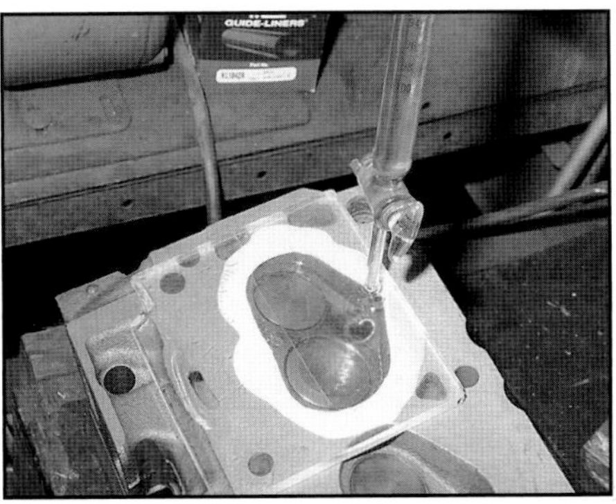

Combustion chamber size is calculated with a graduated scale filled with fluid. Using clear glass over the chamber as shown, using white grease as a seal, we fill the chamber with fluid. When we have completely filled the chamber, we check the amount of fluid used. This tells us chamber volume in cubic-centimeters.

Piston deck height is determined using a TDC indicator as shown. The amount of piston deck height contributes to clearance volume.

Horsepower & Torque

We've long been led to believe horsepower is what power is all about. But horsepower is rooted more in Madison Avenue advertising rhetoric than fact. In the power picture, horsepower doesn't count for much. What counts most is torque, and where in the rev range our engine makes the most of it. The truth is, engines make torque when we feed fuel and air into combustion chambers and squeeze the mix. A good friend of ours, John Baechtel of Westech Performance in Ontario, California, said it best when he said, "Torque is the grunt that gets us going, and horsepower is the force that keeps us moving..." Well said, John, and oh so very true.

Engines are doing their best work when they reach peak torque, where they are making the most grunt. John tells us that when an engine is below the torque peak, it has more than enough time to completely fill the cylinder with air and fuel. He adds that when engine RPM rises above the torque peak, there isn't enough time to completely fill the cylinders with air and fuel.

The power we feel from an engine's spinning crankshaft is torque multiplied by engine speed (RPM) to produce a number that tells us something about the engine's output. This theory dates back to steam engines and an inventor named James Watt. Watt invented the steam engine long ago in the 1800s. Watt's theory was a simple one. It compared the work his steam engine could do with the same work an equal number of horses could do. Watt determined a single horse could pull a 180-pound load 181 feet in one minute's time. This formula figured out to 32,580 lbs/ft per minute. Watt rounded it off to 33,000 lbs/ft per minute. He divided this figure by 60 seconds, which worked out to 550 lbs/ft per second. And this became the standard for one horsepower.

As a result of Watt's calculations long ago, horsepower has become a measure of force in pounds against a distance in feet for the brief period of one minute. Then, we take this formula and

Other Power Considerations

When we're planning for power, we rarely stop to consider how power gets wasted in an engine's design and construction. Friction is the power pick-pocket hiding in all sorts of placed inside our engines. Most of the friction occurs at the pistons and rings. Some of it gets lost at the bearings and journals. Yet more of it gets consumed at piston wrist pins, lifters and bores, cam lobes and lifters, rocker arm fulcrums, and valvestems.

Our mission during the engine build needs to be finding a compromise between having tolerances that are too loose and too tight. Piston-to-cylinder-wall clearances are critical in order to have good cylinder sealing without too much friction and drag. The same is true for rod and main bearing clearances.

Another power-tap issue is engine breathing. You want an induction system that helps your engine breathe well at the RPM range it is designed and built for. This means the appropriate intake manifold and carburetor. Go too small on carburetor sizing, and you restrict breathing. If ports don't match in terms of size, you restrict breathing. Opt for cylinder heads

Even overtorquing main and rod bearing caps can result in frictional losses not to mention engine damage.

Bearing clearances have an effect on frictional power losses. This is where close attention must be paid to crankshaft machining issues.

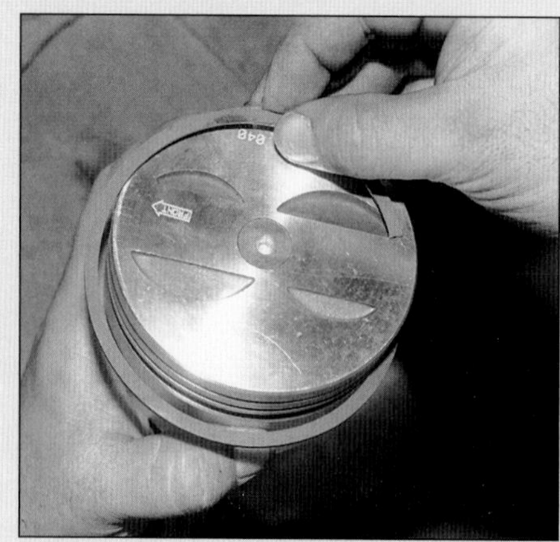

To keep piston-to-cylinder-wall clearances in check, we have to ascertain proper ring size and gap. Piston ring end gap depends on how the engine will be used, as do piston to cylinder wall clearances.

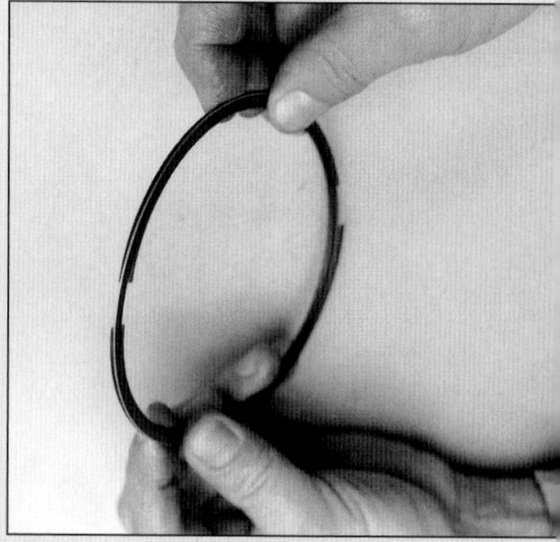

Using the right piston rings helps the engine make power. Some rings are designed for better sealing and less drag. You want excellent cylinder sealing without the penalty of drag.

Vhen we think of frictional losses, we lon't often think of valves and guides, ut huge losses happen here. Closely heck valve and stem clearances during our headwork. It's a good idea to run alves and guides a tad loose, without acrificing oil control and valve seat ntegrity.

vhere port sizing is too limited for your lisplacement and you restrict breathing. One example would be stock 289/302 eads on a 355ci stroker. This brings comression to mind immediately. Run too nuch compression and you kill power vith detonation.

On the exhaust side, you want a scavnging system that makes sense. You don't ave to have long-tube headers for great reathing. Shorty headers will do the job ust as well, and without the shortcomings of long-tube headers. Go too large on header tube size and you hurt torque. Go too small and you hurt power on the high end. This is where your exhaust system has to work hand-in-hand with the heads, camshaft, and induction system.

Balancing can either make or break an ngine. Detailed dynamic balancing llows an engine to spin with fury. In roper balance, an engine revs smoothly nd quickly. When we have imbalance ssues, vibration abounds, which loses us ower and reliability.

Flat tappet lifters create plenty of friction, which is why a roller tappet camshaft makes more sense in a high-performance engine.

Heat kills power. To make power, we have to make the best use of heat where it counts – in the combustion chamber. Did you know chrome-plated oil pans and valve covers hold heat inside the engine? They also stay hot long after shutdown. You want components like oil pans, valve covers, and intake manifolds that get rid of heat. Cast aluminum is the best heat-sink there is, short of copper.

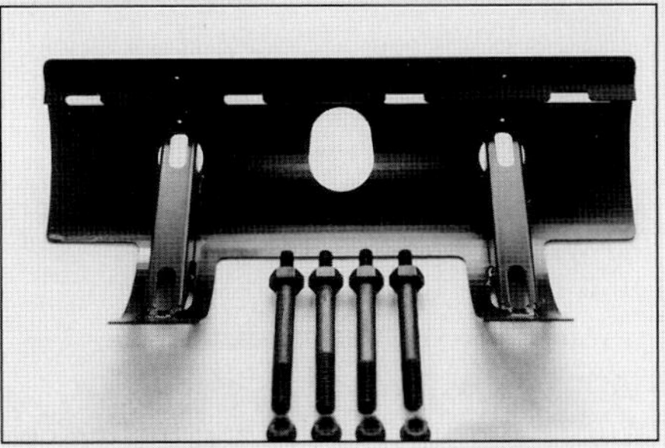

Oil windage is another issue that will cost you power. Oil that is picked up and slung around the crankshaft and rods causes a frictional loss of its own. Windage trays and pan baffles keep oil where it belongs – away from the spinning crankshaft.

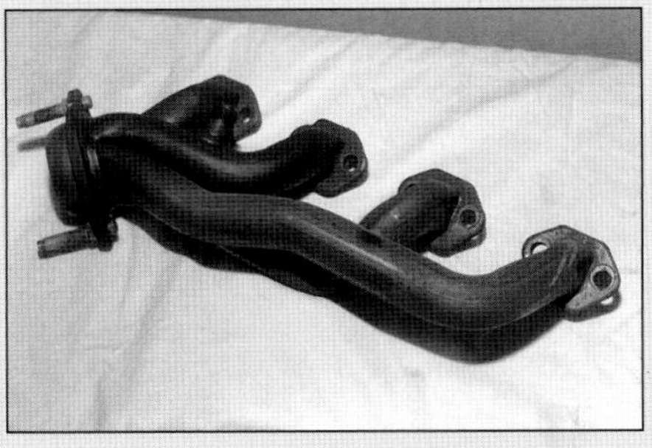

Exhaust headers and mufflers create their own set of power losses. Factory shorty headers sure look like headers, but they're very restrictive. This costs you torque. The engine has to be able to breathe to make power. Aftermarket shorty and long-tube headers reduce restriction.

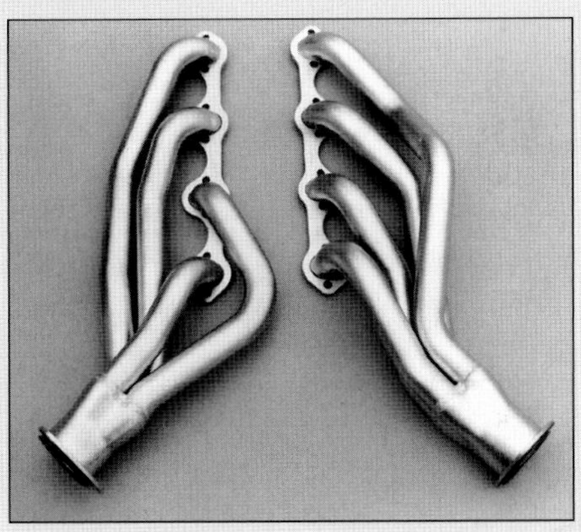

apply it to an engine's crankshaft at each journal throw to arrive at horsepower. This is based on the number 5252.

Torque and RPM are divided by 5252. And torque and horsepower always equal at 5252. If you are able to solve this equation at 5,252 rpm, RPM cancels out, ultimately leaving horsepower equal to the torque figure. In fact, if you work this out on a graph, the torque, horsepower and RPM lines should always intersect.

When we look at torque alone, it is the measure of an engine's work. Horsepower is a measure of how quickly the engine does the work. Torque comes mostly from displacement and stroke. This means the real power we derive from an engine comes in the torque curve. The broader the torque curve, the better our power package. A broader torque curve comes from making the most of the fuel/air mixture across a broader RPM range. This is best accomplished with a longer stroke and a larger bore. And this is what strokers are all about. Strokers are about making the most torque across the broadest range. Truth is, we're never going to get the best of everything, even with fuel-injected engines. Our engines need to be planned and built based on the way we're going to use them. What we choose in terms of a camshaft, cylinder heads, and induction system determines how our engine will perform.

Making Real Stroker Power

There are plenty of myths about making power, especially in the Ford camp. Folklore tells us it's easier to make power with a Chevrolet than a Ford. But this is pure nonsense. You can make just as much power with a Ford for the same amount of money you can a Chevrolet. What gives the Chevrolet an advantage is numbers. Chevys are simply more commonplace than Ford. But even this is changing because Ford's popularity has grown dramatically in recent years. When it comes to seat-of-the-pants performance, there's no black magic here, just the simple physics of taking thermal expansion and turning it into rotary motion.

Quick Power With Nitrous Oxide

Meet John Da Luz of JMC Motorsports in San Diego, California. John has always been passionate about power, but understands the consequences of power handled irresponsibly.

Nitrous oxide, or "squeeze," is popular today for those looking for quick and easy power (50 to 150 horsepower) on demand. It makes boatloads of power at the touch of a button, but nitrous can be very harmful to an engine that isn't properly prepared and tuned. Nitrous will severely damage your pistons and rings if it is not used properly. It can and does hammer rod bearings, resulting in severe wear. It is also hard on main bearings due to these severe loads. And no matter what the nitrous oxide optimist club will tell you about laughing gas, nitrous can and does shorten engine life. So don't be drawn into believing it's a magic horsepower pill without consequences. If you're going to be using nitrous oxide, be prepared for its shortcomings. Accept the fact that nitrous will shorten engine life no matter how it is used. The more aggressively you use nitrous, the shorter your engine will live.

So what, exactly, is nitrous oxide, an what does it do? Nitrous is a physics lesso in how to generate greater amounts o power from the fuel/air charge we intro duce to the combustion chambers. Nitrou Oxide is a very simple gas composed of tw nitrogen atoms attached to one oxyge atom. Chemists call it N_2O. Contrary t what you may believe about N_2O, it is no a poisonous gas, nor is it harmful to th atmosphere. This doesn't mean you shoul breathe it, however. Because N_2O is a asphyxiant, it can suffocate you if inhale in heavy quantities. It would have a simila affect on you as carbon dioxide (CO_2 called oxygen deprivation.

Nitrous makes for great bolt-on horse power. NOS, for example, offers us kit that deliver various levels of power. Bu remember, too much nitrous equa engine destruction. All that power at th punch of a button has a price calle reduced engine life. Below is a pisto damaged by nitrous.

Quick Power With Nitrous Oxide (continued)

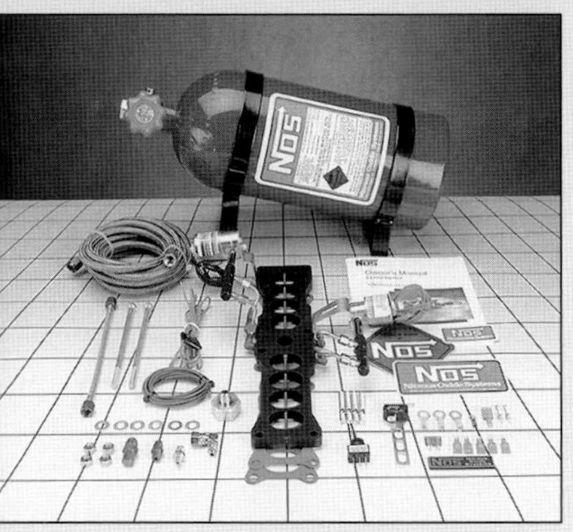

'his is the NOS Big Shot nitrous plate for .0L and 5.8L small blocks with electronc fuel injection. This system can net you p to 300 additional horsepower with he right engine prep and tuning.

Nitrous Oxide is available in three basic rades: medical, commercial, and high-purity. The medical grade is what's commonly nown as "laughing gas," which used by lentists and surgeons. It has to be very pure or human consumption. You must be icensed as a medical professional to get it. Commercial grade nitrous oxide is what we

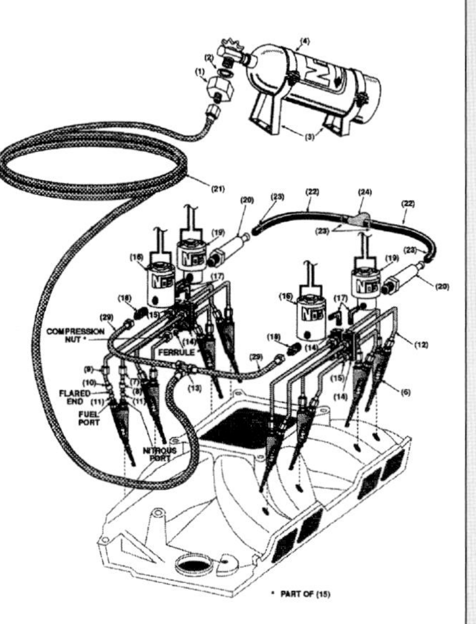

'his is a typical port-injected nitrous setp from NOS.

use in our engines for performance gains. High-purity is also a medical grade nitrous oxide that is extremely pure, resulting in it being priced and controlled accordingly.

The commercial grade nitrous oxide is marketed as Nytrous+ and sold by the Puritan-Bennett Corporation. You can find it all across the country. It is a mix of 99.9% nitrous oxide and 0.01% sulfur dioxide. Puritan-Bennett adds the sulfur dioxide to give its N_2O gas odor just like we experience with natural gas.

When you buy nitrous oxide, it is pumped into a storage tank that you provide the supplier. You need an appropriate tank capable of holding at least 1,800 pounds per square inch (psi). To play it safe, your tank(s) must have a visible certification date from within the past five years. Inside the tank, nitrous oxide exists in liquid form. As it leaves the tank, it becomes a gas. When it leaves the tank quickly, it leaves very cold, just like refrigerants and propane. To be a liquid, there has to be enough pressure inside the tank to turn the nitrous oxide into a liquid. Unpressurized, nitrous oxide exists as a gas. For nitrous oxide to become a liquid in an unpressurized environment, the ambient temperature has to be –127 degrees F. At 70 degrees F, nitrous oxide needs to be pressurized to 760 psi to become a liquid. Warm things up to 80 degrees F and you need 865 psi to make nitrous oxide a liquid.

The use of nitrous oxide to make power is nothing new. In World War II, it was used to help aircraft engines make more power. The principle then was much the same as it is now. Nitrous oxide was stored under pressure in tanks. Nitrous oxide stored under pressure must be anchored securely in the interest of safety. We stress safety because a carelessly handled nitrous oxide bottle with nearly 1,000 psi of pressure behaves like a bomb if the bottle fails. It can explode, maiming or killing you.

To get the nitrous we need for performance use on demand, we meter this gas from the bottle via electrical solenoids that are fired when we hit the button. Of course, it involves more than this. Nitrous oxide should be administered on demand at a time when it is safe to do so. Too much nitrous oxide and not enough fuel can destroy an engine. For one thing, nitrous oxide should never be administered to the intake ports unless the throttle is wide open. Set up properly, the throttle should close a nitrous oxide solenoid switch when in the wide-open position. Closing the switch activates the nitrous oxide solenoid, releasing the nitrous oxide into the intake manifold.

This is a typical nitrous carburetor plate fogger located between the carburetor and manifold, available from Wilson Manifolds.

So how do we get nitrous oxide into the intake ports? We do it a number of ways, depending on how the engine is set up. Carbureted engines get their nitrous oxide diet through a fogger plate located beneath the carburetor. Pin the butterflies and the nitrous oxide fogs the intake plenum, adding to the fuel/air mixture en route to the chambers. Carbureted engines may also use nozzles at each intake port to administer the nitrous oxide. The nice part about this design is being able to tune each cylinder bore based on the needs of that cylinder. On carbureted engines, the center ports typically receive more fuel and air than the perimeter ports. The outers tend to run more lean than the centers, which is very critical when you are running nitrous oxide.

Quick Power With Nitrous Oxide (continued)

Port fuel-injected engines also use nozzles off of a common tube manifold to administer nitrous oxide at each port. Like its carbureted counterpart, the port-injected nitrous oxide arrangement can be port-tuned for better performance. This is especially true when you think of your V-8 engine as eight separate engines operating on a common crankshaft.

One popular misconception is that we get power from the nitrous oxide itself. But this isn't true. Nitrous oxide works hand-in-hand with the fuel/air mix to make power in each cylinder bore. Nitrous oxide brings out the best in the fuel. Not only is the nitrous oxide mist cold (good for thermal expansion), it is also loaded with oxygen, which gives the igniting fuel/air mix a bad attitude. It makes the fuel/air mix burn faster, which creates a powerful thermal expansion experience in each combustion chamber.

Where we have to be careful with nitrous oxide is how we feed it to our engines. Perhaps this isn't the best parallel, but nitrous oxide has to be thought of the same way you would cocaine, crystal meth', or nicotine. The more powerful the nitrous oxide experience, the more an enthusiast wants. So we keep feeding our engine more and more nitrous oxide in our quest for power, until it fails under the stress. You must recognize your engine's limits before even getting started on a nitrous oxide diet.

Working With Nitrous Oxide

The first thing to remember with nitrous oxide is that it makes fuel burn faster. This means you must be mindful of what it can do, both productively and counterproductively. All that instantaneous power comes for a reason. As a result, extraordinary attention to detail must be paid on the road to power.

Lets start with engine tuning. Administering nitrous oxide to the combustion chambers should not be done with reckless abandon. Use too much of it and you burn pistons. You have to think of nitrous oxide and your air/fuel mixture just like you would oxygen and acetylene. When we're using oxygen and acetylene to weld or cut steel, we use lots of oxygen to blaze a path through the steel. The same can happen inside your engine when we use too much nitrous oxide. You can burn right through the piston like a cutting torch. And aluminum pistons aren't as forgiving, they melt at 1300 degrees F.

When we're dialing in an engine to run on nitrous, we need not only consider fuel delivery and spark timing, but also compression. Along with compression, we need to consider expected fuel octane rating.

When we are tuning a small-block Ford to run on nitrous oxide, we have to get fuel/air mixture and spark timing where they need to be or face certain destruction. So how do we get there? First, we have to control fuel delivery to where it jibes with the flow of nitrous oxide. If we get too much N_2O and not enough fuel, we overheat the chamber and melt pistons. This means we have to control fuel and nitrous oxide flow to a finite point where we get the most power possible without doing engine damage. This takes practice.

The key to getting the most power from nitrous oxide is getting spark timing, fuel delivery, and peak cylinder pressure going at the same time. Ideally, we light the fuel/air/nitrous mixture at the time when we have peak cylinder pressure, which makes the most of the incoming charge. When everything is working well together, we get a smooth, firm light-off that nets us a lot of power. Things go wrong when the light-off resembles an explosion, exerting a shockwave on the top of the piston. This is the spark knock we hear as a multiple rapping under acceleration.

When fuel, air, and nitrous ignite violently, why don't we net more power from the explosion? The answer is simple. When an engine is running smoothly, we get that quick-fire mentioned earlier in this chapter. A smooth light-off applies pressure to the piston dome, forcing it downward in the cylinder bore, turning the crank and completing the power stroke. Detonation is what occurs when we get a spontaneous light-off, especially from two points in the chamber. The two waves of power collide, causing spark knock or pinging under acceleration. The problem with this kind of light-off is that those violent combustion spikes don't really yield much power.

So how do we safely make the most of nitrous oxide? We should first address the fuel system because we need to have enough fuel to meet the demands of nitrous oxide. Without enough fuel, we toast the engine. The next issue is fuel octane rating. You need to decide what octane rating you expect to use. Next is ignition timing. Where does yours need to be? And finally, too much compression with nitrous will cause destructive detonation. Getting each of these elements dialed in is crucial to productive performance.

Compression has to be thought of two ways – static and dynamic. Static compression is the compression ratio we often think of. This is the swept volume above the piston, with the piston at bottom dead center, versus the clearance volume left when the piston is at top dead center. If we have 100cc of volume with the piston at bottom dead center and 10cc left with the piston at top dead center, then we have a static compression ratio of 10.0:1 – 100cc to 10cc.

Dynamic compression is what happens with the engine operating. This is the kind of compression that happens with pistons, valves, and gasses in motion through the

Quick Power With Nitrous Oxide (continued)

ngine. We get dynamic compression when ve are huffing lung-fulls of air through the ngine during operation. With the engine unning, we are pumping more volume hrough the cylinders and chambers than we vould simply hand-cranking the engine. This actually increases the compression ratio, vhich means dynamic compression is higher han static compression. This means you eed to consider the dynamic compression atio as your engine's actual compression figire when you're planning nitrous oxide.

With the issue of compression out of he way, we will address camshaft selection vhen using nitrous oxide. Nitrous-burning ngines need different camshafts than those hat are naturally aspirated or supercharged. Dynamic compression ratio, mentioned arlier, is affected by camshaft profile. A amshaft profile with a short duration will give us greater dynamic compression. When ve lengthen the duration, we tend to lose lynamic compression.

On the exhaust side, duration is a very mportant issue with nitrous. Because the uel/air/nitrous charge coming in expands vith fury during ignition, it needs a way to scape when the exhaust valve opens. We eed a longer exhaust valve duration with itrous for good scavenging and thorough xtraction of power.

While we're thinking about exhaust alve duration, we must also remember overlap in all of this. Less overlap equals nore dynamic compression. More overlap quals less dynamic compression. Overlap s that process in the power cycle where the xhaust valve is closing and the intake valve s opening. The incoming charge helps scavnge the outgoing hot gasses through the overlap process. What this means is simple. t means the exhaust valve needs to open arlier in the cycle and stay open longer for dequate scavenging.

Fuel octane plays into the power rocess because we need to understand vhen and how the fuel will ignite. The igher the fuel octane rating, the more lowly it ignites and burns, which reduces the chances of detonation and pre-ignition. With a higher octane rating, we get a smooth, more predictable light-off in the chamber. When we opt for a lower fuel octane rating, we get a more unstable fuel that will light quickly and causing pinging. When we throw nitrous oxide into the equation, we can count on a quick light that can be violent in nature. This is why a higher octane rating is so critical to a cohesive performance package.

With the issues of fuel octane and compression behind us, we're ready to address the all-important air/fuel mixture. This is called the air/fuel ratio. We do this by adjusting jet size in the carburetor or controlling fuel injector pulse width. Jet size and pulse width both determine how much fuel we're going to throw in the chamber.

If your tuning effort involves a carburetor, you have to get jet sizing down to a science that will help your engine live on nitrous oxide. As a rule, carbureted engines live happily with an air/fuel ratio of 12.5:1 to 13.0:1. This is where we have just the right amount of air and fuel to make power. If we go any leaner, we can cause engine damage. We will also lose power. Any richer and we lose power as well.

When we're working with fuel-injected engines, we can control fuel mixture by reprogramming the electronic control module or changing injector size. With nitrous, we typically go up on injector size and fine tune from there. Too large is better than too small. Factory fuel injection systems run a fuel manifold pressure of 30-45 psi. If you're running nitrous oxide, you're going to need a lot more fuel pressure to get the job done safely. Around 80 psi is considered the norm for nitrous oxide and electronic fuel injection. This is when you need to step up to high-pressure Earl's hoses and fittings.

Ignition timing is the next big hurdle because it can kill an engine as quickly as a lean fuel mixture or too much compression when we're running nitrous. We want the spark to occur in advance of peak cylinder pressure because it takes time for the fuel/air/nitrous mixture to ignite. Under normal circumstances, without nitrous, we want full spark advance around 36 to 41 degrees before top dead center. Exactly where the spark occurs depends on how the engine is equipped and how it performs at full spark advance at 3,500 rpm. Because each and every engine is different, full advance is going to vary from engine to engine.

When we throw nitrous oxide into the equation, we have an air/fuel/nitrous mixture that is going to ignite more rapidly than the conventional fuel/air mix. The pros suggest retarding the ignition timing to approximately 12 degrees BTDC because the air/fuel/nitrous mixture ignites much more quickly. With the full spark advance at 36-41 degrees BTDC, we would waste the engine in short order. Retard timing to 12 degrees BTDC and go from there. Twelve degrees BTDC at 3,500 rpm needs to be your baseline, then slowly advance ignition timing from there. Test it out at wide-open throttle under a load, beginning at 12 degrees BTDC, then advance from there one degree at a time.

With the basics out of the way, there are other points to consider when running nitrous. To be effective, fuel has to atomize (vaporize) properly. This means the fuel has to mist as it enters the intake manifold and,

Engines fitted with nitrous oxide injection need forged pistons. Cast and hypereutectic pistons will not hold up well on a steady diet of nitrous. Much of it depends on how much nitrous you're going to throw at your engine. Forged pistons are good life insurance.

Quick Power! (concluded)

ultimately, the combustion chamber. Problem here is, nitrous comes out of the fogger or nozzle ice cold. This makes it very difficult to atomize the fuel effectively. When nitrous comes out of the fogger or nozzle at a frigid –100 degrees F, fuel tends to exist as large droplets, rather than the mist we need for good ignition and combustion.

Nitrous oxide system manufacturers have dealt effectively with the issue of fuel atomization by designing systems that allow the gasoline to atomize with the nitrous oxide fog or mist. The finer we can get the mist, the more power we're going to pull from the mixture. So, the objective is to keep the fuel in suspension as long as possible.

How Much Fuel?

There is a formula that will make it easier to prepare your fuel system for nitrous operation. The air to fuel ratio in a naturally aspirated engine should be between 12.5:1 and 13.0:1. This is a range where engines are happiest and make the most power. Things change dramatically when we introduce nitrous oxide to the air/fuel mixture. We need way more fuel to both make power and prevent engine damage.

Most nitrous experts we have consulted suggest a nitrous to fuel ratio of 5.0:1 as a starting point for engine tuning. Starting here means going decidedly rich, but it's the safest approach going. Begin at 5.0:1 and steer your tuning toward 6.0:1 for optimum results. If your power goal is, for example, 500 horsepower on nitrous oxide, you're going to need 37.94 gallons an hour or 0.63 gallons a minute to run happily on nitrous oxide. Obviously, we're not going to stay on nitrous oxide for one hour, but it gives you a good idea about how much fuel you're going to need.

CarTech Books publishes an excellent nitrous oxide book (SA-50), authored by respected and well-known automotive writer, Joe Pettitt. For more detailed information on nitrous oxide, pick up this book at your favorite bookstore.

Look what improper nitrous tuning did to this 5.0L High Output SEFI engine. When you closely examine the main and rod bearings, along with the crankshaft rod journals, it is apparent someone fed this engine a lot of nitrous and a whole lot of detonation. This is what happens when you don't have all of the tuning elements tied together.

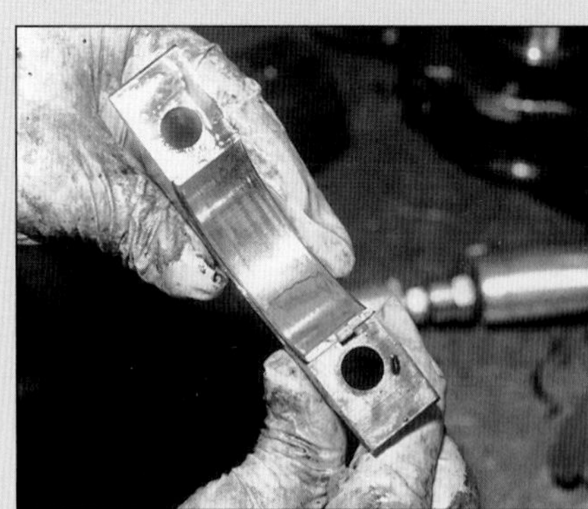

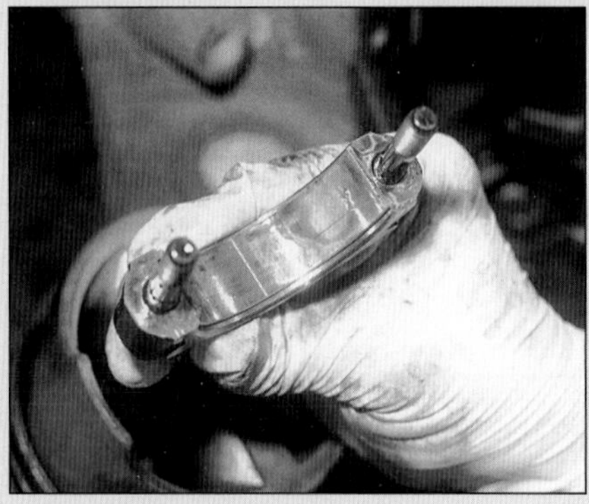

To learn how to make power, we have to understand how power is made inside an engine to begin with. How much power an engine makes depends on how much air and fuel we can pump through the engine, plus what we do with that fuel and air mixture during that split-second it lives and dies in the combustion chambers.

We have to think of an internal combustion engine as an air pump. The more air and fuel we can pump through the cylinders, the more power we're going to make. This is why racers use big carburetors, manifolds, heads, superchargers, turbochargers, and nitrous oxide. Racers understand this air pump theory and practice it with reckless abandon, – sometimes with catastrophic results. But good racers also understand the too much of good thing theory. Sometimes it can cost you a race – sometimes an engine.

Getting power from our air pump takes getting liberal amounts of air and fuel into the chambers, then squeezing the mixture as hard as we can without damaging the engine. When we raise compression, we increase the power our mixture yields. It is the intense heat of compression coupled with the ignition system spark that launch the yield of energy from our mixture. The more compression we have, the greater the heat we have to ignite the mixture.

Problem is, when there's too much compression and the resulting heat, the air/fuel mixture can ignite prematurely resulting in pre-ignition and detonation. So we have to achieve the right compression ratio to get the most from the fuel we have. Today's street fuels won't tolerate much over 10.0:1 compression. This means we have to look elsewhere for answers in the power equation, like more aggressive camshaft profiles, better heads, port work, hotter ignition systems, exhaust headers that breathe better, state-of-the-art intake manifolds and carburetors, even electronic fuel injection where we never thought of using it before.

The thing to remember about gasoline engines is this: The fuel/air mixture does not explode in the combustion chambers, it lights off just like your gas furnace or water heater. Because the mixture is compressed and ignited, i lights-off more rapidly. Combustion in a piston engine is just that, a quick fire that sends a flame front across the top of the piston. Under ideal circumstances, the flame front will travel smoothly across the piston dome, yielding heat and pressure that act on the piston and rod uniformly to create rotary motion at the crankshaft.

A bad light-off that originates at two opposing points in the chamber is pre-ignition or detonation, which we were talking about earlier. The opposing light-offs collide creating a shock that hammers the piston dome, which is the pinging or spark knock we hear under acceleration. The objective is to get a smooth, quick fire, with the flame front traveling in one direction for maximum power. Call this power management.

Power management is having the right balance of ignition timing, fuel mixture, compression ratio, valve timing events, and even external forces like blower boost or nitrous input. All of these elements have to work together if we're going to make productive power. Let's talk about some of the elements we need to make power.

For one thing, the science of making power must tie in with your intended vehicle usage. And that's where most of us get it wrong all too often. In our quest for stroker torque, we sometimes forget how the vehicle is going to be driven and used. If you are building a stroker to go drag racing, the way you build your engine is going to be different than the guy who builds one for trailer towing. By the same token, road racing engines should be constructed differently than drag racing powerplants.

So how do we approach each engine's mission? Street engines for the daily commute need to be designed for good low and mid-range torque. Drag racing engines need to make power at mid to high-RPM ranges. Road racing engines need to be able to do it all – down low, in the middle, and at high RPM – because they're going to be in all of these ranges while racing. Engines scheduled for trailer towing need plenty of low-end torque. They also need to be able to live comfortably at mid-range, when we're going to be pulling up a grade.

One More Thing ...

Anytime you're going to raise your engine's stress level by using nitrous oxide, supercharging, or turbocharging, you should remember the importance of cylinder sealing. Opt for only the best competition head gaskets you can find. Be prepared to spend more than $100.00 for a set. If you're going to blow a ton of squeeze or boost into the chambers, think seriously about O-ringing the block for adequate cylinder sealing.

Camshaft & Valvetrain Basics

The camshaft and valvetrain directly determine not only an engine's personality, but how reliably an engine will perform throughout its service life. When it comes to camshafts, there are probably more misconceptions then there are facts. We're here to dissolve most of the myths and get you headed in the right direction on your stroker project.

To understand how to pick a camshaft and valvetrain, you must first understand how it all works. Choosing a camshaft profile is rooted in how we want an engine to perform. Are we building a streetable stroker where low and mid-range torque are important, or are we building a high-revving racing engine that makes peak torque in the high revs?

A camshaft manufacturer's catalog lists dozens of camshaft types for the same type of engine. This is where it gets mighty confusing for the novice. We see words like lift, duration, lobe separation, base circle, lobe centerline angle, and valve overlap. It is important to know what this information means and how will it affect your engine's performance.

Camshaft Shop Talk

What separates one camshaft from another is called profile. Profile is lobe design, dimension and positioning, when it opens the valve, when it closes the valve, how long it keeps the valve open, and how much it opens the valve. All of these factors play into how the engine will perform.

Lift is the maximum distance that a camshaft lobe will open a valve. **Duration** is how long the lobe will keep the valve open. **Lobe Separation** or **centerline** is the time or duration between intake and exhaust valve action. **Overlap** plays into lobe separation because it is the period when the exhaust valve is closing and the intake valve is opening. The **Ramp** is the ascending or descending side of the cam lobe coming off the base circle when lift begins to occur. **Flank** is the ascending or descending portion of the lobe past the base circle nearest maximum lift. The camshaft's **Base Circle** is the portion of the lobe that doesn't generate lift. The bottom-most portion of the lobe is called the **Heel**.

Flat tappet camshafts work differently than roller tappet camshafts, which means we have to think differently with each type. Flat tappet camshafts limit what we can do with lobe profile if we want streetability. If we want an aggressive profile with flat tappets, we can only go so far with a street engine, or suffer with poor drivability (rough idle and low manifold vacuum). If you want an aggressive profile in a street engine, we suggest stepping up to a roller camshaft, which can handle the aggressive profile better using roller tappets.

Street Cam Facts

Based on everything we've seen in 50 years of experience, the best street performance cams are ground with a lobe separation between 108 to 114 degrees. When we keep lobe separation above 112 degrees, we improve drivabil-

Supercharging

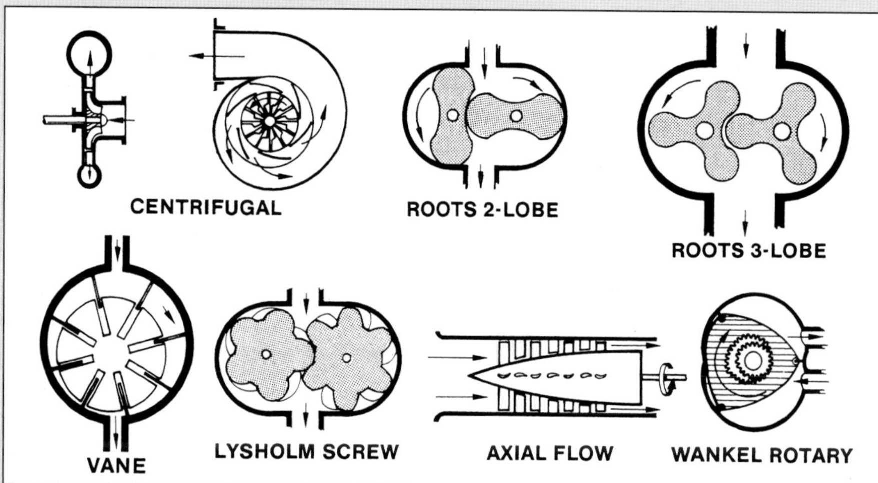

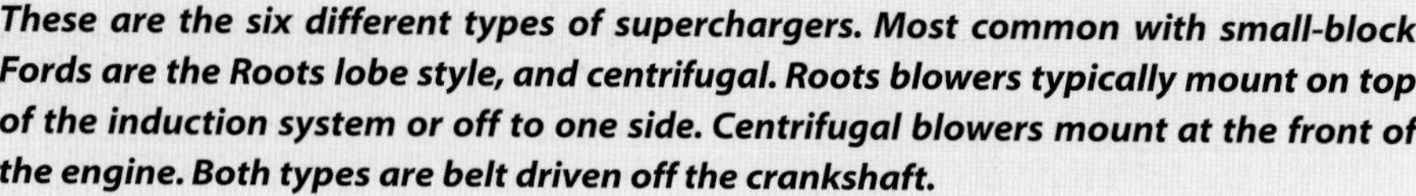

These are the six different types of superchargers. Most common with small-block Fords are the Roots lobe style, and centrifugal. Roots blowers typically mount on top of the induction system or off to one side. Centrifugal blowers mount at the front of the engine. Both types are belt driven off the crankshaft.

Here's a view of the Roots blower opened up for your inspection. The interlocking three-lobe rotors move a lot of air.

Supercharging, like nitrous oxide injection, was conceived of a long time ago to extract as much power as possible from a given displacement. Unlike nitrous oxide, supercharging is more involved, yet easier to tune and manage. It is easier to tune because you know you're getting into trouble before getting there. Knowing you're in trouble comes from the sound of detonation. Superchargers and turbochargers don't come on as strong as quickly as nitrous. For the most part, they cannot damage the engine as quickly as nitrous, because you can come off the power in time to prevent engine damage. There is also a safety device, called a wastegate, designed to prevent excessive boost with superchargers and turbochargers. With nitrous oxide, damage and certain engine death are instantaneous if you deliver too much of it without enough fuel, or with too much ignition timing.

Supercharging and turbocharging both accomplish the same objective. They each force air into the cylinders to make the most of a combustion power cycle. They mechanically increase cylinder pressure , which, given enough fuel, makes more power. Superchargers are driven by the engine's crankshaft. Turbochargers are driven by exhaust gas pressure. A supercharger's compressor, driven by the crankshaft, moves the air we're feeding into the intake manifold. A turbocharger's compressor, driven by exhaust gas pressure, does the same thing.

Superchargers give engine nearly immediate power. The power comes on stronger with RPMs. With the increase in RPMs, the compressor turns faster, forcing more air pressure into the intake manifold, which gives us the power. We prevent overpressure by fitting the supercharger with a wastegate, which vents excessive pressure.

Turbochargers take a certain amount of time to give us induction pressure when we step on the gas. This is called turbo lag. Since it takes the turbocharger time to spool up during acceleration, there is a certain amount of lag before we get the boost or pressure, and the resulting power. Turbochargers have a wastegate, which also bleeds excessive boost pressure and prevents engine damage.

There are six basic different types of superchargers: centrifugal, rotary, axial flow, Roots two and three-lobe, vane type, and Lysholm screw. Probably the most common type we see out there on small and middle-block Fords are centrifugal and Roots blowers. Centrifugal types are typically hung on the front of the engine, driven by the crankshaft pulley. Roots blowers, also driven by the crankshaft pulley, are normally an integral part of the intake manifold, with the carburetor mounted immediately upwind of the blower. With fuel injection, the throttle body is mounted in any number of locations before the Roots blower's intake. Fuel injectors are positioned in each of the intake ports, downwind of the Roots blower.

This is one example of a centrifugal blower on a Ford. The Paxton VR and SN superchargers, like the one shown here, force air through a carburetor (inside the shell on top of the manifold) to help an engine make greater amounts of power.

Supercharging (continued)

Which type of supercharger should you choose and why? This is hard to answer because everyone has different expectations and needs. Which supercharger you choose is going to depend on your needs. Roots and centrifugal superchargers both have significant purposes. We choose the Roots blower for different purposes than we choose a centrifugal huffer. Lets talk about the Roots blower first.

The Roots lobe-type supercharger has served many purposes during its service lifetime. Probably the most common Roots supercharger duty has been to feed hungry Detroit two-stroke diesel engines. You've undoubtedly heard the term "6-71 blower" in hot-rodding circles. Detroit two-stroke diesel engines, once manufactured by General Motors, are named based on displacement, number of cylinders and cylinder arrangement. The Detroit 6V-71, for example, is a V-6, with 71 cubic inches of displacement per cylinder. A Detroit 8V-92 is a V-8, with 92 cubic inches per cylinder. The Detroit 6-71 is an in-line six, with 71 cubic inches per cylinder. So when you see a huge 6-71 blower atop a well-fed small-block Ford, it's a blower originally designed for huge, heavy-duty Detroit diesels that power semi-trucks. Detroit two-cycle diesel engines have been in steady service since the 1930s. They're smoky and noisy. You've probably seen untold thousands of them over your lifetime in city busses, heavy trucks, fire trucks, stationary water pumping stations, and hundreds of other places. Since they are a two-stroke design, they fire on every revolution of the crankshaft, which makes them real screamers.

What makes a Roots blower effective is its positive displacement design, which a Detroit two-stroke diesel engine needs for proper ingestion of air and scavenging of exhaust gasses. This kind of positive displacement design provides plenty of cylinder pressure when and where it counts in a high-performance V-8 engine.

We speak of positive displacement when discussing Roots blowers because their very design doesn't allow much, if any air to escape en route to the chambers. Roots blowers have two and three-lobe rotor designs where rotors interlock to ensure consistent airflow into the engine.

This is a cutaway of a Paxton supercharger. Air is drawn in through the intake at the center of the impeller and thrust outward through a pressure housing to an outlet and tubing.

Ford has been using the Roots design on factory production engines for many years, beginning with the 1989 3.8L Essex V-6 Thunderbird. Today, it is used atop the 5.4L SOHC V-8 engine in the Lightning and Harley-Davidson F-150 trucks, for example. This reliable, highly successful supercharger will work quite well on your small-block Ford.

A more common type of supercharger is the centrifugal type we see and hear at a lot of Ford events on newer 5.0L and 4.6L Mustangs. It's that familiar whistle associated mostly with the Vortech and Paxton superchargers. Instead of the interlocking rotors used in the Roots positive displacement supercharger, centrifugal superchargers employ a fan that draws air into its center and rings it outward into a duct where it enters the intake manifold. Centrifugal force is defined by The American Heritage Dictionary as "the component of an apparent force or a body in curvilinear motion, as observed from that body, that is directed away from a curvature or axis of rotation."

To make this easier to understand, centrifugal force is the energy of a spinning object that tends to throw the object, or parts of the object outward. In this case, air is the object we sling outward from the spinning fan (compressor). The compressor takes the air in through its center and blows it outward with the whirling blades or fins that thrust it outward into the shell into the intake tube. Not only does the compressor move the air outward from its center, it also squeezes the air in the shell, feeding it to the

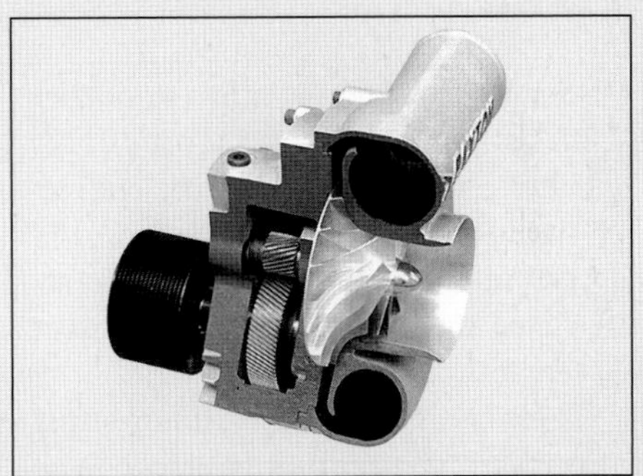

This is the high-tech Paxton Novi centrifugal supercharger for small-block Fords. Thanks to its roller bearing design and step-up gearing, it gets the job done reliably.

Supercharging (concluded)

intake tube. Think of the centrifugal style blower like your hairdryer where air is drawn into one side and blown out the other side. A hairdryer is a compressor of sorts. Even the humble blower in your Ford's air conditioning system compresses air to some degree before it exits your dashboard outlets. Even your home vacuum cleaner has a compressor, most of which are of a centrifugal blower design. The best vacuum cleaner example we can think of is an old-fashioned Kirby upright vacuum cleaner with a centrifugal blower.

Turbochargers are like the centrifugal supercharger because they work much the same way. Instead of being belt-driven, they're driven by a turbine that is propelled by hot exhaust gasses. As we accelerate, hot exhaust gasses drive the turbocharger's single-stage turbine, which drives the centrifugal compressor.

This is a cutaway of the Powerdyne supercharger, which has a quiet belt-drive inside the case instead of gears.

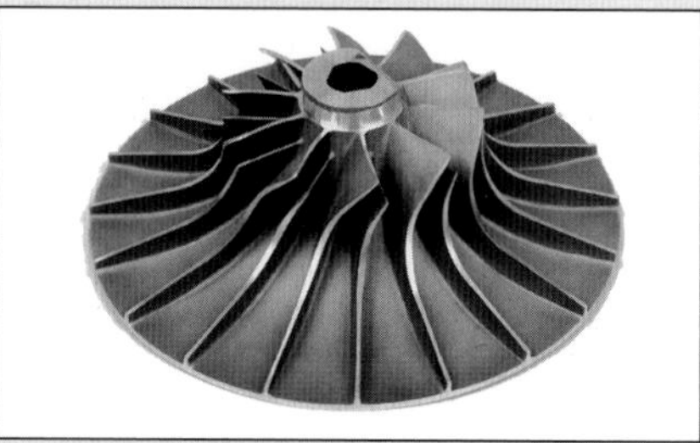

This is a typical centrifugal supercharger impeller. As you can see, air is drawn in through the center of the impeller and spun out through the blade tips.

The Vortech V1 for the 5.0L small block has a high-output T-trim impeller, with a water to air aftercooler. The result here is more power.

ity because the engine idles smoother and makes better low-end torque. This is what we want from a street engine. Any time lobe separation is below 108 degrees, idle quality and streetability suffer. But there's more to it than just lobe separation.

Compression and cam timing must be considered together because one always affects the other. Valve timing events directly affect cylinder pressure. Long intake valve duration reduces cylinder pressure. Shorter duration increases cylinder pressure. Too much cylinder pressure can cause detonation (pinging). Too little and you lose torque. You can count on cam manufacturers to figure stock compression ratios into their camshaft selection tables, which makes choosing a camshaft easier than it's ever been. Plug your application into the equation and you will be pleased with the result most of the time.

The greatest advice we can offer the novice is to be conservative with your cam specs if you want reliability and an engine that will live a long time. Keep with a conservative lift profile (under .500 inch). High-lift camshafts beat the daylights out of a valvetrain. And they put valve to piston clearances at risk. Watch duration and lobe separation closely, which will help you be more effective in camshaft selection. Instead of opening the valve more (lift), we want to open it longer (duration) and in better efficiency with piston timing (overlap or lobe separation).

Always keep in mind what you're going to have for induction, heads, and exhaust. The savvy engine builder understands that in order to work effectively, an engine must have matched components. Cam, valvetrain, heads, intake manifold, and an exhaust system must all work as a team or you're just wasting time and money. If you're going to use stock heads, which we expect with a budget stroker engine, your cam profile need not be too aggressive. Opt for a cam profile that will give you good low and mid-range torque. Torque doesn't do you any good on the street when it happens at 6500 rpm. Choose a cam profile that will make good torque between 2500 and 4500 rpm. Otherwise, you're just wasting engine.

The thing to remember with camshaft selection is how the cam will work with your engine's cylinder heads. We need to take a close look at valve lift with a particular head and determine effect. Some camshafts will actually lose power with a given head because there's too much lift or duration. This is why we want to understand a cylinder head before choosing a camshaft. You want to seek optimum conditions with any cylinder head/camshaft combination. This means having to do your homework before making a decision.

What type of fuel do you intend to run in your engine? This also affects camshaft selection. We can actually raise compression if we're running a mild camshaft profile or using a higher octane fuel. It all has to work together. Camshaft timing events must be directly tied to compression ratio. The longer our duration, the lower the cylinder pressure and resulting compression. The shorter the duration, the less air we're going to bring into the cylinder, which also affects compression. Our objective needs to be the highest compression without detonation, which will harm the engine. With this in mind, we want the most duration possible without compression extremes. Duration is what gives us torque, as long as compression is sufficient.

Valve overlap, as we have stated earlier, is the period between exhaust stroke and intake stroke when both valves are slightly open. This occurs to improve exhaust scavenging. It improves exhaust scavenging by allowing the incoming intake charge to push remaining exhaust gasses out via the closing exhaust valve. Were the exhaust valve completely closed, we wouldn't get scavenging. The greater the overlap in a street engine, the less torque the engine will make down low where we need it most. This is why we want less valve overlap in a street engine and more in a racing engine, which will make its torque at high RPM. Increased valve overlap works best at high RPM.

Street engines need 10 to 55 degrees of valve overlap to be effective torque powerhouses. When valve overlap starts wandering above 55 degrees, torque on the low end begins to go away. A really hot street engine will need greater than 55 degrees of valve overlap, but not too much greater. To give you an idea of what we're talking about, racing engines need 70 to 115 degrees of valve overlap.

For a street engine, we want valve overlap to maximize torque, which means a conservative approach in the first place. Push overlap as far as you can without compromising torque. We also have to figure in lift and duration with valve overlap to see the complete power picture.

Lobe separation angle is another area of consideration in street cam selection. This camshaft dynamic is chosen based on displacement and how the engine will be used. Rule of thumb is this. Consider lobe separation based on how much displacement and camshaft you're going to be using. The smaller the valves, the tighter (fewer degrees) lobe separation should be. However, tighter lobe separation does adversely affect idle quality. This is why most camshaft manufacturers spec their cams with wider lobe separations than the custom grinders.

Duration in a street engine is likely the most important dynamic to consider in the selection process. We increase duration whenever less lift is desired. Why? Because we get airflow into the cylinder bore two ways – lift and duration. We can open the valve more and for less time to get airflow. Or we can open the valve less and keep it open longer via duration to get airflow. Each way will have a different effect on performance. Desired duration should be determined by how much cylinder head and displacement you have, and how the engine will be used. Excessive duration hurts low-end torque, which is what we need on the street. So we have to achieve a balance by maximizing duration without a loss in low-end torque. We do this by using the right heads with proper valve sizing. Large valves and ports don't work well at all for street use. Mix

SA DESIGN

Camshaft Terminology

Lift is the maximum amount a valve-lifter-pushrod combo can be raised off the base circle. Lift is measured in thousands of an inch (.000"). Lobe profile determines how quickly this occurs. It can either be smooth or abrupt depending on lobe profile.

Duration is the amount of time the valve is open beginning when the valve unseats. By this, we mean the number of degrees the camshaft will rotate when cam lift begins. Duration typically begins at .004-inch of cam lift or when the lifter begins to ride the ramp coming off the base circle. "Duration at fifty" means duration begins at .050 inches of cam lift. Duration at fifty is the industry standard for determining camshaft lobe duration. When you're reading camshaft specs, duration at fifty is the spec you will see.

Lobe Separation (also known as lobe centerline) is the distance (in degrees) between the intake lobe peak and the exhaust lobe peak. Lobe separation generally runs between 102 and 114 degrees (camshaft degrees).

Intake Centerline is the position of the camshaft in relation to the crankshaft. For example, an intake centerline of 114 degrees means the intake valve reaches maximum lift at 114 degrees after top dead center (ATDC).

Exhaust Centerline is basically the same thing as intake centerline. It is when the exhaust valve reaches maximum lift before top dead center in degrees (BTDC).

Valve Overlap is the period of time when both the intake and exhaust valve are both open to allow for proper cylinder scavenging. Overlap occurs when the exhaust valve is closing and the piston is reaching top dead center. The intake charge from the opening intake valve pushes the exhaust gasses out. Valve overlap is also known as lobe separation. Camshaft grinders can change lobe separation or valve overlap to modify the performance of a camshaft. Sometimes they do this rather than change lift or duration.

Adjustable Valve Timing is being able to dial in a camshaft by adjusting valve timing at the timing sprocket. By adjusting the valve timing at the sprocket, we can increase or decrease torque. Advance valve timing and you increase torque. Retard valve timing and you lose torque.

Degreeing a camshaft begins with getting the timing marks at 12 and 6 o'clock as shown.

Piston top dead center is determined with a piston stop as shown.

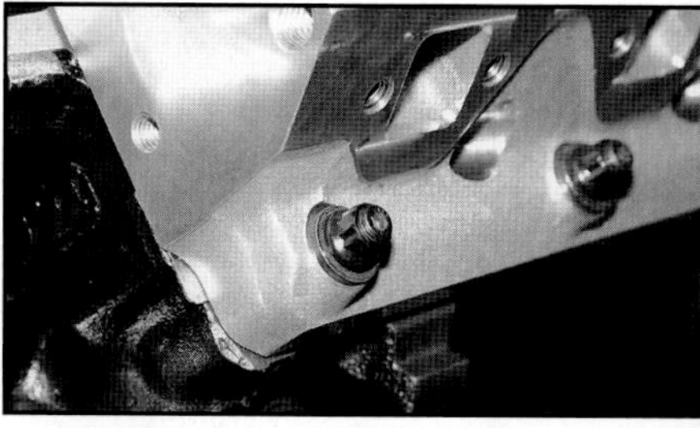

Piston TDC can also be determined by placing your thumb over the spark plug hole and bringing the piston to TDC. When air stops traveling out of the spark plug hole, the piston is at top dead center. You may also check this with a piston stop that screws into the spark plug hole.

in too much duration and you have a real slug at the traffic light.

So what does this tell us about duration? Plenty. We want greater duration whenever displacement and valve sizing go up. Increasing duration falls directly in line with torque peak and RPM range. And this does not mean we necessarily gain any torque as RPM increases. It means our peak torque simply comes in at a higher RPM range. For example, if our engine is making 350 ft-lbs of torque at 4500 rpm and we increase duration. We may well be making that same amount of torque at 5200 rpm. In short, increased duration does not always mean increased torque.

Compression has a direct effect on what our duration should be. When we're running greater compression, we have to watch duration closely because it can drive cylinder pressures too high. Sometimes we curb compression and run greater duration depending on how we want to make power. When we have greater duration, our engine is going to make more power on the high end and less on the low end. This is why you must carefully consider duration when ordering a camshaft. Higher compression with a shorter duration helps the engine make torque down low where we need it most in a street engine. The thing to watch for with compression is detonation and overheating. Maximum street compression should be around 10.0:1.

Valve lift is an issue we must think about as it pertains to an engine's needs. Small blocks generally need more valve lift than big blocks. As we increase lift, generally we increase torque. This is especially important at low and mid-RPM ranges where it counts on the street. Low-end torque is harder to achieve with a small block because these engines generally sport short strokes and large bores. Your objective needs to be more torque with less RPM if you want your engine to live longer. Revs are what drain the life out of an engine more quickly.

To make good low-end torque with a small block, we need a camshaft that will offer a combination of effective lift and duration. As a rule, we want to run a longer intake duration to make the most of valve lift. We get valve lift via the camshaft to be sure. But, rocker-arm ratio is the other half of the equation. The most common rocker arm ratio is 1.6:1, which means the rocker arm will give the valve 1.6 times the lift we have at the cam lobe. When we step up to a 1.7:1 ratio rocker arm, valve lift becomes 1.7 times that which we find at the lobe.

When we're calculating valvetrain specs, it is best to achieve a balance all around. If you run a high-lift camshaft with a 1.7:1 rocker-arm ratio, you may be getting too much lift, which means excessive wear and tear. It is best to spec on the side of conservatism, especially if you're building an engine for daily use. Whenever you opt for an aggressive camshaft with a lot of lift, you're putting more stress on the valvestem, guide, and spring. The constant hammering of daily use with excessive lift is what kills engines without warning.

We will take this excessive wear logic a step further. It is vital that you ascertain proper centering of the rocker arm tip on the valvestem tip when you're setting up the valve train. We do this by using the correct length pushrod for the application. Buy a pushrod checker at your favorite speed shop if ever you're in doubt. A pushrod checker is little more than an adjustable pushrod that you can use to determine rocker-arm geometry. If the pushrod is too long, the tip will be under-centered on the valvestem, causing excessive side loads toward the outside of the cylinder head. If the pushrod is too short, the rocker-arm tip will be over-centered, causing excessive side loading toward the inside of the head. In either case, side loads on the valvestem and guide cause excessive wear and early failure. This is why we want the rocker-arm tip to be properly centered on the valvestem for smooth operation.

One accessory that will reduce valvestem tip wear and side loading is the roller-tip rocker arm. Roller-tip rocker arms roll smoothly across the valvestem tip, virtually eliminating wear. Stamped steel, roller-tip rocker arms are available at budget prices without the high cost of extruded or forged pieces.

Dual-Pattern Camshafts

You've undoubted heard the term "dual-pattern" camshaft. A dual-pattern camshaft runs different profiles on the

Using a dial indicator as shown, we learn the valve-timing events. At a given number of degrees of crankshaft rotation, shown at the degree wheel, the intake valve opens. This is how we confirm camshaft specifications. But this is only the beginning.

At a given number of degrees of crankshaft rotation, the exhaust valve opens.

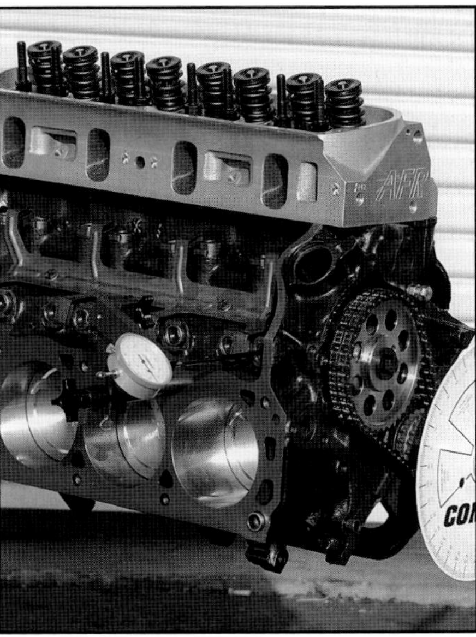

With a degree wheel, we can also determine crankshaft integrity. We do this by determining when each piston reaches top dead center. This tells us a lot about crankshaft journal indexing.

intake and exhaust side. We tend to run dual-pattern profiles whenever we're pushing the revs up. Typically, a dual-pattern camshaft will run a shorter exhaust valve duration due to less time required to scavenge the exhaust gasses at high RPM. It is also beneficial whenever we're running nitrous, supercharging, or turbocharging, where exhaust scavenging is rapid and furious. Running a dual-pattern camshaft on the street doesn't make much sense because we lose torque and fuel economy at low and mid-RPM ranges. Keeping the exhaust valve open longer is what helps a street engine.

Racing Camshafts

If you're building an engine for racing, it is a different picture than we find with street engines. Camshaft profile in a racing engine depends upon the type of racing you're going to do, vehicle weight and type, even the type of transmission and rear axle ratio.

Drag racing mandates a different camshaft profile than road or circle track racing. A short track racing engine will need to be able to produce huge amounts of torque in short order, for example. The same is true for a drag racer. These issues teach us something about engine breathing. Breathing effectiveness is determined by camshaft profile.

Lobe separation for the drag racing camshaft should be between 104 and 118 degrees. There is a broad range because drag racing needs can vary quite a bit. This is where you have to custom dial in your application with a camshaft grinder. Most camshaft grinders have computation charts that show the right cam for your application. As your needs change, so must the camshaft profile.

If you're going road racing, lobe separation becomes more specific, probably somewhere in the 106 degree range. Some cam grinders push lobe separation higher for the circle track engine, depending on conditions. Generally, the higher the lobe separation, the broader the torque curve (more torque over a broader RPM range).

Why Degree A Camshaft?

Making power isn't just about a longer stroke, large-port heads, big carburetor, and a lumpy camshaft. It is also about the science of setting up your engine properly. It is important to know why we degree camshafts after they're installed inside an engine, and what this accomplishes.

Degreeing a camshaft is like a Columbo investigation. Call it, "just one more thing, Sir..." in your quest to learn the truth about power. The most basic reason for degreeing a camshaft is to determine that you have the correct grind for the job. Camshaft grinders today employ the most advanced technology available. As a result, few faulty camshafts ever make it to the consumer. However, camshafts do get packaged incorrectly at times, which means you could receive a completely different grind than appears on the cam card and packaging. All the more reason to degree the cam going in.

We degree a camshaft by bolting a degree wheel to the crankshaft, cranking the number one piston to top dead center, and installing a timing pointer. You can get a degree wheel from Comp Cams, Crane Cams, Performance Automotive Warehouse, and any number of other performance shops across the country.

We find top dead center with a bolt-on piston stop that screws into the spark plug hole or at the top of the block with

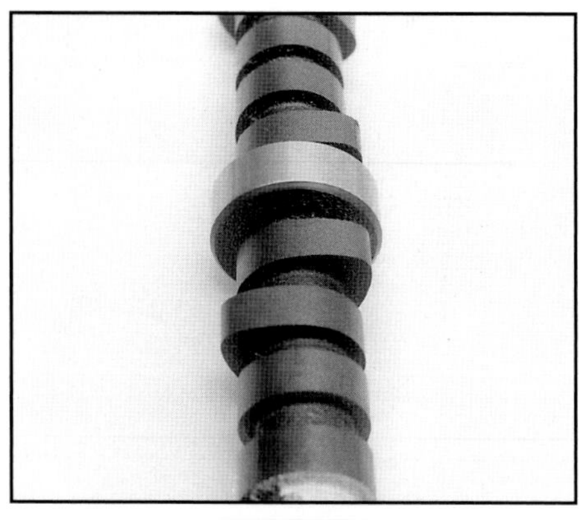

Camshaft design can be confusing. Think of the cam lobe in geographical regions as it travels against the lifter – opening ramp, opening flank, nose, closing flank, closing ramp, then the heel. The base circle is the part of the lobe that doesn't generate lift.

This is a flat tappet camshaft. Notice the cam lobe profile (shape). It is more aggressive by nature even with a stock grind. Streetability suffers when we increase lift and duration, which make the idle rough and erodes manifold vacuum.

Roller camshafts are identifiable by their smooth radiused lobes. Note the shine and more rounded shape. Roller camshafts are more flexible because they allow for a more aggressive amount of lift and duration without disturbing idle quality. Lift can be as much as .540 inch with only minor changes in idle quality.

the head removed. We suggest doing this with the cylinder head removed, which provides the greatest accuracy. Begin this process by turning the crankshaft clockwise until #1 piston comes up to top dead center. With the cylinder head installed, hold your thumb over the spark plug hole and listen to the air being forced out by the piston. The air will stop when you reach top dead center.

At this point, both timing marks on the crank and camshaft sprockets should be in alignment at 12 and 6 o'clock. Install the degree wheel next and align the bolt-on timing pointer. With all of this accomplished, the number one piston should be at top dead center, with the degree wheel and pointer at zero degrees. This becomes our base point of reference. Everything from here on out becomes BTDC (before top dead center) or ATDC (after top dead center). The intake valve will open at a given number of degrees after top dead center and close at a given number of degrees before top dead center. The exhaust valve will open at a given number of degrees before top dead center and close a given number of degrees after top dead center. Much of this depends on valve overlap.

Induction

Just as the camshaft and valvetrain determine an engine's personality, so does the induction system. With electronic fuel injection, planning and execution is pretty straightforward because manufacturers have done most of the work for you. Most of it is boiler-plate where components are designed specifically to work together in harmony. Manufacturers walk you right through the process with a package of components that will work well together. You can even fine tune it to work well with your particular application.

For those of you who choose carburetion, your job as an engine performance planner becomes more involved. Because carburetion is decidedly involved just by itself, we're going to address it first. Carbureted street engines need long intake runners in order to produce good low and mid-range torque. Longer intake runners are found in dual-

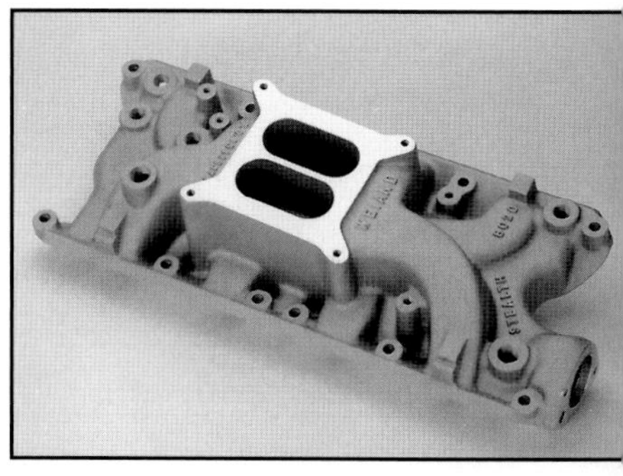

Street engines need to produce good low end torque. To get there, they need a dual plane intake manifold like this Weiand Stealth cast-aluminum high-rise manifold. The Stealth has long intake runners which help the engine make torque at lower RPM ranges.

plane intake manifolds like the Edelbrock Performer and Weiand Stealth. Installing an aftermarket manifold like the Performer or Stealth improves performance because it improves airflow velocity into the combustion chambers. This is likely one of the best modifications you can make to a street engine without selling off the farm.

It is easy to be lulled into believing a larger carburetor, more aggressive camshaft, and large-port heads will make more power. But this isn't always true, especially in budget street engines. Induction, camshaft, and heads should always synch with your performance mission. What's more, you want your engine to survive while making all that power. Your engine build plan needs to include a common sense approach that involves the right selection and packaging of parts for best results.

If you're building a driver for the daily commute, you're going to have to compromise to some degree in terms of performance if you want reliability and some level of fuel economy. We compromise because radical engines don't do well for the daily drive. They also struggle to pass a smog check, depending on where you live. Radical camshaft profiles give the engine a rough idle, which can be frustrating in traffic and make it virtually impossible to pass a smog check. Loud mufflers can cause hearing damage and make for an annoying drive. They can also get you a ticket for noise pollution in

Swap meets offer a wealth of used high-rise dual and single-plane manifolds. The older Cobra high-rise manifolds were based on the Edelbrock F4B high-rise of the 1960s and 1970s. They don't always come cheap, but they offer a period-specific look.

some communities. A high compression ratio can cause overheating when traffic comes to a stop. Over-carburetion fouls spark plugs and pollutes the air.

This brings us to another valid point – air pollution. Environmentalists and performance enthusiasts don't get along, but it is our responsibility as performance enthusiasts to build and tune our engines for cleaner emissions and better human health. This doesn't mean you have to go out and buy catalytic converters and a smog pump. It does mean you need to package your induction and ignition systems for optimum emissions performance at the tail pipe. To sum it up, clean up your performance act.

A big 750 or 850cfm carburetor looks good and works well at the drag strip, cruising spot, and car show. However, these are not practical carburetors for everyday street use where clean

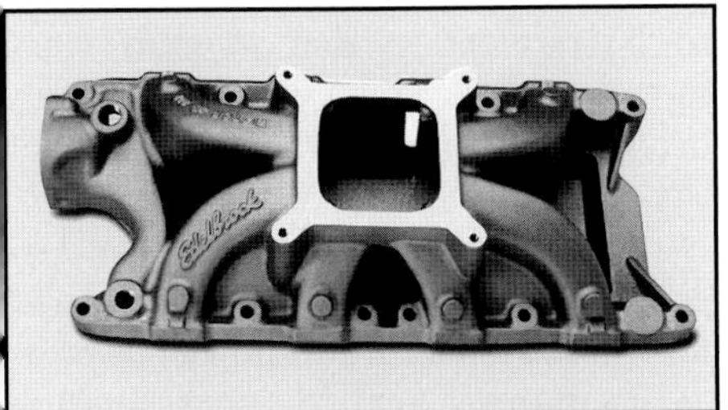

High-revving engines that do most of their work at high RPM need a deep-breathing single-plane manifold with shorter intake runners. A single-plane manifold helps the engine make torque at high revs.

emissions and some level of fuel efficiency are important. We want carburetor size and engine mission to be compatible for optimum performance and cleaner emissions. If you think this clean emissions issue is a lot of nonsense, consider the last time you were behind a hopped up vintage muscle car or street rod in traffic. The obnoxious exhaust gasses made your eyes water, didn't they? Think of the other guy and clean up your filthy tailpipe emissions. And consider this, if your vehicle falls under the guidelines of state emission laws and smog checks, the law doesn't give you a choice. Clean up your exhaust emission or face revocation of your license plates in some states.

Building an environmentally responsible engine doesn't have to be difficult either. Carbureted engines are not going to burn as clean as their fuel-injected counterparts. If you can run electronic fuel injection, do so for cleaner air. Do so for your own health and for the sake of others who breathe. If you can't, be conservative in your performance plan and dial in the right size carburetor.

Instead of a 750 or 850cfm carburetor, opt for a 600 or 650cfm carb and see how your engine performs. A carburetor that's too small will quickly become apparent in the absence of torque as RPM increases. Large carburetors give us more torque on the high end. Smaller carburetors do well on the low end. Choosing the right amount of carburetion is often trial and error.

Keep proper carburetor jetting in mind too. Jets that are too large will make the engine run rich or fat, watering the eyes of those who have to follow you. Jets that are too small can be harmful if you're leaning on it hard and lean detonation burns a hole in a piston. Again, fine tune carburetor and jet sizing for best results. And always err on the side of rich versus lean for longer engine life. If you really want to make a lasting impression on the community, go for a smog check each time you make a carb/jet change and see what it does for emissions. Cleaner air is up to all of us.

Dual-plane, high-rise manifolds don't always have to be new ones

Although you are probably inclined to top your stroker with a Holley, Demon, Edelbrock, or Carter carburetor, the most reliable carburetor going is the factory Ford Autolite 4100 four-barrel. It is available in sizes ranging from 480cfm to 600cfm. With vacuum secondaries, it makes a great street carburetor for daily use. However, this is not a racing carburetor.

This is the Race Demon carburetor from Barry Grant. Available in sizes ranging from 650 to 850 cfm, the Race Demon offers outstanding performance and is easy to tune.

either. Vintage Cobra and Edelbrock dual-plane, high-rise manifolds yield the benefits of low-end torque and high-RPM breathing, and they can be found at swap meets. They do well on the street in stop and go driving, and they yield plenty of power when it's time to rock. Single-plane intake manifolds like the Edelbrock Torker, Torker II, Tarantula, and even the Streetmaster are not good street manifolds because they're designed to make torque at 3000 to 7000 rpm. However, we see them on a wide variety of street engines where a good dual-plane manifold would work much better.

Long intake runners and a dual-plane design are but two reasons why

Carburetor Sizing Quick Reference Chart

Engine Displacement	Suggested Carburetor Size
260 to 310ci	500 cfm 4V (600 cfm if fitted with high-performance camshaft and heads)
310 to 355ci	500–600 cfm (600–650 cfm if fitted with high-performance camshaft and heads)
355 to 390ci	600–650 cfm (650–700 cfm if fitted with high-performance camshaft and heads)
390 to 450ci	650 cfm (700–750 cfm if fitted with high-performance camshaft and heads)

we can achieve good low and mid-range torque from a carbureted engine. We also want cool air both ahead of the carburetor and beneath it. To get cool air before the carburetor, we need to source cool air from outside. Underhood air is much hotter than the ambient air outside. If we can drop the intake air temperature by 50 to 80 degrees F, this will make a considerable difference in thermal expansion inside the combustion chamber. We can net nearly 10 percent more power this way.

We get cooler air with a hood scoop or a ram-air scoop at the leading edge of the vehicle. Ram air can be sourced through the radiator support or beneath the front bumper. Ram-air kits can be sourced from Summit Racing Equipment, Performance Automotive Warehouse (PAW), or your favorite speed shop. The choice is yours.

Getting cool induction air after the carburetor requires closing off the manifold heat passages from the exhaust side of the cylinder head. We do this during intake manifold installation by installing the manifold heat block-off plates included in most intake manifold gasket kits. Manifold heat is needed only when the outside air is really cold. A cold intake manifold does not allow the fuel to atomize as well as it does in a hot manifold, which causes hesitation and stumbling. We curb this problem by adjusting the choke to remain on for a longer period of time. Then, when the engine is warm, we still have a cool manifold that offers us better performance.

A popular myth is that we make more power by removing the air cleaner. The thing is, removing the air cleaner allows dirt and grit inside your engine, which shortens engine life. We want a low restriction air cleaner that will effectively filter out dirt while allowing healthy breathing at the same time. K&N air filters meet the mission effectively, but they don't come cheap. They can be washed and reused, which actually saves you money long term because K&N claims these filters can last a million miles. What's more, they outperform the nearest competitor by a wide margin. A K&N air filter is money well spent in terms of performance and longevity. The new K&N filter with a separate filter in the lid improves breathing even more.

One of the biggest mistakes enthusiasts make is over-carburetion. It may surprise you to know engines don't need as much carburetion as you might think. The formula is simple, and without a lot of complex engine math. Small blocks ranging from 221 to 302ci need no more than 500cfm for street use. The 351W and 351C need from 500 to 600cfm. Big blocks displacing 352 to 390ci need 600 to 650cfm. Larger displacements of 406 to 428ci need from 650 to 750cfm. These numbers may sound modest, but they're all a healthy street engine needs. We have to laugh whenever we see a mildly modified street 302ci small-block with a 750cfm Holley double-pumper. This is way too much carburetor.

The exception to our carburetion formula is racing applications. When we're going racing, our engine needs more carburetor if it's going to make torque. Small-blocks can tolerate 600 to 650cfm in racing applications. Higher displacement applications up to 390ci need 700 to 850 cfm. Beyond 390ci, we need 850 to 1050 cfm. Performance tuning is where we learn how much carburetor we're going to need.

Over-carburetion on a street engine wastes fuel and pollutes the air. Too much fuel can be as bad for an engine as not enough. Too much fuel washes precious lubricating oil off the cylinder walls and fouls spark plugs. Your performance objective should also include being environmentally responsible. Plan and tune for cleaner air, not just power. Performance today is a two-way street – efficiency and power. With efficiency, we get power and clean air.

Through the years, we have seen and used a wide variety of carburetors on Ford V-8s. Although the Holley 1850, 4150, and 4160 are legendary performance carburetors, they don't enjoy the reliability of the Autolite 4100 – that plain Jane four-throat carburetor Ford installed on a wide variety of V-8s from 1957-1966. The 4100 is very reliable and it offers the same level of performance we're used to with the Holley. Holley carburetors struggle with bowl leakage and metering block difficulties. Metering block passages tend to clog easily, causing idle and driveability problems. We don't see these problems with the Autolite 4100.

Some Holley carbs perform well for years while others tend to be high maintenance. The 1850, 4150, and 4160 tend to be challenging due to their small metering block passages that can easily become clogged. This is a problematic issue common to Holley carburetors.

For most street engines, we suggest a Holley with vacuum secondaries for a smooth transition into high power. Vacuum secondaries work better in street use because they function only when we need them – at wide-open throttle. Mechanical secondaries make more sense in racing use because they come into play more quickly in a linear fashion.

Our message here for the street buff is simple. Be realistic about how your engine will be used and don't kid yourself. Most of your driving will be normal stop and go with open highway tossed in for good mix. Weekend drag racing will be the exception, not the rule. Build an engine you can live with on a daily basis, then make tuning changes for weekend fun. You need an intake manifold and carburetor that will give you good acceleration and driveability coupled with clean emissions. Companies like Edelbrock and Weiand have done extensive research to improve the performance of their products including improved emissions. Good dual-plane street manifolds like the Performer and Stealth get the job done nicely.

The Autolite 4100 mentioned earlier, available in sizes ranging from 480 to 600 cfm, is a better street performance carburetor than the Holley from a reliability standpoint. It delivers plenty of power on demand and will go for years without much in the way of service. The only exception to this rule is California with its destructive oxygenated fuels that harm older fuel systems. You can expect failing gaskets, seals, and rubber hoses with the California fuel additive MTB. For California vehicles, we suggest hard lining your fuel system between the fuel pump and carburetor and the use of steel reinforced hoses where necessary to prevent fuel leakage and fires.

When your performance requirements mandate something more aggressive than the Autolite 4100, opt for that weekend Holley racing experience with a simple carb swap when you want to go racing. Holleys and Autolite are easily interchanged in an afternoon, which enables you to live peacefully with both.

Where carbureted induction systems become tricky is late-model 5.0L High Output V-8 engines because we must build an engine that will pass both a visual and tailpipe emissions smog check. Although you might be tempted to dig your heels in on this one, your goal should always be cleaner emissions for the daily driver.

Choosing A Casting

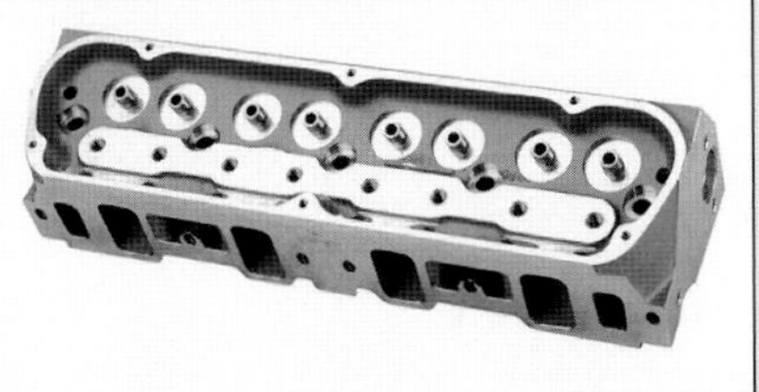

Choosing a block or cylinder-head casting is a matter of knowing what to look for. Seasoned engine builders we know have certain castings they favor and others they like to stay away from. When it comes to cylinder blocks, the word on the street is simple. Builders like older blocks from 1962 through the mid-1970s. It appears Ford went through a period during the late 1970s into the early 1980s where flawed castings seem to be epidemic. Core shift, cracking, and other irregularities seem to plague Ford castings of the period. But this theory isn't completely in stone. Each prospective casting needs close inspection before you should proceed further.

Whenever you are shopping for a block casting, also keep bore size in mind. Ascertain bore size before laying down the cash. Despite what a lot of builders will tell you, it is rarely a good idea to bore a small-block Ford beyond .060-inch oversize. Limit your overbore to .040-inch oversize maximum. If you have found a .040-inch oversize block, move on. A .030-inch oversize block can be honed out to .040-inch oversize.

Another area of concern is line bore. It is a good idea to check the line bore of any prospective block casting. This isn't always possible. It is a good idea to get a guarantee with any casting you buy. Make sure you have the option of returning a flawed casting if it is proven irregular or damaged beyond repair. Irregular line bores can be bored and/or honed to take out the irregular alignment.

While you're at it, make sure the block deck has never been milled. This can be accomplished by sonic-checking, which tells you the thickness of the deck. Thin decks should be passed up. You need room for minor mill work if the deck is warped. And if you're going to blow squeeze or supercharge your stroker, there must be room at the deck for o-ring grooves.

Cylinder Heads

When we think of the camshaft and valvetrain as our engine's frontal lobe, it becomes easier to understand how an engine's personality is formed. Nothing determines an engine's personality more than the camshaft and valvetrain. With this in mind, what will cylinder heads do for an engine's personality? Cylinder heads have to synch with the engine's camshaft profile. It all has to be a cohesive, working package.

There is little point in fitting your small-block Ford with a radical camshaft if the cylinder heads won't allow the camshaft to work to its greatest potential. By the same token, why bother with 2.02-inch intake valves if you're running a mild street camshaft. Camshaft and cylinder head must work shoulder-to-shoulder for best results.

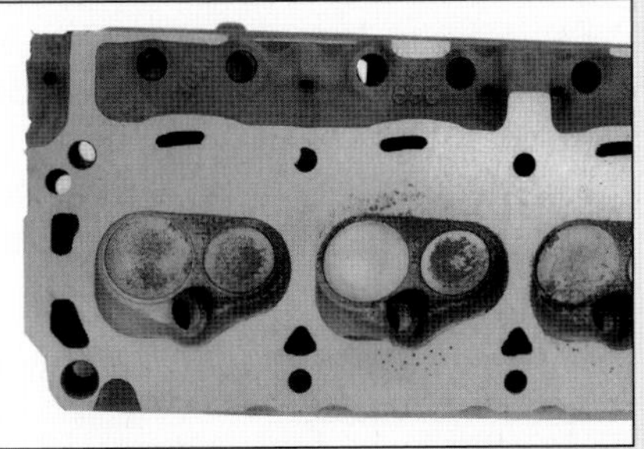

The 1962-1973 289/302 head has 57cc chambers for a healthy compression ratio. One exception to this pattern is the 1968 302-4V head (not pictured), with 53cc chambers for even greater compression. Ford controlled the compression with flat-top and dished pistons. Flat-tops yielded around 10.0:1 compression. Dished pistons dropped the compression by one point to 9.0:1.

Choosing A Casting (continued)

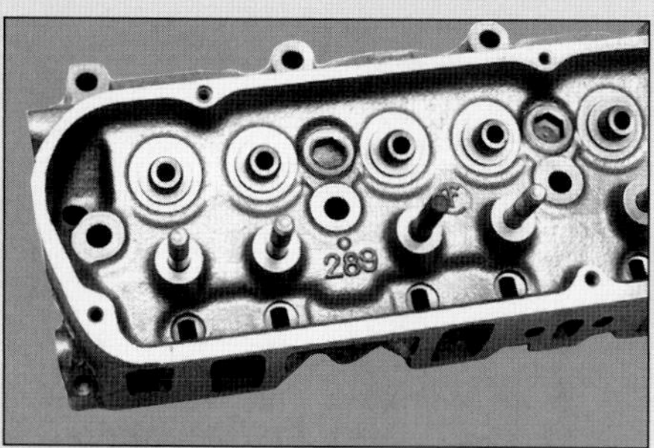

The 1963-67 289 High Performance head is a rare casting useful to restorers only. Port and valve size are the same as the 289-2V/4V casting. What makes the Hi-Po head distinctive is valve spring pockets and screw-in rocker arm studs for stability at high revs. Spend your money wisely on the right factory heads and a port job, or good aftermarket heads that will yield more power.

So how do we match up cylinder heads and camshaft? First, what can you afford in the cylinder head department? If you are limited to factory castings, such as 351W cylinder heads, there remains a lot you can do. A good port job, coupled with larger valves, makes for a respectable cylinder head.

Despite everything you're going to learn about porting 289/302 heads in this book, you're going to find the 1969-71 351W head with a 60cc chamber is the best factory casting for a 289/302 build-up. The 351W

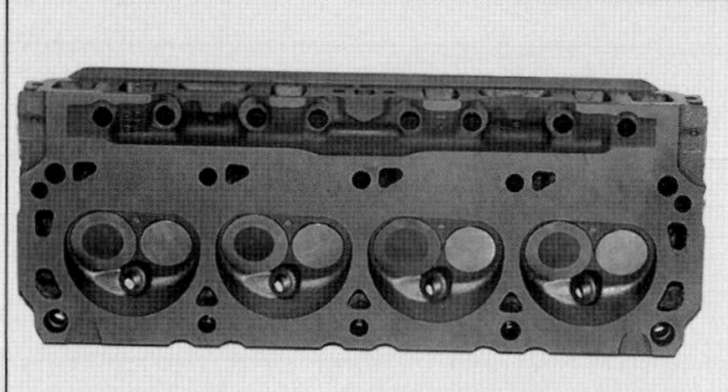

Small-block Ford heads after 1973 had larger chambers for reduced compression. They also have hardened exhaust valve seats for use with unleaded fuels. From 1975-up, these heads have smaller 14mm spark plugs.

head offers larger intake and exhaust valves, and larger ports. This is a decision that is easy to make. Probably the greatest challenge will be finding 1969-71 351W head castings.

Another thing to consider in selecting a cylinder head is desired compression ratio. Because you are reading this book, we presume you are considering a stroker. A stroker has compression considerations due to the increased stroke. If you're going to supercharge or blow nitrous through the engine, compression becomes even a greater issue to be considered carefully. You can adjust compression with proper piston selection, or you can search for the right cylinder head combustion chamber size. As the 1970s progressed, chamber sizes grew larger in

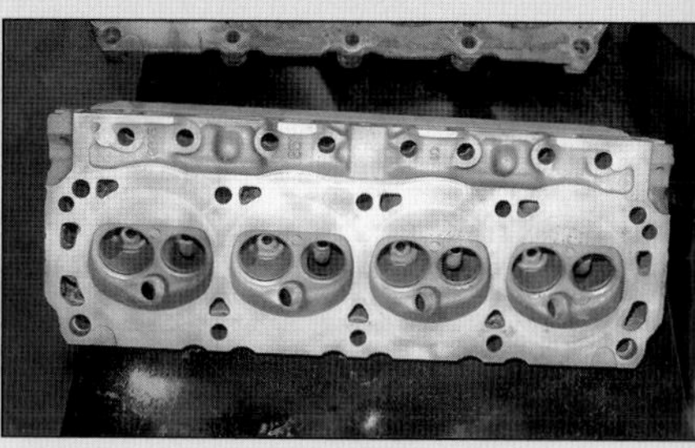

The best factory head for 289/30 engines is the 1969-1973 351W head wit larger ports and valves. This head pro vides good, affordable power when afte market heads are priced out of reach.

Pressed-in rocker arm studs should b replaced with screw-in studs wit pushrod guide plates if you are goin with factory heads.

stock castings because compression ratio dropped. Chamber sizes generally increasec to 69cc and higher to get compression down

Small-Block Ford Factory Cylinder Head Identification Chart

(Bold Indicates High Performance or Change in Valve/Port Size)

Cubic Inch Year	Casting Number	Chamber Size	Valve Size	Port Size
221ci 1962-63	C2OE-A C2OE-B C2OE-C C2OE-D C2OE-E C3OE-A	45–51cc	1.59″ Int. 1.39″Exh.	1.76″ x 1.00″ Int. 1.24″ x 1.00″ Exh.
255ci 1980-81	E0SE-AB	53.6–56cc	1.68″ Int. 1.46″ Exh.	N/A
260ci 1962-63	C2OE-F C3OE-B	52–55cc	1.59″ Int. 1.39″ Exh.	1.76″ x 1.00″ Int. 1.24″ x 1.00″ Exh.
260ci 1964	C4OE-B	52–55cc	1.67″ Int. 1.45″ Exh.	1.76″ x 1.00″ Int. 1.24″ x 1.00″ Exh.
289ci 1963-67	C3AE-F C3OE-E C3OE-F C4AE-C	52–55cc	1.78″ Int. 1.45″ Exh.	1.94″ x 1.04″ Int. 1.24″ x 1.00″ Exh.

Choosing A Casting (continued)

Cubic Inch Year	Casting Number	Chamber Size	Valve Size	Port Size
	C5DE-B			
	C6DE-G			
	C6OE-C (Thermactor)			
	C6OE-E (Thermactor)		63cc	
	C6OE-M			
	C7OE-A (Thermactor)			
	C7OE-B (Thermactor)			
	C7OE-C			
	C7OZ-B (Thermactor)			
	C7ZE-A (Thermactor)			
	C8OE-D (Thermactor)			
	C8OE-L (Thermactor)			
	C8OE-M (Thermactor)			
289ci	**C3OE**	**52–55cc**	1.78" Int.	1.94" x 1.04" Int.
1963-67	**C4OE-B**		1.45" Exh.	1.24" x 1.00" Exh.
High	**C5OE-A**			
Perf.	**C5AE-E**			
289ci	**C7ZZ-B**	**52–55cc**	1.78" Int.	1.94" x 1.04" Int.
1963-67			1.45" Exh.	1.24" x 1.00" Exh.
Service Head				
302ci	C7OE-C	69cc	1.78" Int.	1.94" x 1.04" Int.
1968-78	C7OE-G		1.45" Exh.	1.24" x 1.00" Exh.
	C8OE-F (4V)			
	C8OE-J			
	C8OE-K (Thermactor)			
	C8OE-L (Thermactor)			
	C8OE-M	58.2cc		
	C8AE-J			
	C8DE-F			
	C9TE-C (Truck Head)			
	D0OE-B			
	D1TZ-A (Truck Head)			
	D2OE-BA			
	D5OE-GA			
	D5OE-A3A			
	D5OE-A3B			
	D7OE-DA			
	D8OE-AB			
302ci	D9AE-AA	67.5–70cc	1.78" Int.	1.94" x 1.04" Int.
1979-84			1.46" Exh.	1.24" x 1.00" Exh.
302ci	**E5AE-CA**	67–70cc	1.78" Int.	1.94" x 1.04" Int.
1985			1.46" Exh.	1.24" x 1.00" Exh.
302ci	**E6AE-AA**	62–65cc	1.78" Int.	1.94" x 1.04" Int.
1986			1.46" Exh.	1.24" x 1.00" Exh.

Cubic Inch Year	Casting Number	Chamber Size	Valve Size	Port Size
302ci	**E5TE-PA**	62–65cc	1.78" Int.	1.94" x 1.04" Int.
1987-93	**E7TE-PA**		1.46" Exh.	1.24" x 1.00" Exh.
302ci	**F3ZE-AA**	60–63cc	1.84" Int.	
1993			1.54" Exh.	
Cobra				
302ci	**F4ZE-AA**	60–63cc	1.84" Int.	
1994-95			1.54" Exh.	
Cobra				
302ci	**F1ZE-AA**	63–66cc	1.84" Int.	
1996-97			1.46" Exh.	
Explorer				
302ci	**F7ZE-AA**	58–61cc	1.84" Int.	
1997-2000			1.46" Exh.	
Explorer				
302ci	**C9ZE-A**	61–64cc	2.23" Int.	2.50" x 1.75" Int.
1969-70	**C9ZE-C**	58cc	1.71" Exh.	2.00" x 1.74" Exh.
Boss 302	**D0ZE-A**		2.19" Int.	2.50" x 1.75" Int.
	D1ZE-A		1.71" Exh.	2.00" x 1.74" Exh.
351W	C9OE-B	60cc	1.84" Int.	1.94" x 1.76" Int.
1969-84	C9OE-D		1.54" Exh.	1.24" x 1.00" Exh.
	D0OE-C	69cc		
	D0OE-G		1.78" Int.	1.94" x 1.04" Int.
	D5TE-EB (Truck)		1.45" Exh.	1.24" x 1.00" Exh.
	D7OE-A			
	D8OE-A			
	D8OE-AB			
351W	E5AE-CA	67–70cc	1.78" Int.	1.94" x 1.04" Int.
1985-86			1.45" Exh.	1.24" x 1.00" Exh.
351W	E7TE-PA	62–65cc	1.78" Int.	1.94" x 1.04" Int.
1987-95			1.45" Exh.	1.24" x 1.00" Exh.
351C	D0AE-E	74–77cc	2.04" Int.	2.02" x 1.65" Int.
1970-74	D0AE-J	61–64cc	1.67" Exh.	1.84" x 1.38" Exhaust
	D0AE-G (4V)		2.19" Int.	2.50" x 1.75" Intake
	D0AE-H (4V)		1.71" Exh.	2.00" x 1.74" Exhaust
	D0AE-M (4V)	74–77cc		
	D0AE-N (4V)	61–64cc	2.04" Int.	2.02" x 1.65" Int.
	D0AE-R (4V)		1.67" Exh.	1.84" x 1.38" Exh.
	D1AE-AA (2V)		2.19" Int.	2.50" x 1.75" Int.
	D1AE-CB (2V)		1.71" Exh.	2.00" x 1.74" Exh.
	D1AE-GA (4V)		2.19" Int.	2.50" x 1.75" Int.
	D1ZE-DA (CJ)	**73–76cc**	1.71" Exh.	2.00" x 1.74" Exh.
	D1ZE-B (Boss)	**64–67cc**	2.19" Int.	2.50" x 1.75" Int.
	D2ZE-A (HO)	**73–76cc**	1.71" Exh.	2.00" x 1.74" Exh.
	D3ZE-AA (CJ)	**73–76cc**		

Choosing A Casting (continued)

Aftermarket Cylinder Heads

The aftermarket brings us so much in terms of choice today. There has never been a better selection of cylinder heads available in Ford performance history. Ford Racing Performance Parts (FRPP) has done its homework when it comes to availability and choice. Choice ranges from the stock-appearing cast iron and aluminum GT-40 head casting all the way up to a Yates-style NASCAR head.

Few aftermarket companies are more committed to Ford performance than Edelbrock. Because the Edelbrock family races Fords, their research and development people have spent a lot of flow bench and dyno time developing small-block Ford cylinder heads for virtually every need out there.

Across Los Angeles from Edelbrock is Airflow Research (AFR). Like Edelbrock, AFR has spent a lot of time developing some of the best small-block Ford cylinder heads on the market. In fact, no one offers a broader selection of cylinder heads for small-block Fords than AFR. You can custom dial-in your cylinder head selection by simply visiting AFR's website and examining its selection of castings.

The most basic AFR street head is the 165cc, available in two styles – street emission legal, and street/strip, without the manifold heat passages. The 165 is an easy bolt-on head void of valve clearance issues thanks to its 1.90-inch intake valves. Because chamber sizes range from 58 to 61cc, you can dial in your AFR purchase for your particular application. Older 289 and 302 engines want the smaller 58 chambers. Newer applications like the larger 61cc chamber. The AFR 185cc has larger 2.02-inch intake valves and the same duo of chamber sizes at 58 or 61cc.

The AFR 165cc and 185cc castings are excellent street and strip heads. Castings designed for street and strip don't have the intake manifold heat passages necessary for good warm-up and cleaner emissions. AFR street heads have the manifold heat passages, which improve cold start performance.

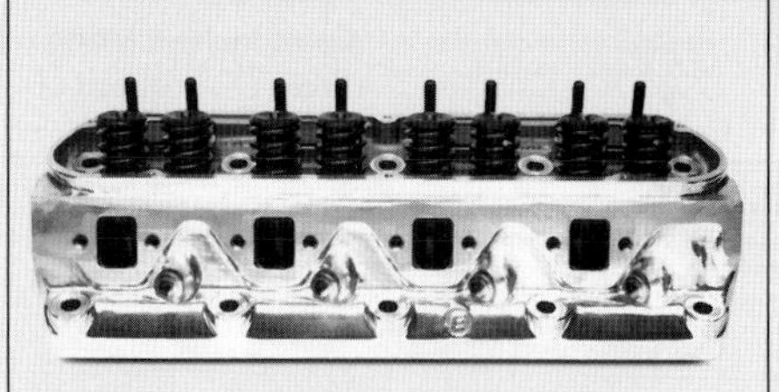

This is the Edelbrock Performer RPM cylinder head (#60329) with 1.94-inch intake and 1.60-inch exhaust valves. With 60cc chambers, this is a nice head for early and late-model small-block Fords alike.

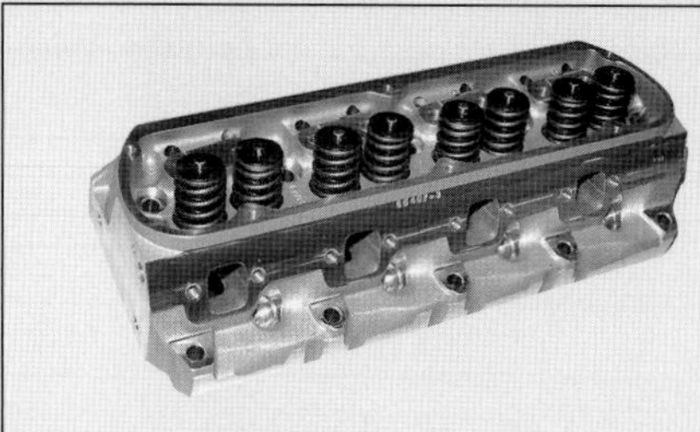

AFR cylinder head technology begin with the AFR 165cc head with 1.94-inc intake and 1.60-inch exhaust valves Chamber volumes include 58, 61, o 69cc. This is a street legal head fo smog-check applications.

When we step up to the AFR 205 and 225cc heads, we're looking at race head designed more for high-RPM use and breathing. The 205 and 225cc heads do their best work at high RPM. These head are also designed more for higher displacements between 331 and 392ci. This mean they work quite well on stroked 302 and 351W based engines. Both heads have huge 2.08-inch valves, which can present piston and cylinder clearance issues in some applications.

What can AFR heads do for your small-block? Take a look at the flow bench numbers compiled by AFR. These number were observed at 28-inches of water with 1 7/8-inch exhaust pipe.

AFR Flow Bench Results

AFR Head/Number	Intake Flow	Exhaust Flow
AFR 165cc Street Head AFR 165cc Street/Strip	250cfm @ .600" Valve Lift	191cfm @ .600" Valve Lift
AFR 185cc Street Head AFR 185cc Street/Strip	277cfm @ .600" Valve Lift	191cfm @ .600" Valve Lift
AFR 205cc Race Head	308cfm @ .600" Valve Lift 314cfm @ .700" Valve Lift	231cfm @ .600" Valve Lift 236cfm @ .700" Valve Lift
AFR 225cc Race Head	315cfm @ .600" Valve Lift 325cfm @ .700" Valve Lift	250cfm @ .600" Valve Lift 255cfm @ .700" Valve Lift

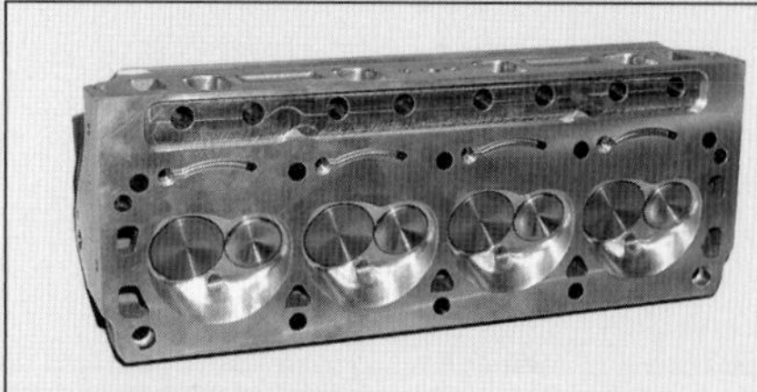

The AFR 185cc aluminum head is an outstanding street head with 2.02-inch intake and 1.60-inch exhaust valves Piston-to-valve clearance is critical here because the 2.02-inch intake valve don't always clear. Check this issue out before buying.

Choosing A Casting (continued)

Aftermarket Cylinder Head Quick Reference Guide

Manufacturer	Type/Number	Intake Valve	Exhaust Valve	Chamber Size
AFR	Street 165cc	1.90″	1.60″	58 or 61cc
AFR	Street/Strip 165cc	1.90″	1.60″	58 or 61cc
AFR	Street 185cc	2.02″	1.60″	58 or 61 cc
AFR	Street/Strip 185cc	2.02″	1.60″	58 or 61cc
AFR	205cc SBF Race Head	2.08″	1.60″	60 or 71cc
AFR	225cc SBF Race Head	2.08″	1.60″	60cc
Edelbrock	Performer #60319 Bare #60329 Assem.	1.90″	1.60″	60cc
Edelbrock	Performer #60349	2.02″	1.60″	60cc
Edelbrock	Performer #60279 Assem. Loc-Wire	2.02″	1.60″	60cc
Edelbrock	Performer #60219 Bare #60229 Assem. Non-Emissions	1.90″	1.60″	60cc
Edelbrock	Performer #60249 Bare #60259 Assem. Non-Emissions	2.02″	1.60″	60cc
Edelbrock	Performer #60259 Assem. Loc-Wire	2.02″	1.60″	60cc
Edelbrock	Performer #602159 Polished	2.02″	1.60″	60cc
Edelbrock	Performer 5.0L/5.8L #60369 Bare #60379 Assem.	1.90″	1.60″	60cc
Edelbrock	Performer 5.0L/5.8L #60289 Assem. Loc-Wire	1.90″	1.60″	60cc
Edelbrock	Performer 5.0L/5.8L #60389 Bare #60399 Assem.	2.02″	1.60″	60cc
Edelbrock	Performer 5.0L/5.8L #60299 Assem. Loc-Wire	2.02″	1.60″	60cc
Edelbrock	Victor Jr. #77169 Bare #77179 with valves only #77189 with valves, springs and keepers. #77199 with valves, springs and keepers for mechanical roller cams.	2.05″	1.60″	60cc
Edelbrock	Victor Jr. #77389 Bare	2.05″	1.60″	70cc
Edelbrock	Victor Jr. CNC #61269 Bare Std. Exhaust Pattern	2.10″	1.60″	60cc
Edelbrock	Victor Jr. CNC #61279 Bare J302 Pattern	2.10″	1.60″	60cc
Edelbrock	Glidden Victor CNC #61099 Bare	N/A	N/A	56cc
Edelbrock	Glidden Victor CNC #77099 Bare For 9.2″ Blocks with 9.5″ manifold.	N/A	N/A	56cc
Edelbrock	Victor Ford #77219 Bare	N/A	N/A	47cc
Edelbrock	Chapman Victor CNC 276cc Head #61299 Bare	N/A	N/A	60cc
Edelbrock	Chapman Victor CNC 255cc Head #77289 Bare	N/A	N/A	50cc
Edelbrock	Chapman Victor CNC 255cc Head #77299	N/A	N/A	61cc
FORD	GT-40 "Turbo-Swirl" Aluminum M-6049-Y302 (Bare Head) M-6049-Y303 (Complete)	1.94″	1.60″	64cc
FORD	GT-40X "Turbo-Swirl" Aluminum M-6049-X302 (Bare Head) M-6049-X303 (Complete)	1.94″	1.54″	64cc
FORD	GT-40X "Turbo-Swirl" Aluminum M-6049-X304 (Bare Head) M-6049-X305 (Complete)	1.94″	1.54″	58cc
FORD	Sportsman Short Track Cast Iron M-6049-N351	2.02″	1.60″	64cc
FORD	"Z" Head Aluminum	2.02″	1.60″	64cc
TRICK FLOW	Twisted Wedge Aluminum TFS-51400002	2.02″	1.60″	61cc
TRICK FLOW	Twisted Wedge	2.02″	1.60″	61cc

Choosing A Casting (concluded)

Aftermarket Cylinder Head Quick Reference Guide (continued)

Manufacturer	Type/Number	Intake Valve	Exhaust Valve	Chamber Size
	Aluminum TFS-51400003			
TRICK FLOW	Track Heat Aluminum TFS-52400010	2.02"	1.60"	61cc
TRICK FLOW	Track Heat Aluminum TFS-52400011	2.02"	1.60"	61cc
TRICK FLOW	R-Series Aluminum TFS-52400001	2.08"	1.60"	61cc
TRICK FLOW	R-Series Aluminum TFS-52400101	2.08"	1.60"	61cc
TRICK FLOW	R-Series Aluminum TFS-52400201	2.08"	1.60"	61cc
TRICK FLOW	R-Series Aluminum TFS-52400100	2.08"	1.60"	61cc
TRICK FLOW	R-Series Aluminum TFS-52400200	2.08"	1.60"	61cc
TRICK FLOW	High Port Aluminum TFS-51700001	2.02"	1.60"	64cc
TRICK FLOW	High Port Aluminum TFS-51700002	2.02"	1.60"	64cc
WORLD PRODUCTS	Windsor Jr. Cast Iron 053030 (Bare)	1.94"	1.60"	58cc
WORLD PRODUCTS	Windsor Jr. Cast Iron 053030-1 (Hydraulic)	1.94"	1.60"	58cc

Manufacturer	Type/Number	Intake Valve	Exhaust Valve	Chamber Size
WORLD PRODUCTS	Windsor Jr. Cast Iron 053030-2 (Hydraulic Roller)	1.94"	1.60"	58cc
WORLD PRODUCTS	Windsor Jr. Cast Iron 053030-3 (Solid Roller)	1.94"	1.60"	58cc
WORLD PRODUCTS	Windsor Jr. Lite Aluminum 023030 (Bare)	1.94"	1.60"	58cc
WORLD PRODUCTS	Windsor Jr. Lite Aluminum 023030-2 (Hydraulic Roller)	1.94"	1.60"	58cc
WORLD PRODUCTS	Windsor Jr. Lite Aluminum 023030-3 (Solid Roller)	1.94"	1.60"	58cc
WORLD PRODUCTS	Windsor Sr. Lite Aluminum 023020 (Bare)	2.02" 1.60" 64cc		
WORLD PRODUCTS	Windsor Sr. Lite Aluminum 023020-2 (Hydraulic Roller)	2.02"	1.60"	64cc
WORLD PRODUCTS	Windsor Sr. Lite Aluminum 023020-3 (Solid Roller)	2.02"	1.60"	64cc
WORLD PRODUCTS	Roush 200 Cast Iron 053040 (Bare)	2.02"	1.60"	64cc
WORLD PRODUCTS	Roush 200 Cast Iron 053040-1 (Hydraulic)	2.02"	1.60"	64cc
WORLD PRODUCTS	Roush 200 Cast Iron 053040-2 (Hydraulic Roller)	2.02"	1.60"	64cc
WORLD PRODUCTS	Roush 200 Cast Iron 053040-3 (Solid Roller)	2.02"	1.60"	64cc

The Edelbrock Street Legal Performer is also available with larger 2.02-inch intake valves. This head is also designed for 351W strokers.

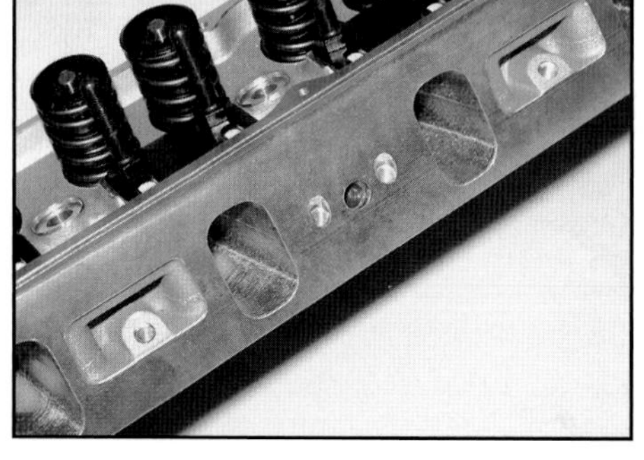

The AFR 205cc head raises performance a notch with 2.08-inch intake and 1.60-inch exhaust valves. Chamber sizes include 60cc and 71cc. This is a good street/strip head that lives well on top of strokers. It is perfect for your 331 to 392ci stroker.

Ford Casting Identification

Ford makes it easy for enthusiasts to identify corporate castings. Please understand that Ford casting numbers aren't always the same as part or engineering numbers. Identifying a casting is a matter of knowing what Ford part and casting numbers mean. Here's what you can expect.

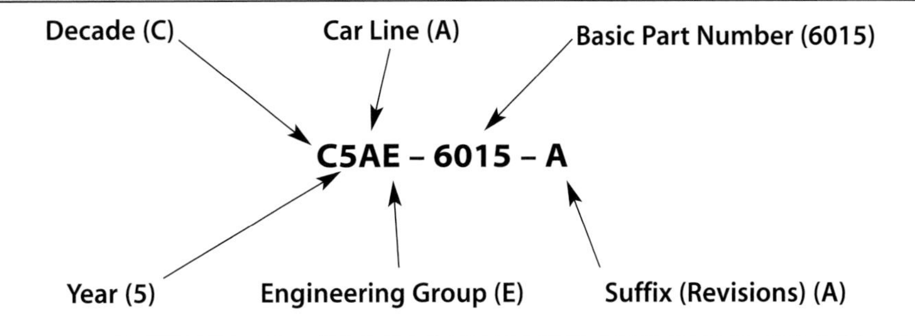

Typical Ford Part/Casting Number

It's easy to identify Ford castings once you understand the system because there's not only a casting number, but a casting date code that tells you exactly when the piece was cast. Not only that, a date code is stamped in the piece, which tells us the date of manufacture. With these two date codes, we know when the piece was cast and when it was ultimately manufactured.

Ford part numbers can be found in the Ford Master Parts Catalog on microfilm at your Ford dealer or in one of those obsolete 900-pound parts catalogs from the good old days. Because Ford has made a great many parts for vintage Fords obsolete, these part numbers don't always exist in present day dealer microfilms. This is called "NR" or "not replaced" which means it is no longer available from Ford. However, casting numbers on parts tell us a lot about the piece.

Here's how a typical Ford part/casting number breaks down.

- First Position indicates **Decade** (<u>C</u>5AE-6015-A):
  - B = 1950-59
  - C = 1960-69
  - D = 1970-79
  - E = 1980-89
  - F = 1990-99
- Second Position indicates **Year of Decade** (C<u>5</u>AE-6015-A):
- Third Position indicates **Car Line** (C5<u>A</u>E-6015-A):
  - A = Ford
  - D = Falcon
  - G = Comet, Montego, Cyclone
  - J = Marine & Industrial
  - M = Mercury
  - O = Fairlane & Torino
  - S = Thunderbird
  - T = Ford Truck
  - V = Lincoln
  - W = Cougar
  - Z = Mustang
- Fourth Position indicates the **Engineering Group** (C5A<u>E</u>-6015-A):
  - A = Chassis Group
  - B = Body Group
  - E = Engine Group

  If the item is a service part, the fourth position then indicates the applicable division as follows.
  - Z = Ford Division
  - Y = Lincoln-Mercury
  - X = Original Ford Muscle Parts Program
  - M = Ford Motorsport SVO or Ford-Mexico
- Four Digit Number indicates the **Basic Part Number** (C5AE-<u>6015</u>-A):

  The basic part number tells us what the basic part is. For example, "6015" in the example above is a cylinder block. The number "9510" is carburetors, and so on. Each type of Ford part, right down to brackets and hardware, has a basic part number. This makes finding them easier in the Ford Master Parts Catalog.
- The last character is the **Suffix** (C5AE-6015-<u>A</u>):

  The suffix indicates the revision under the part number. "A" indicates an original part. "B" indicates first revision, "C" second revision, "D" third revision, and so on. During Ford's learning curve with emissions in the 1970s, it was not uncommon to see "AA", "AB" and so on in cylinder head casting suffix.

Date Codes

Date codes can be found two ways in Ford castings. When the four-character date code is cast into the piece, this indicates when the piece was cast at the foundry. When it is stamped, this indicates the date of component manufacture.

5 A 26

Year (5)/Month (A)/Day (26)

Typical Date Code

Another area of interest to Ford buffs is where the piece was cast or forged. With Ford engines, we've seen three foundry identification marks. A "C" circled around an "F" indicates the Cleveland Iron Foundry. "DIF" indicates Dearborn Iron Foundry. "WF" or "WIF" indicates Windsor Iron Foundry. Single and double digit numbers typically indicate cavity numbers in the mold.

Ford Small-Block Engine Block Information

(Bold Indicates High Performance)

Displacement Years Available	Casting Number (6015)	Part Number (6015)	Bore Size	Deck Height	Other Information
221ci 1962-63	C2OE-G	C4OZ-B	3.50″	8.206″	Five-bolt bell.
221ci 1962-63	C3OE-A	C4OZ-B	3.50″	8.206″	Five-bolt bell.
260ci 1962-64	C3OE-B	C4OZ-B	3.80″	8.206″	Five-bolt bell.
260ci 1962-64	C3OE-C	C4OZ-B	3.80″	8.206″	Five-bolt bell.
260ci 1962-64	C4OE-B	C4OZ-B	3.80″	8.206″	Five-bolt bell.
260ci 1962-64	C4OE-D	C4OZ-B	3.80″	8.206″	Five-bolt bell.
260ci 1962-64	C4OE-E	C4OZ-B	3.80″	8.206″	Five-bolt bell.
289ci 1963-64	C3AE-N	C4AZ-B	4.00″	8.206″	Five-bolt bell.
289ci 1963-64	C4OE-C	C4AZ-B	4.00″	8.206″	Five-bolt bell.
289ci 1963-64	C4OE-F	C4AZ-B	4.00″	8.206″	Five-bolt bell.
289ci 1963-64	C4AE	C4AZ-B	4.00″	8.206″	Five-bolt bell.
289ci 1963-64	C4DE	C4AZ-B	4.00″	8.206″	Five-bolt bell.
289ci 1963-64	**C3OE-B**	**C4OZ-E**	4.00″	8.206″	**High Perf.** Five-bolt bell.
289ci 1963-64	**C4OE-B**	**C4OZ-E**	4.00″	8.206″	**High Perf.** Five-bolt bell.
289ci 1965-67	C5AE-E	C5AZ-E C5OZ-D C7OZ-C	4.00″	8.206″	Six-bolt bell.
289ci 1965-67	C5OE-C	C5AZ-E C5OZ-D C7OZ-C	4.00″	8.206″	Six-bolt bell.
289ci 1965-67	C6AE-C	C5AZ-E C5OZ-D C7OZ-C	4.00″	8.206″	Six-bolt bell.
289ci 1965-67	**C5AE-E**	**C5OZ-D**	4.00″	8.206″	**High Perf.** Six-bolt bell.
302ci 1968-69	C8OE-A	D1TZ-E D2OZ-C D1ZZ-C	4.00″	8.206″	Extended cylinder skirts "302" in valley
302ci 1968	C8TE-B	D1TZ-E	4.00″	8.206″	Truck block
302ci 1969	C9TE-C	D1TZ-E	4.00″	8.206″	Truck block
302ci 1970-74	D1OE-AA	D1TZ-E D2OZ-C D1ZZ-C	4.00″	8.206″	8.229″ deck height in 1973-76
302ci 1971-74	D1TE-AA	D1TZ-E D2OZ-C D1ZZ-C	4.00″	8.206″	Truck block
302ci 1974	D4DE-AA		4.00″	8.206″	8.229″ deck height in 1973-76
302ci 1975-77	D5ZY-AA		4.00″	8.206″	8.229″ deck height in 1973-76
302ci 1978-79		D8VE-AA	4.00″	8.206″	
302ci 1980-82		E0AE-DD	4.00″	8.206″	
302ci 1983-84		E2AE-KA	4.00″	8.206″	
302ci 1985		E5AE-HA	4.00″	8.206″	Roller Tappet Block
302ci 1986-93		E6SE-DC	4.00″	8.206″	Heavier Block
302ci 1994-01		E7TE-PA	4.00″	8.206″	
351W 1969-70	C9OE-B	C9OZ-B D1AZ-E	4.00″	9.480″	
351W 1971-74	D2AE-BA	C9OZ-B D1AZ-E	4.00″	9.480″	9.503″ deck height in 1974
351W 1971-74	D4AE-AA	C9OZ-B D1AZ-E	4.00″	9.480″	9.503″ deck height in 1974
351W 1975-84	D4AE-DA	C9OZ-B D1AZ-E	4.00″	9.503″	
351W 1985-86		E5AE-CA	4.00″	9.503″	
351W 1987-00		E7TE-PA	4.00″	9.503″	
302ci 1969-70	**C8FE**	**D1ZZ-B** **D1ZZ-C**	4.00″	8.209″	**Boss 302** 302 Tunnel-Port block
302ci 1969-70	**C9ZE**	**D1ZZ-B** **D1ZZ-C**	4.00″	8.209″	**Boss 302**
302ci 1969-70	**D0ZE-B**	**D1ZZ-B** **D1ZZ-C**	4.00″	8.209″	**Boss 302**
351C 1970-71	D0AE-A	D0AZ-D	4.00″	9.206″	2-bolt main
351C 1970-71	D0AE-C	D0AZ-D	4.00″	9.206″	2-bolt main
351C 1970-71	D0AE-E	D0AZ-D	4.00″	9.206″	2-bolt main
351C 1970-71	D0AE-G	D0AZ-D	4.00″	9.206″	2-bolt main
351C 1970-71	D0AE-J	D0AZ-D	4.00″	9.206″	2-bolt main
351C 1970-71	D0AE-L	D0AZ-D	4.00″	9.206″	2-bolt main
351C 1972-74	D2AE-DA	D0AZ-D	4.00″	9.206″	2-bolt main
351C Australian		**D6HM-L**	4.00″	9.206″	
351C 1971	**D0AE-B** **D0AE-D** **D0AE-F** **D0AE-H**		4.00″	9.206″	**4-bolt main**
351C 1971	**D1ZE-A** **D1ZE-B**	**D1ZZ-D**	4.00″	9.206″	**Boss 351 4-bolt main**
351C 1971-74	**D2AE-CA**	**D1ZZ-A** **D3ZZ-A**	4.00″	9.206″	**Cobra Jet**
351C 1972	**D2AE-EA**	**D1ZZ-D**	4.00″	9.206″	**High Output 4-bolt main**

Five Bolt vs. Six Bolt Bell Housing

Although it is unlikely you will stumble across a block with the five-bolt bellhousing pattern, it is easy to get mixed up and buy the wrong block. The 221, 260, and 289 blocks from 1962-1964 all had five-bolt bellhousing patterns. Ford enlarged the bellhousing bolt pattern to six bolts in 1965 to reduce noise, vibration, and harshness. This six-bolt bellhousing pattern has been the standard ever since with 289, 302, 351W, and 351C engines. If you're building a 1963 Fairlane or 1964 1/2 Mustang with the original transmission, then you want a block with the five-bolt bellhousing pattern. The 221 block will have 3.50-inch bores. The 260 has 3.80-inch bores. The 289 block will have 4.00-inch bores.

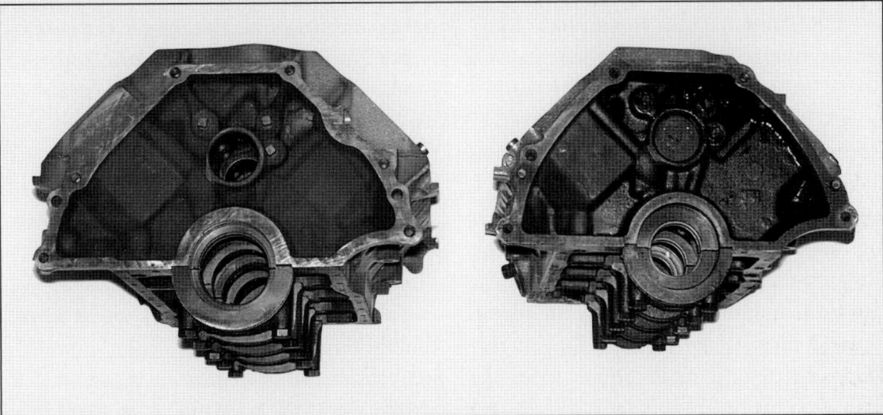

Here are the two small-block bellhousing bolt-patterns you can expect to find for 221/260/289ci blocks. On the left is the six-bolt pattern common from late-1964-up. On the right is the smaller five-bolt pattern common between 1962-64. With this pattern is a narrow transmission bolt-pattern.

Aftermarket Engine Blocks and Sources

Manufacturer	Type/Number	Bore	Main Size	Deck Height
Ford Racing	Stock 5.0L Iron Block M-6010-A50	4.00"	2.248"	8.206"
Ford Racing	Sportsman 302 Iron Block M-6010-B50	4.000"	2.2480"	8.200"
Ford Racing	Siamese Wet Sump 302 Iron Block M-6010-R302 Replaces A4 Block	4.00"	2.248"	8.200"
Ford Racing	Siamese Wet Sump 302 Iron Block M-6010-S302 Taller Deck Height	4.00"	2.248"	8.700"
Ford Racing	Wet or Dry Sump 302 Aluminum Block M-6010-F302	4.00"	2.248"	8.200"
Ford Racing	Wet or Dry Sump 302 Aluminum Block M-6010-F8.7 Taller Deck Height	4.00"	2.248"	8.700"

Manufacturer	Type/Number	Bore	Main Size	Deck Height
Ford Racing	Wet or Dry Sump 351 Aluminum Block M-6010-X351	4.00"	2.749"	9.200"
Ford Racing	Wet or Dry Sump 351 Aluminum Block M-6010-X352	4.00"	N/A	9.200"
Ford Racing	Wet or Dry Sump 351 Aluminum Block M-6010-Z351 Taller Deck Height	4.00"	2.749"	9.500"
Ford Racing	Non-Siamese Bore 351 Cast Iron Race Block Wet or Dry Sump M-6010-M351	4.00"	2.749"	9.200"
Ford Racing	Non-Siamese Bore 351 Cast Iron Race Block Wet or Dry Sump M-6010-N351 Taller Deck Height	4.00"	2.749"	9.500"

How Much Rod?

Undoubtedly, you've heard of "long-rod" strokers. What are the benefits of a longer connecting rod? Is going with a longer connecting rod worth the cost? Opting for a longer connecting rod does make a difference in power because it improves combustion efficiency. A longer rod improves combustion efficiency by allowing the piston to dwell longer at the top of the cylinder bore. When the piston stays at the top of the bore longer, this allows us to pull more power from the same amount of air and fuel. The longer the connecting rod, the longer the piston is permitted to stay at both the top and bottom of the cylinder bore. This allows us more time to extract energy from the fuel/air charge.

Speed-O-Motive, as one example, offers a variety of long-rod stroker kits designed to make the most of your small-block power project. Lets use a 351W engine as one example. In box-stock form, the 351W has a 5.956-inch long connecting rod. It has been proven that you can stroke the 351W to as much as 429ci in a factory block. We can fit as much as 6.580-inches of connecting rod into a 351W stroker. This gives us 0.62-inch more rod, not to mention more dwell time.

Internal combustion engines tend to waste approximately 70 percent of the heat energy they create. Allowing the piston to dwell longer at the top of the bore enables us to capture some of the wasted heat energy, which is absorbed by the coolant or lost out the tail pipe.

Dampen the Vibes

Ford used a number of harmonic balancers over the small-block Ford's production life. From 1962-1969, a three-bolt balancer was used. In that period, there was a narrow balancer for 221, 260, 289-2V, and 289-4V engines. The 289 High Performance engine received a wide three-bolt balancer, plus a counterweight. In 1968-1969, the 289 and 302 engines received a wider three-bolt balancer that was marked differently than the narrow 1962-1967 balancer. Beginning in 1970, small-block Fords received a four-bolt balancer that was used well into the early 1980s. With the onset of serpentine belt drive came a new generation of four-bolt balancers for 5.0L and 5.8L engines.

Late-model 5.0L and 5.8L engines employ this four-bolt balancer designed for serpentine belt drive and crank trigger.

The 1962-69 three-bolt balancer.

The 1970-up four-bolt balancer.

HOW TO BUILD A STROKER

This chapter is dedicated to good, solid, reliable engine building technique. Producing this book and others here in Southern California, we've been in the company of some of the best engine builders in the world. One of them is John Da Luz of JMC Motorsports in San Diego. John has been building automobiles and the engines that power them for more than 25 years. He enjoys an extraordinary track record as a seasoned engine builder. His experience lives in virtually every kind of racing venue in the world, including top fuel.

We have also had the good fortune of knowing Mark Jeffrey of Trans Am Racing in Gardena, California, who possesses a wealth of experience as a seasoned engine builder, most of it with Fords. These two gentlemen are going to show us the way to solid, reliable power from a small-block Ford.

Engine building technology has made considerable advances over the past 30 years. We've learned that it's the small details that can make or break a project. The two biggest details we can think of are checking clearances and triple-checking your work. Far too many of us learn the hard way because we're not attentive enough to detail. We learn when an overlooked rod bolt fails half way down the track. And we learn when a carelessly seated valve keeper escapes at high revs, destroying the piston and cylinder wall in less than a second. These are the important details we don't want you to miss during your budget engine build.

Far too many engine projects fail because there wasn't proper planning. Planning is the most effective engine-building tool you can have. We waste time and money when we don't think about what we want the engine to do. Part of building an engine is knowing exactly what you can afford, then not giving in to ego and the temptation. And that's the mistake a lot of us make along the way. We want to impress our peers. But these are the wrong reasons to build an engine. Don't build an engine to impress anyone beside yourself, because you alone will have to live with the result.

Most of us overbuild our engines. We build more engine than our Ford needs, which costs unnecessary time and money. For example, you're building a classic Mustang and you want it to be

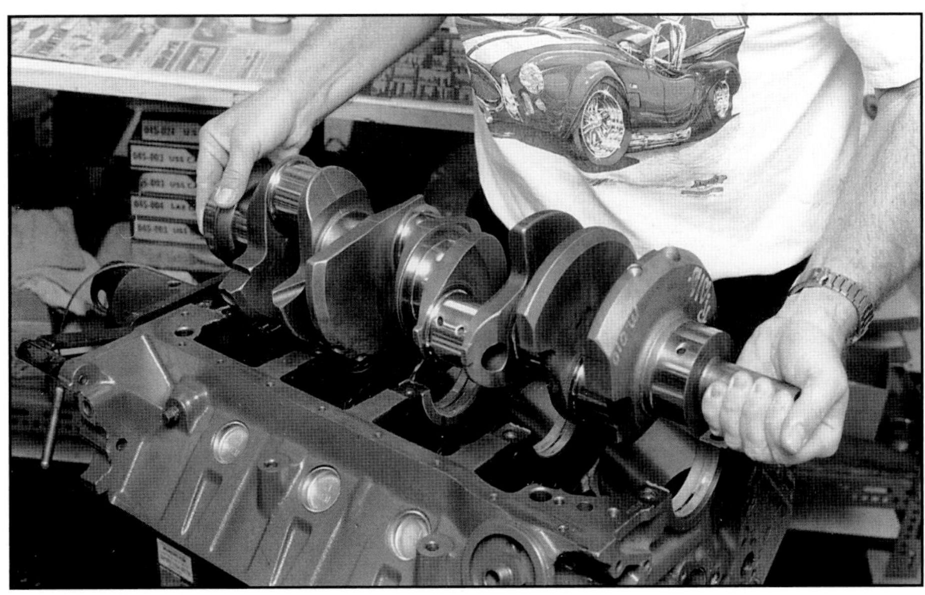

Building a solid, reliable stroker small-block takes very close attention to detail. Clearances need to be checked and rechecked. Make sure rods, pistons, and crankshaft counterweights clear the block and oil pumps.

fast. You're thinking of building a 351W stroker displacing 427 cubic inches. Future plans include fuel injection and a supercharger. Just imagine, the power of a big-block in a lightweight classic. Maybe it is more than your Mustang (and your driving skills) can handle. You don't have to worry about impressing us. We've been there too. And we understand the drawbacks of overbuilding. This is why we're sharing the cold, hard facts of engine building with you.

Too many enthusiasts build more engine than a car can safely handle. When we infuse big displacement power into a lightweight Mustang, Falcon, or Fairlane, we're not thinking enough about the engine and vehicle as a package. Most of us get it backwards. We build a powerful engine, then we wonder how to manage all that power safely and effectively. Build the car first, then the engine, because too much power in an unprepared platform can get you killed. A well thought-out platform will have good brakes, a handling package, traction enhancement, the right tires and wheels, a rear axle that can take the punishment, and a mature driver who understands all of this.

Not all of us can afford a Sears Craftsman rollaway, but this should be your ultimate goal. Start with a good top box for starters that you can sit on the workbench, then move into the bottom rollaway box later. Craftsman offers you options, like the side-saddle box shown here. You can grow with Craftsman, one step at a time.

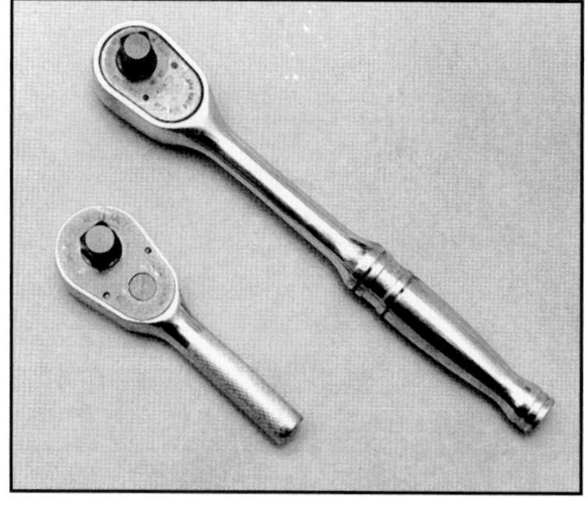

When you shop for tools, think flexibility and ease of use. Here are two variations on the humble ratchet. The short ratchet gets into places the longer piece cannot. Start with the basics, then add as your needs dictate.

Our goal is to teach you how to build a reliable engine that you can afford that will make the power you need. No matter what the formula is, one basic formula holds true. Performance level is tied directly to budget. The greater the budget and know-how, the faster you're going to go. You're not going to make a 600 horsepower small-block for $2500. Keep your expectations and planning realistic. Then go work your plan with perseverance. Lets get started.

Tools Of The Trade

It is easy to get carried away in the tool department at any department store. That first trip to Sears is often like your first trip to the speed shop. You lay down the credit card and come home with a wealth of goodies. But they don't always apply to building an effective engine. It is easy to waste money in all of the excitement.

We suggest Sears Craftsman tools because they have a lifetime warranty, a great reputation, and there's a Sears store in nearly every area of the world. The Craftsman warranty is a no nonsense, no fine print warranty. Bust a socket and Sears will replace it with no questions asked. Strip out a ratchet and Sears will hand you a new one or rebuild your old one. Sears Craftsman tools are the best tool value there is. Yes, they're costly going in, but they remain the best tool value going. The next best tool value going is Husky in the bang-for-the-buck department. You can find Husky tools at nearly any home improvement or hardware store for even less money than Craftsman, yet with the same no nonsense lifetime warranty.

Here's what you need to get started:

- Set of Common and Phillips Head Screwdrivers
- Set of combination wrenches (1/4", 5/16", 11/32", 3/8", 7/16", 1/2", 9/16", 5/8", 11/16", 3/4", 7/8", 15/16" and 1")
- 3/8" Drive Socket Set (3/8", 7/16", 1/2", 9/16", 5/8", 11/16", 3/4")
- 3/8" Deep Well Sockets (3/8", 7/16", 1/2", 9/16", 5/8", 11/16" 3/4")
- 1/2" Drive Socket Set (7/16", 1/2", 9/16", 5/8", 11/16", 3/4", 7/8", 15/16", 1", 1 1/16", 1 1/8" and 1 1/4")
- 1/2" Drive Deep Well Sockets (7/16", 1/2", 9/16", 5/8", 11/16", 3/4", 7/8", 15/16", 1", 1 1/16", 1 1/8" and 1 1/4")
- 1/2" Drive Breaker Bar
- Pliers
- Needle Nose Pliers
- Diagonal Cutting Pliers
- C-Clip Pliers
- Set of Vice Grips (and we mean Vice Grip brand only!)
- Set of Punches
- Small and Large Hammers
- A Five-Pound Sledge Hammer
- Torque Wrench (optional, but a great investment)
- Drill and Bits (spend the money and opt for high quality bits)
- Putty Knife or Gasket Scraper
- Hack Saw (use 24 teeth per inch for best results with metal)
- Magnetic Bolt Tray
- Large Top Chest or Heavy Duty Tool Box with drawers

This list is suggested to get you started and will last you the rest of your life with care. Tools are something you can pass along because, with proper

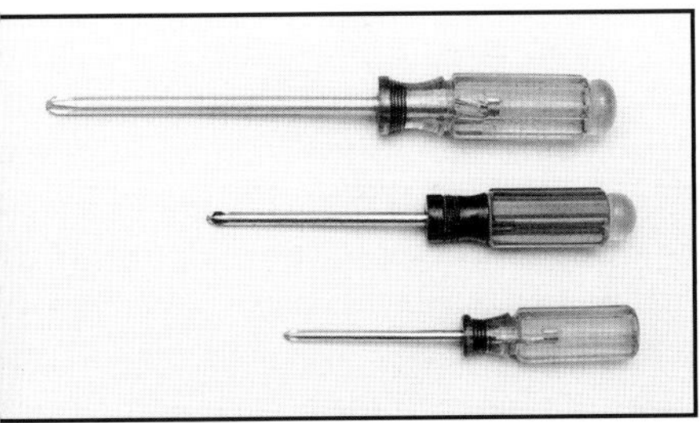

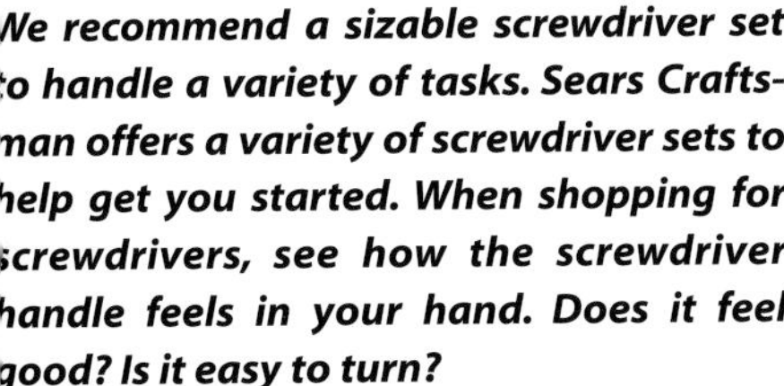

We recommend a sizable screwdriver set to handle a variety of tasks. Sears Craftsman offers a variety of screwdriver sets to help get you started. When shopping for screwdrivers, see how the screwdriver handle feels in your hand. Does it feel good? Is it easy to turn?

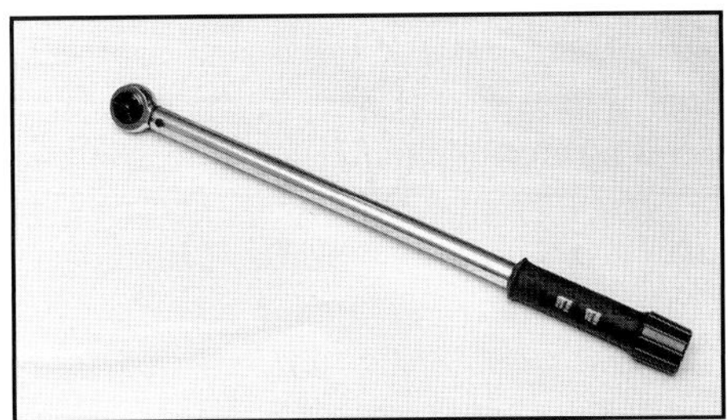

If you're going to assemble an engine, you must have a good quality torque wrench. This is a high-end Sears Craftsman breakaway torque wrench. It clicks when the desired torque is reached. There are more affordable beam-type torque wrenches available.

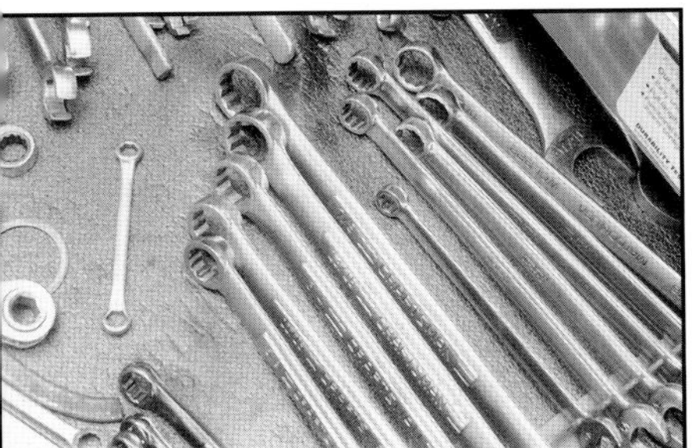

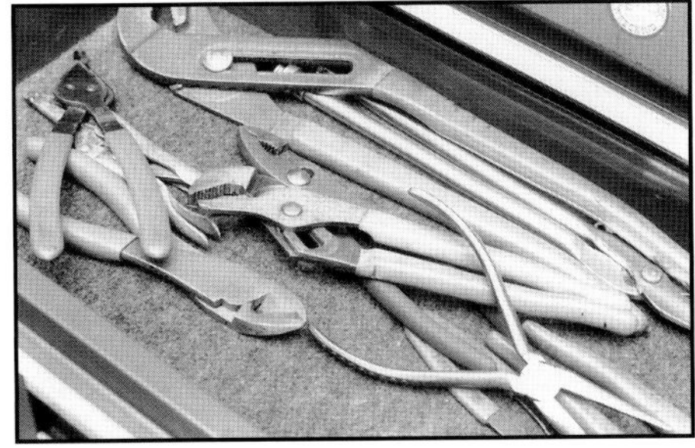

Organize your tool storage right from the start. Every tool should have its place where you know where it is at a glance. When you are finished, return the tool to its proper location. Few things are more frustrating than tools we cannot find.

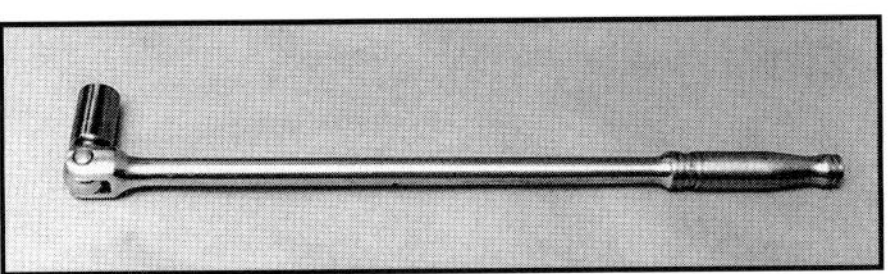

Engine teardowns need a 3/8-inch or 1/2-inch drive breaker bar. Breaker bars give you solid mechanical advantage when it's time to loosen a main bearing cap or cylinder head bolt.

care, they will last several lifetimes. Most of us buy socket sets, but we forget to go for the deep well sockets, which you will need in the course of an engine build. And one other thing – opt for six-point sockets, not 12-point. A six-point socket won't strip a bolt head and provides a firm grip. Make sure your socket sets have at least two extensions – one 3-inch and one 7-inch. Spring for the universal adapter as well for easy access. If you can afford it, buy a matching set of 12-point shallow and deep well sockets because they do have a purpose with some engine applications.

When you're shopping screwdrivers, hold them in your hand first. You want a screwdriver that feels good in your hand and offers adequate grip comfort and mechanical advantage. If your hand slips around the handle, then it is a poor design. The tip should be super tough tool steel that will not strip out or break. Cheap screwdrivers always strip out and break. Go the extra mile and invest wisely now in a screwdriver that will last you a lifetime. Another idea is to buy screwdrivers with bright orange handles for visibility and safety. This lessens the chance of leaving tools where they don't belong.

We push the idea of quality tools because there really is a difference. Low-buck wrench sets you can buy for nine bucks won't get the job done effectively. A cheap forging or casting will strip out and leave you hanging on a Sunday afternoon when you need it most. With Sears Craftsman, Husky, MAC, or Snap-On tools, you get a lifetime warranty you can count on. And it's a warranty that's good for as long as the tool exists – for you, your child, your grandchild, great grandchild, and more. MAC and Snap-On tools tend to be very expensive and available only off a truck at better garages everywhere, which makes Craftsman and Husky better a better value and easier to find. Husky doesn't get enough air-time, but it is one of the best bargains for the money. It costs less than Craftsman, Snap-On, or MAC, and you still get a lifetime warranty.

Proper tool care once you've made the investment is what assures you reliability from here on out. Keep your tools clean and serviceable. Lubricate ratchets periodically with engine oil or white grease for best results. Drill bits should be sharpened periodically. And when you're using a drill, run the bit slow and keep it wet with lubrication while drilling. Drill bits begin to squeak whenever they're dull. Invest in a drill bit sharpener or find a reliable shop in town that sharpens drill bits. Just about any-

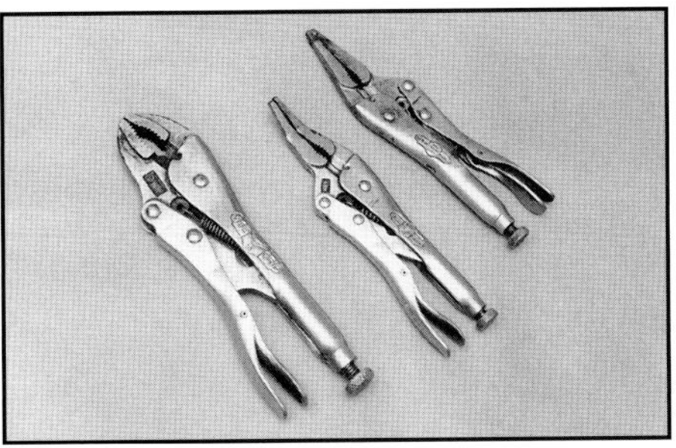

Vice Grip brings us a wide variety of ways to hold onto our work. You need a variety of Vice Grip pliers in your arsenal, not to mention a C-clamp or two.

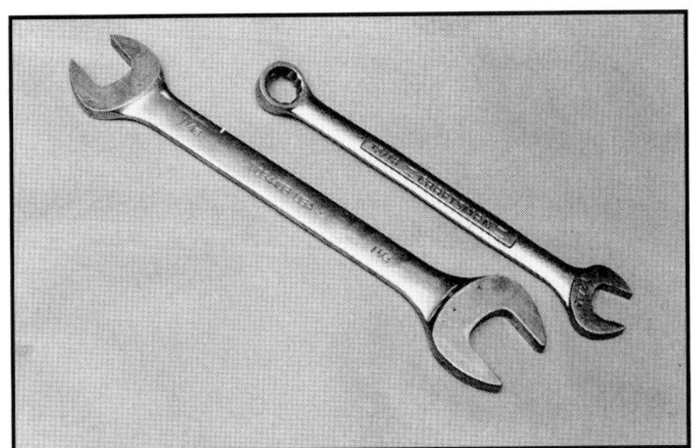

When we speak of wrenches, opt for the combination wrench on the right. The combination wrench gives you the benefit of a box or open-end wrench.

one who sharpens lawnmower blades and chain saws can sharpen your bits.

Know when it's time to retire worn-out tools. Tools that are not serviceable can be dangerous. A loose hammerhead, for example, could accidentally rearrange someone's dental work. Cracked sockets, worn wrenches, busted screwdriver handles, stripped ratchets, and other forms of serious tool deterioration are reasons to invest in fresh equipment. Remember, it is about your safety and the integrity of your work.

Tools To Rent

These are the tools you're going to use only during an engine build and probably won't need again until the next build.

- Torque Wrench
- Piston Ring Compressor
- Harmonic Balancer Puller
- Valve Spring Compressor
- Freeze Plug Driver
- Seal Driver
- Thread Chaser
- Small Grinder (if you port your own heads)
- Easy Outs (for broken bolts in blocks and heads)
- Engine Hoist
- Engine Stand
- Dial Indicator

Torque wrenches typically are either beam or breakaway types. We suggest the breakaway type that clicks when the specified torque is reached. What's more, learn how to properly use a breakaway torque wrench. Two things are important to remember about torque wrenches. Never use a torque wrench to remove a bolt or nut – ever. You will disturb the calibration. And secondly, never over-torque a fastener. When you torque a fastener, you are stretching the bolt stock. Too much torque and you stress the fastener. Specified torque readings are there to ensure fastener integrity.

Piston ring compressors are available in different forms. The most common type you will be able to rent is an adjustable type. There is also a ratcheting type that makes piston installation a snap. Custom sized billet ring compressors are costly and not for the novice.

Harmonic balancer pullers are a borderline rental item. This is a tool you may use again and again. They don't cost that much to buy, which is what makes them a borderline item. Balancer pullers also make great steering wheel pullers. Look for the multi-purpose in any tool you're thinking about renting. If you expect to use the tool again, it may well be worth the investment now.

There are two basic types of valve spring compressors – one you use in the shop on a cylinder head in the raw (looks like a huge C-clamp) and one you use with the head installed (more like a pry bar used only for ball/stud fulcrum rocker arm applications). For engine rebuilding, you're going to need the C-clamp type. You can sometimes pick these up at a discount house for less than it would cost to rent one for several days.

Freeze plug and seal drivers are one of those borderline items you could use again and again. You can also use a like-sized socket as a driver on the end of an extension. This saves money, but could damage the socket. Don't be a tool abuser.

Thread chasers are a vital part of any engine build because you want clean threads. Clean threads yield an accurate torque reading when it's time to reassemble the engine. It's a good idea to chase every bolt hole. When a thread chaser is outside of your budget, use Grade 8 bolts and other fasteners with WD-40 to chase the threads. This may sound crude, but it will save you money and get the job done. What's more, no one knows you did it but you will have clean threads.

Tools should be rented only at the time you intend to use them. Don't rent every tool mentioned here at the same time because you're not going to use all of them at the same time. Thread chasing, for example, should be performed when the block returns from the machine shop clean, machined, and ready for assembly. Machine shops that are on the ball will have already chased your threads. Remember that thread chasing is time consuming. Machine shops don't generally do this unless asked and paid for the service.

Engine stands are one of those purchase/rent questions because renting can sometimes cost you more than simply buying, and engine stands can be cheap depending on where you buy. Harbor Freight Salvage has some of the best values going at $50 to $100 for a stand you will have for the rest of your life.

The decision to rent or buy tools boils down to how often you will use the tool and how long you will need the tool during your engine build. Any time you're going to need the tool longer than 1-3 days, you're probably better off buying. If you have to buy, look on the bright side. You can always loan it to friends or sell it after your engine is finished. Keeping it makes it a useful piece of community property among friends.

Keep A Clean, Organized Shop

We cannot stress enough the importance of keeping a clean, organized shop. Do your engine teardown work where you can catalog everything and keep it in its rightful place. Keep engine parts and fasteners in jars or plastic containers

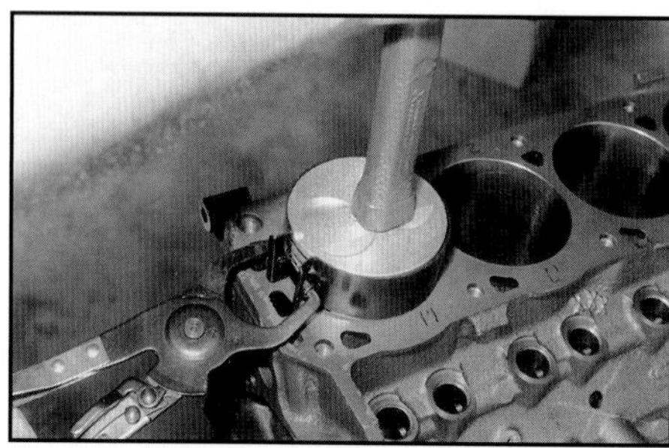

Piston ring compressors are necessary to proper engine assembly. Adjustable types are more affordable than size-specific billet types. For the novice, Saturday afternoon engine builder, the adjustable type makes more sense.

that are labeled with a marker. Haul the block, heads, crankshaft, and connecting rods to a machine shop immediately upon disassembly. This avoids any confusion and keeps you rolling. If you cannot afford the machine shop at the time, leave the engine assembled until you are ready. We speak from experience on this one because too much is lost both mentally and physically once the engine is disassembled. Keep disassembly, cleaning, machine work, and assembly as cohesive as possible.

It is always a good idea to keep an engine project organized from planning to completion. Know what you're going to do and when you're going to do it. Then get busy and see your engine project through to completion. Nothing's more discouraging than a disassembled engine that's going nowhere because you didn't have a plan or the money.

When it is time to assemble the engine, you must have a hospital-clean environment. Even simple house dust (which is actually dead human skin cells, hair, and other forms of decaying matter) will damage an engine's mating surfaces. House dust will score bearings, journals, and cylinder walls. We're not kidding either. Whenever you're not working on the engine, keep it covered inside a plastic trash bag. When you are assembling parts, clean them first with brake cleaner or compressed air to remove any dust. Avoid engine assembly on a windy day, which generates its share of dust. Automotive bodywork and sheet metal repair create harmful dust that will damage engine parts. Keep this kind of work away from your engine. If the gardener is out there mowing the lawn and edging the sidewalks, keep your engine covered. Make sure engine assembly lube and oil are pure and clean. Stray matter in either of these elements will damage your engine. Always keep one thing squarely in mind. Any kind of stray matter, no matter how small, will damage your engine.

When it is time for engine assembly, everything should be in proper order. Pistons should be matched to each bore. This means each bore should have been mic'ed and honed to the piston. In short, each piston should be a custom fit. Each piston should be numbered to the bore that was honed for the match. All piston rings should have been custom gapped for each bore. All of your engine's critical parts should be laid out on the workbench in order for error-free assembly.

Take organization to extremes. Number each cylinder with a magic marker at the block deck. Lay pistons and rods out on the bench in cylinder number order. Study the valve reliefs in the pistons. You would be amazed how many engine builds we've witnessed where the pistons were installed backwards. Closer attention to detail during assembly could have avoided the inconvenience of disassembly. Valve reliefs always go toward the top of the block with small-block Fords (except 351C).

Keep a can or two of brake cleaner on your workbench to last-minute clean parts during assembly. This eliminates any chance of dust particles and stray matter getting where they don't belong. Keep plenty of engine oil and assembly lube close by. Keep these items covered.

Getting Started

Unless you are starting with brand new castings and forgings, you're going to be dealing with disassembly, cleanup, and inspection of parts with your engine build. In any case, you will be dealing with inspection, even with new parts. Just because parts are new doesn't mean they are right. This is a very critical phase. Overlooking a substandard part can lead to unnecessary engine failure. We have seen new parts that were improperly machined and sized, not

Once you have removed the intake manifold and valve covers, both easy tasks, remove the rocker arms and pushrods. Small-block Fords have three basic kinds of rocker arm types. See the accompanying table. If you are going to reuse the rocker arms and valves, keep each rocker arm and valve in the same location.

Small-Block Ford Rocker Arm Types

S-A DESIGN

Rocker Arm Type	Years Affected	Details
Fully Adjustable	1962 – May 8, 1966	Pushrod guide cast in head
Rail Style	May 8, 1966 – 1967	Rocker arm tip has rails, which keep the tip on the valvestem. Integral pushrod guide in head deleted.
Rail Style with Positive Stop	1968-1977	Not adjustable. Just tighten and forget it.
Bolt-Fulcrum *	1978-present	Not adjustable. Bolt and fulcrum instead of ball and stud.

**351C, 351M & 400M Midland engines with hydraulic lifters have the bolt/fulcrum, stamped steel rocker arm. The Boss 351 (1971) and 351C High Output (1972) have stud-mounted, adjustable, stamped steel rocker arms.*

machined at all, improperly packaged, and more. Unless parts are washed and closely inspected, it is easy to make a critical mistake and use them when they need to go back in the box. So what to do first?

Remove the cylinder heads next using a 1/2-inch drive breaker bar and the appropriate socket. Sometimes, cylinder heads need help with a pry bar or large screwdriver.

Remove the cam plate and gently slid the camshaft out as shown.

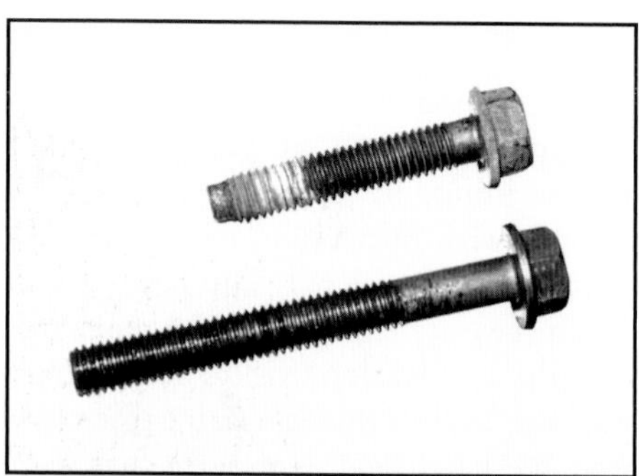

Head bolts need to be inspected closely for distortion and weaknesses. It is generally a good idea to replace them with ARP bolts for engine integrity. New bolts are cheap engine life insurance.

Remove all accessory drive pulleys and the harmonic balancer. Use a puller for the harmonic balancer. It is best to replace the balancer, using a new one with your stroker kit.

Disconnect each connecting rod and gently push the piston/rod assembly ou through the top of the block.

Remove lifters. If you're dealing with a roller block, remove the spider, then the dog bones and lifters. Since you are building extra power with a stroker, we suggest replacing the lifters. Specify a complete new roller camshaft kit, which will include roller tappets, dog bones, and spider. Don't throw the spider and dog bones away, however.

Remove the water pump and timing cover, then the timing set.

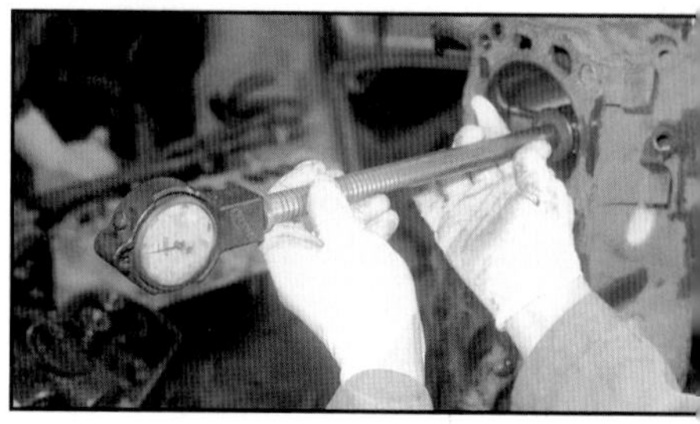

Each bore is checked for sizing anc taper. Anytime taper is more than .011 inch, it must be bored. Although For small blocks have been bored .060-inch oversize, we don't recommend this. Limit your overbore to a maximum of .040-inch oversize.

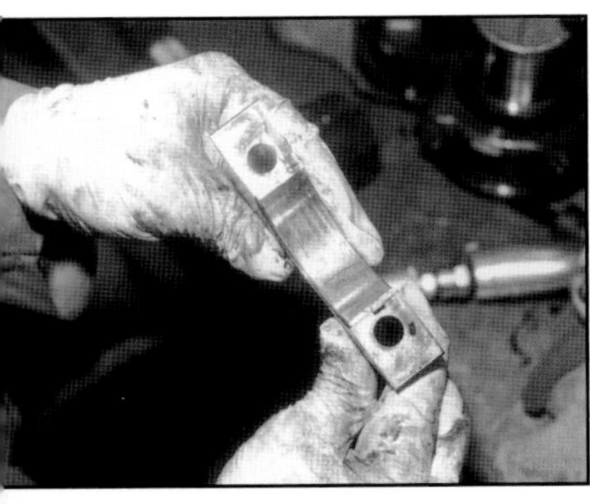

Wear patterns in bearings tell us a lot about a block's integrity, not to mention the condition of its internals. Unusual wear patterns may indicate the need for line boring or a replacement crankshaft. Examine these areas closely during disassembly.

The very first step in a build project after disassembly is cleaning. All parts must be cleaned thoroughly. All block plugs must be removed and passages checked for obstructions and debris. Oil galleys need to be wire brushed. Rust needs to be removed from the water jackets, especially if it impedes passages.

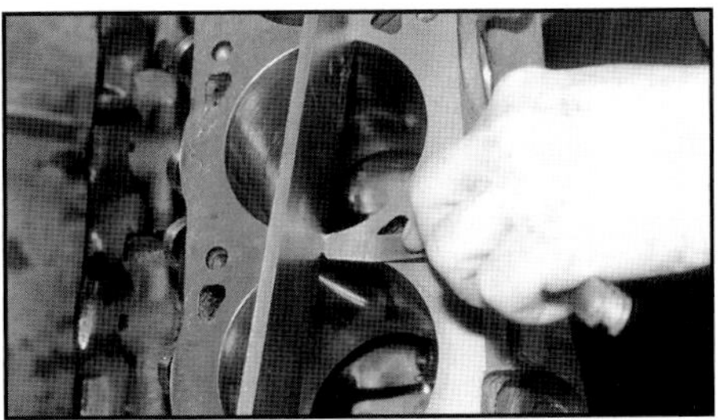

Surfaces must be checked for warping with a straightedge as shown. Any irregularities should be milled smooth.

Small-block Fords should never be bored more than .060-inch oversize. Those going for super big-inch small-blocks take them .060-inch, but we strongly advise against it. Whenever you go .060-inch oversize, you risk getting into the water jacket. Overheating also becomes an issue because we raise compression. Limit your overbore to .040-inch oversize maximum.

Pressed-in oil galley plugs in the front of the block should be replaced with screw-in plugs for safety and security.

Your build should always include brass freeze plugs, which are corrosion resistant.

Cleveland and Midland oiling systems need help because main bearings tend to be oil starved. A screw-in restrictor like this one is installed between the main and cam bearing journals to keep the mains bathed in oil. It reduces excessive oil flow to the cam bearings, which keeps oil plentiful at the mains.

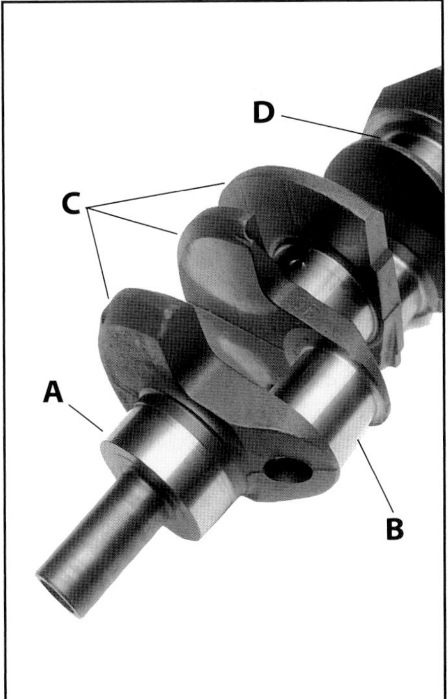

Although any stroker kit you purchase will already have this area handled, it is important for you to understand the crankshaft. Main journals (A) and rod journals (B) should be machined and polished for a smooth marriage with new bearings. Counterweights (C) are dynamic balanced to weigh the same as the reciprocating weight (piston and rod assembly). Small-block Ford thrust journals (D) are located mid-crank. The thrust journal accepts side loads, which keeps the crank centered in the block.

Small-Block Ford Crankshaft Identification

Engine	Crankshaft Type	Ident.	Center-To-Center	Stroke
221, 260, 289ci	Nodular Iron	1M	1.435-inches	2.87-inches
302ci	Nodular Iron	2M	1.500-inches	3.00-inches
Boss 302	Forged Steel	D0ZE-A or TFE-8	1.500-inches	3.00-inches
351W	Nodular Iron	3M	1.750-inches	3.50-inches
351C	Nodular Iron	4M	1.750-inches	3.50-inches
351M	Nodular Iron	4M	1.750-inches	3.50-inches
400M	Nodular Iron	5M	2.000-inches	4.00-inches

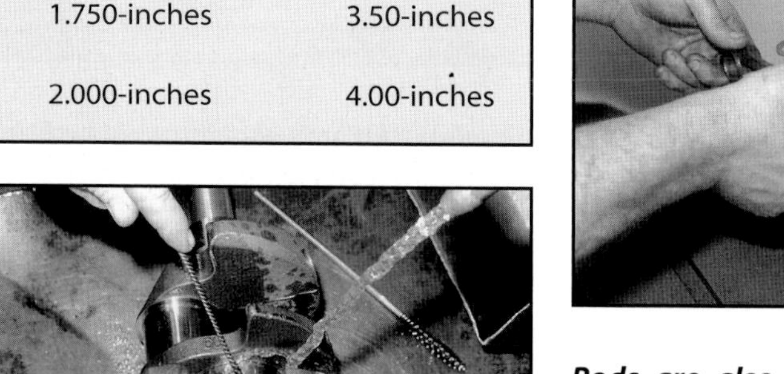

Small-block Ford crankshafts are identified by stamped markings on the first counterweight. This is a 3M crank for the 351W V-8.

Crankshafts are machined as necessary and polished during the build process. Stroker kits arrive at your doorstep machined and ready for installation. Because we are born skeptics, we strongly suggest checking all tolerances before assembly. Just because it is new out of the box doesn't mean it's right.

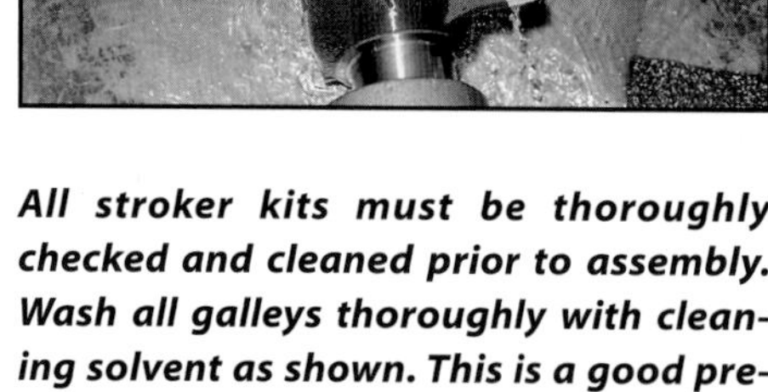

All stroker kits must be thoroughly checked and cleaned prior to assembly. Wash all galleys thoroughly with cleaning solvent as shown. This is a good precaution because even the smallest particle of iron or steel can ruin bearings on the first pass.

When used or box-stock connecting rods are employed in a stroker kit, they receive new, often larger bolts for strength. The rods are also shotpeened for additional strength.

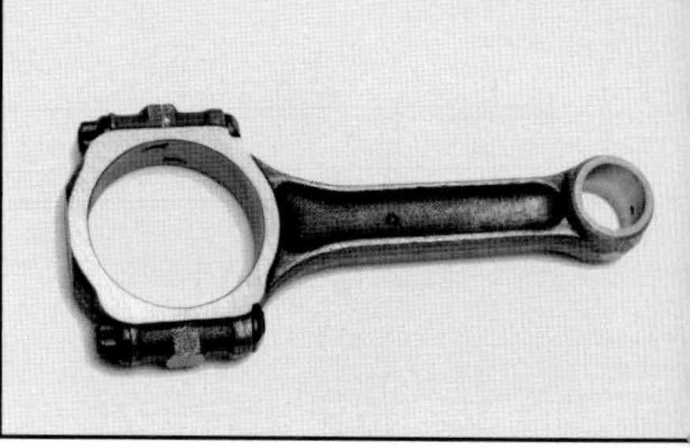

Stroker kits typically have connecting rods outside of the factory stock arena. Budget kits might have something like a Chrysler 360 rod, for example. This is a stock Ford 302 rod. The more affordable stroker kits use stock I-beam rod forgings from a variety of other applications, like Chevy and Chrysler engines.

Rods are also reconditioned, meaning the large end is machined to a perfect circle. Over time and use, the large end of a connecting rod becomes egg-shaped. Reconditioning the rod makes it round again. The crosshatch pattern inside the large end holds the rod bearing better.

When all of the components have been machined, they are dynamic balanced as shown. Dynamic balancing weighs each piston and rod assembly, and gets all of them weighed to the lightest unit in the set. The crankshaft is spun as shown to determine counterweight mass. Each counterweight is drilled to remove weight, getting the weight down to that of the lightest counterweight, matched to the lightest piston and rod assembly.

Harmonic balancers should be in serviceable condition. This means the outer ring should be solid on the rubber and hub. If the rubber is deteriorated, replace the balancer. Always be sure to properly match a balancer to the stroker kit. Ascertain how the stroker kit is balanced. Is it a 28-ounce offset or 50-ounce offset? Small-block Fords prior to 1982 were 28-ounce offset balanced. From 1982-up, they are 50-ounce offset balanced. Check this out before purchasing a balancer. Always include the balancer and the flywheel/flexplate with dynamic balancing.

New oil pumps should always be blueprinted. Few of them come from the manufacturer ready to install. Go that extra mile and check all clearances. Check the relief valve for smooth operation and cleanliness.

Any stroker kit worth its weight will have crankshaft journal oil holes that are chamfered for improved oil flow. If it doesn't arrive this way, have your machine shop do it.

An important part of your oiling system program should be proper oil return. Oil drain holes in the block should allow for a smooth return.

Proper Assembly Technique

With proper selection of castings out of the way, we can get into how to properly assemble an engine using tried and proven technique performed by professionals time and time again. We're not going to show you step by step in this chapter how to assemble an engine. Instead, we're going to show you methods and practices that work.

When it comes to assembly practices, the pros stress two main areas – cleanliness (hospital clean!) and triple-checking your work. Never assemble an engine in the same area where it is torn down. Even the minute amounts of dirt, dust or grit can stop an engine cold. Ordinary house dust can score bearings and cylinder walls. Keep your work covered when you're not working. Keep the area clean.

We stress double and triple checking your work because it actually saves you time. If it's inconvenient to check it two or three times, consider the inconvenience involved in a nuisance tear down because there's oil consumption or having to pick up the pieces of a scattered engine because a rod bolt was missed during the torquing process. Check it thrice and sleep better.

Engine building really is an exact science where every detail must be covered to ensure success. Even with all details covered, it is no guarantee an engine will stay together. It is those troublesome areas we cannot see that can fail when least expected. This means you must be attentive to everything you have control over in the build process.

Engine assembly areas must be hospital clean. Did you know ordinary house dust can score bearings and cylinder walls?

All torque readings should be double and triple checked. If this seems redundant, consider the time involved in building another engine because you scattered this one all over the roadway.

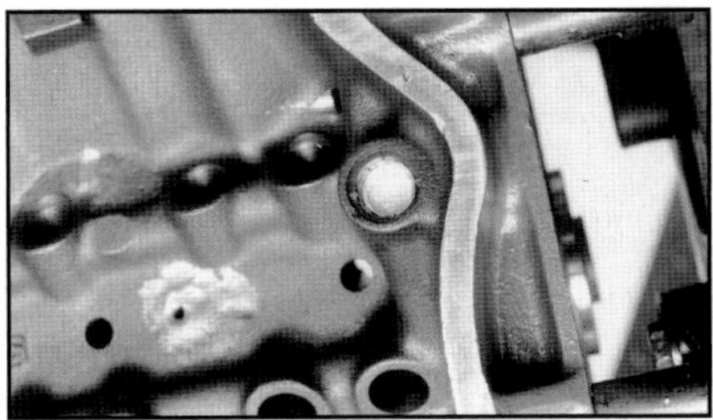

Do you know how often this one gets overlooked? This is the top oil galley plug located at the rear of the block of small-block Fords. Seasoned engine builders sometimes forget this one, which results in zero oil pressure. Make sure yours is installed.

Even new bearings should be examined closely for flaws. Not all of them come from the factory with oil slots correctly positioned. Some are grossly out of alignment, which leads to oil starvation when your engine needs it most. Sometimes, this is the fault of the bearing manufacturer. Other times, it is a flawed block, crank, or connecting rod. In any case, always check oil hole alignment.

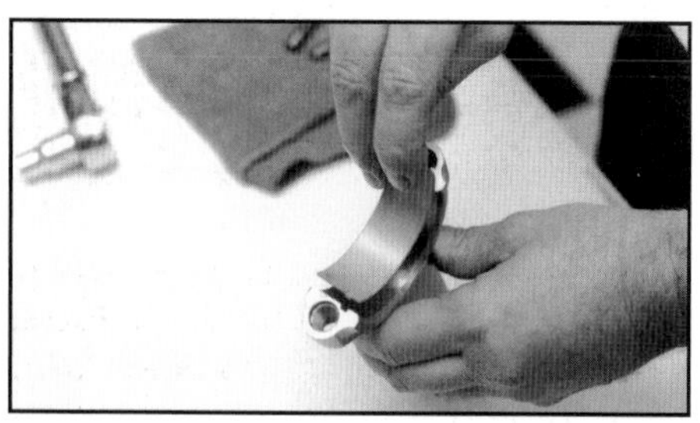

You would be surprised how many times we see this one screwed up. Double check main and rod bearing installation. The little tang fits in the slot. We sometimes get this backwards, and with catastrophic results. Also remember, bearings go in dry. No lubrication between the bearing and connecting rod, nor bearing and block. This practice keeps the bearing firmly anchored. Always lubricate the bearing surfaces with assembly lube, however.

Did you check the line bore? You would be surprised how many don't. Line bore affects power output and engine wear. A flawed line bore puts unnecessary stresses on the crankshaft.

Not only should you check torque and tolerances 2-3 times, you should clean all components 2-3 times to ensure a contaminant free environment. Oil passages in crankshafts can collect metal shavings. Ditto for engine blocks. Be very thorough.

All bearing surfaces should be bathed i engine assembly lube. Some builders us SAE 30 weight engine oil. But engine o doesn't have staying power. You wan generous amount of lubrication durin initial fire-up. Cylinder walls normally ge a splashing of SAE 30 weight engine oil. I the engine is going to be sitting a lon time before fire-up, use assembly lube o the cylinder walls.

Protect cylinder walls and crankshaf journals from nicks and scores by cover ing the rod bolts as shown. Rod bolts ar made a much harder metal than cylinde walls and crankshafts. Just a gentle ta will damage the surface. Cover the ro bolts. You may also use plastic caps, calle "rod bolt condoms" to protect tender sur faces. If these are unavailable, use fue hose of the appropriate size.

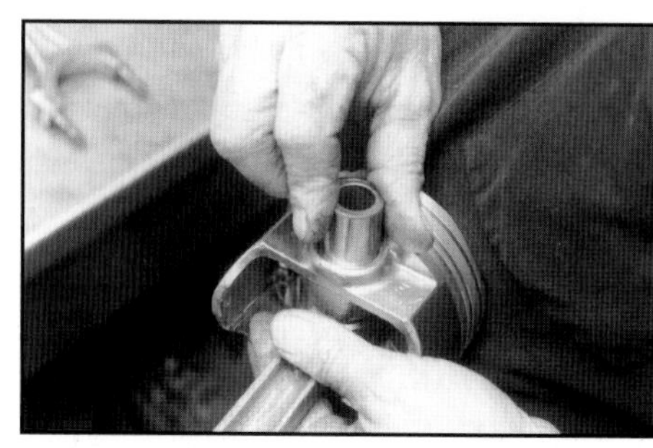

Assume nothing when you receive a stroker kit. Check all tolerances in great detail both before and during assembly. Sometimes, stroker kits get packaged incorrectly or mislabeled, which creates all kinds of grief during assembly. Examine your kit thoroughly at the time of delivery, then it will be ready when it's time for assembly.

Check all connecting rod side clearance and crankshaft end-play. These dimen sions aren't checked often enough.

Not all aftermarket oil pumps will clear the crankshaft counterweight, especially in stroker kits. Make sure the counterweight clears the pump by at least .050-inch. If the pump doesn't clear, do not grind material off of the crankshaft counterweight. Grind the oil pump body enough to clear the pump. Then thoroughly wash the pump in solvent. Seal off pump passages before doing any grinding.

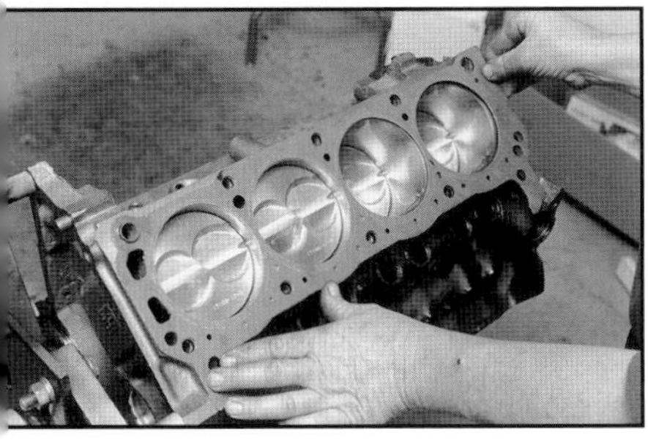

Overheating problems plague small-block Fords because builders install the head gaskets backwards. "FRONT" means FRONT on both sides. Coolant passages in the head gaskets must be positioned at the rear of the block as shown. This enables coolant to circulate through the entire block and heads.

Degreeing A Camshaft

We've been over this once before in Chapter 2, but we're going to touch on it again, just in case you missed it. Why degree a camshaft? Because degreeing a camshaft should always be an integral part of an engine building plan. We degree or dial in a camshaft because this process eliminates all doubt about camshaft, crankshaft, and timing set integrity. It tells us valve timing events and cam lobe specs in great detail. And, believe it or not, cam grinders do make mistakes. Camshafts get packaged incorrectly. And camshafts don't always get ground to the specs on the card. Degreeing in your camshaft is a fact-finding mission.

When we degree a camshaft, we're determining valve timing events as they relate to crankshaft position. The crankshaft makes two complete revolutions for every one revolution of the camshaft. One full revolution of each is 360 degrees. This means the crank turns 720 degrees and the cam 360 degrees. Think of rotation like a pie. Half a turn is 180 degrees. A quarter of a turn is 90 degrees.

Duration is the number of degrees of rotation the camshaft will make from the time the valve begins to open until the time it closes. When we see 244 degrees of duration, this means 244 degrees of camshaft rotation from valve unseat to valve seat. Overlap or lobe separation is the number of degrees between maximum valve lift intake and maximum valve lift exhaust. With all this in mind, we can degree the camshaft timing events in time with piston travel.

When we advance or retard camshaft timing, we do it in the number of degrees of crankshaft rotation. Out of the box camshafts typically have some degree of valve timing advance programmed in by the manufacturer. When we time a camshaft straight up, this means we're keeping the cam in the manufacturer's suggested position on the spec card. Call this point zero or straight up, then advance or retard valve timing from there.

We degree a camshaft using a degree wheel bolted to the crankshaft as shown. Align the degree wheel with crankshaft's top dead center timing mark. Turn the crank and get the #1 piston to top dead center (TDC) using a piston stop for accuracy. Turn the crank, moving the piston down in the bore. Then turn the crank and bring the piston to TDC. Examine the degree wheel. Turn the crank in the opposite direction, then bring the piston back to TDC. Examine the degree wheel again. Split the readings between the two finds to find true TDC. With the piston against the stop, adjust the degree wheel to zero. Double-check the readings.

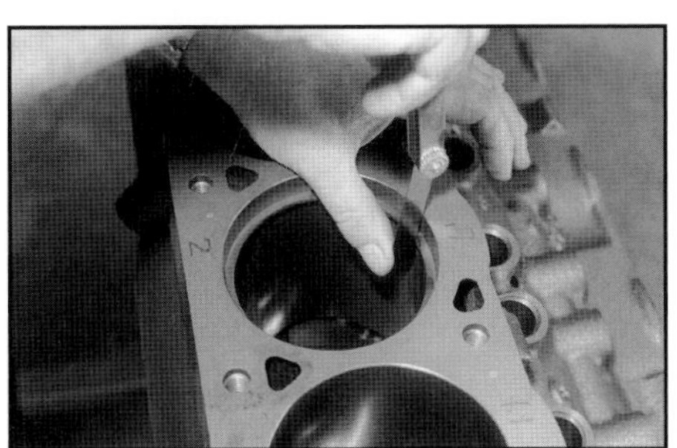

Above and below: All piston ring end gaps should be checked. Never kid yourself. No two sets of rings and cylinder bores are the same dimension.

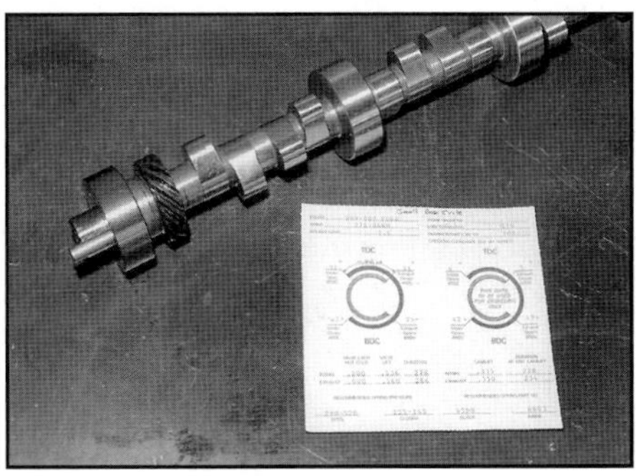

This is a cam card, which contains all of the cam specifications. These specs should jibe with degree events.

Leak Stop!

Few things are more frustrating than a new engine that leaves oil spots on your driveway. This is why you must be as painstaking with leak prevention as you are anywhere else in your stroker build-up.

Whenever possible, use a late-model 5.0L or 5.8L block with the one-piece rear-main seal. The one-piece seal does an extraordinary job of keeping oil inside the engine. It is also very simple to install.

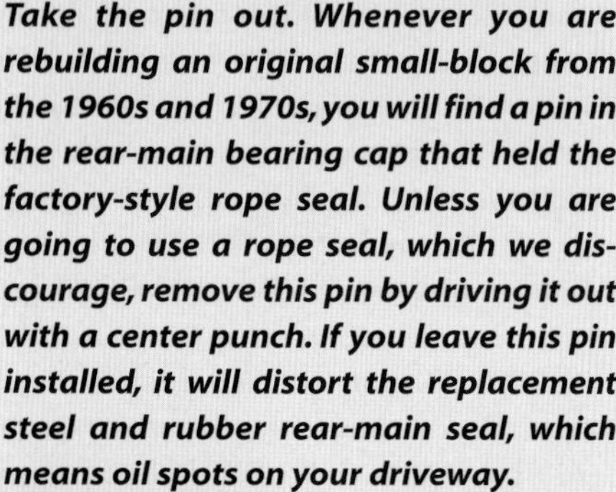

Take the pin out. Whenever you are rebuilding an original small-block from the 1960s and 1970s, you will find a pin in the rear-main bearing cap that held the factory-style rope seal. Unless you are going to use a rope seal, which we discourage, remove this pin by driving it out with a center punch. If you leave this pin installed, it will distort the replacement steel and rubber rear-main seal, which means oil spots on your driveway.

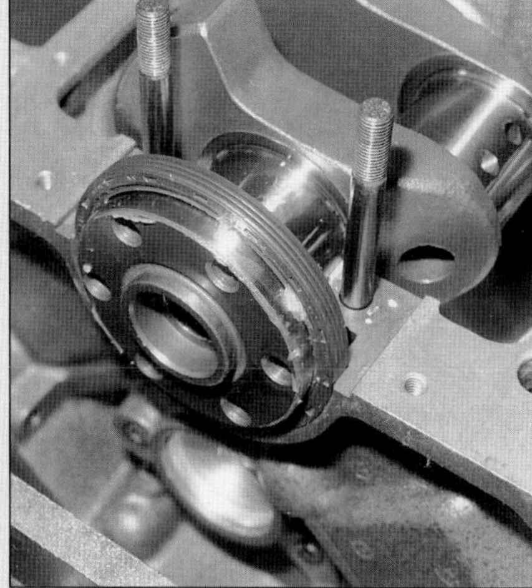

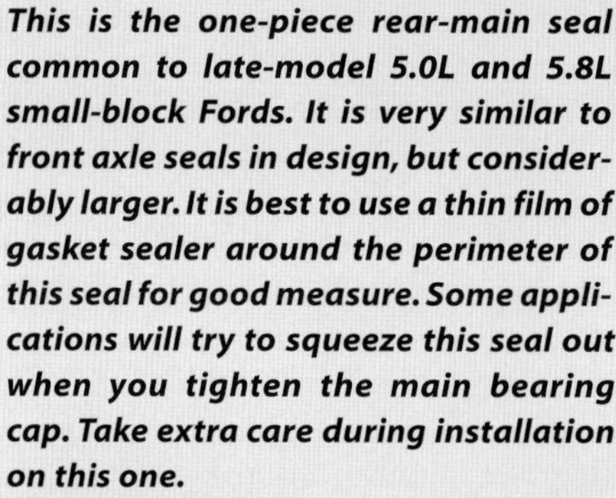

This is the one-piece rear-main seal common to late-model 5.0L and 5.8L small-block Fords. It is very similar to front axle seals in design, but considerably larger. It is best to use a thin film of gasket sealer around the perimeter of this seal for good measure. Some applications will try to squeeze this seal out when you tighten the main bearing cap. Take extra care during installation on this one.

Internal leakage is something we don't often think about, but it can hurt an engine. Where Ford used press-in oil galley plugs behind the timing cover, tap the holes and install screw-in oil galley plugs. One engine builder we know drills a tiny hole in one of the screw-in plugs, which gives the timing chain assembly more oil.

The Right Stuff from Permatex is an outstanding gasket sealer and substitute. Along the intake manifold support rails fore and aft is one favored location for The Right Stuff.

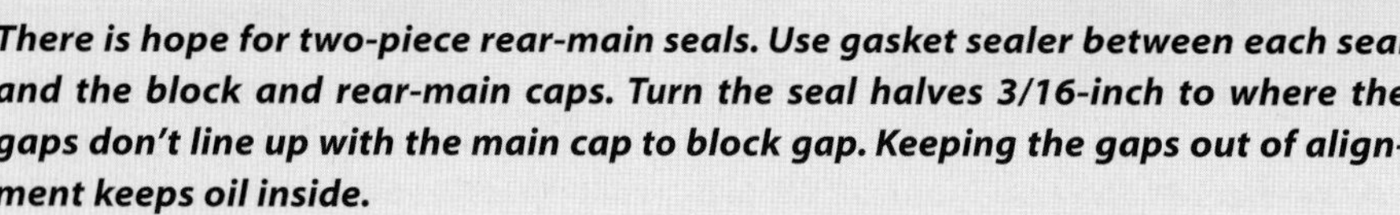

There is hope for two-piece rear-main seals. Use gasket sealer between each seal and the block and rear-main caps. Turn the seal halves 3/16-inch to where the gaps don't line up with the main cap to block gap. Keeping the gaps out of alignment keeps oil inside.

Another area to address is the gap between the rear-main cap and block. Use gasket sealer between the main cap and block as shown.

Valvetrain

Your engine's valvetrain is likely the most tortured collection of moving parts in the engine. At 6000 rpm, valves slam against their seats 3000 times a minute. Exhaust valves not only reciprocate vigorously at half the speed of the crankshaft, they're subjected to combustion temperatures of approximately 1800 to 2000 degrees F. Lifters, pushrods, rocker arms, and valvesprings take a similar amount of punishment. Of all your engine's components, valvetrain components are the most likely to fail. Many a broken valve spring or failed keeper has brought down the mightiest of engines. This is why your attention to this area is vital.

A valvetrain's greatest ally is stability. Valvetrain systems must have matched components for stable operation. This is why camshaft manufacturers have gone more to camshaft kits in recent years to help us choose the right combination of components. Camshaft companies make it easy to package your valvetrain system. Packaging a valvetrain depends on how you want your engine to perform. If you're building a street engine that will be operating in the 2500 – 5500 rpm range, camshaft specifications need to be conservative on the side of torque. The cam should be conservative because we want the engine to make good low-end torque for the street. As a result, lifters, pushrods, rocker arms, and springs need to follow suit. Run a spring that is too soft for your camshaft and your engine will experience valve float (not enough spring pressure to close the valves in a timely fashion) at high RPM. Likewise, run a spring that's too stiff and you can wipe the cam lobes from excessive pressure against the lobe. This is why running matched components is so important.

Lifters

Four basic lifter (tappet) types are used in small-block Fords – flat tappet hydraulic and mechanical, and roller hydraulic and mechanical. Flat tappet lifters were original equipment prior to 1985 when roller tappets debuted inside the 5.0L High Output V-8. Roller tappets found use more and more in Ford factory V-8 engines after 1985. More and more engine builds are witnessing the use of roller tappets because there's less friction, smoother operation, and the ability to run a more aggressive profile without the drawbacks of a radical flat tappet camshaft.

Roller tappets are more costly than flat tappets due to tighter tolerances and a greater number of parts. Their cost puts them outside of the budget engine category, but they're worth every penny in what they save in wear and tear. They also give you the advantage if your desire is to run a more aggressive camshaft profile.

Hydraulic lifters saw more widespread use beginning in the 1960s, although their use dates back to the 1920s. Hydraulic lifters don't require periodic adjustment like a mechanical or solid lifter. As the camshaft and valvetrain wear, hydraulic lifters expand with the wear via oil pressure to take up clearance. This keeps operation quiet and reliability sound. Hydraulic lifters do well until cam lobe and valvestem wear is so excessive the lifter can no longer take up the clearance. Then we hear the tell-tale click or tapping of rocker-arm noise, especially when the engine is cold. Sometimes rocker arm click is a faulty lifter (leaking down hydraulic pressure) or an excessively worn rocker arm. This is especially true with the rail-style rocker arms Ford used from mid 1966 until the 1978 model year. Rail-style rocker-arm tips wear at the valvestem, which eventually leads to the rails digging into the retainer. The first indication of an excessively worn rail rocker arm is that clicking that occurs at any engine temperature.

Lifter and cam lobe wear and failure are rarely caused by a manufacturing defect. They fail because we don't give them a good start when it's time to fire the engine in the first place. Flat tappet camshafts must be broken in properly or failure is inevitable. Moly coat must be applied to the cam lobe and lifter face when you're installing a flat tappet camshaft. The engine must be operated at 2500 rpm for 20-30 minutes after the initial fire-up to properly wear in the lobes. Synthetic engine oil should not be used until after the break-in period. During this period, check the pushrods for rotation.

Roller tappets don't require break-in because rollers and cam lobes enjoy a good relationship to begin with. The lobes are already hardened and rollers provide a smooth ride. Roller tappets can even be reused with a new camshaft if they're in good condition. If you're building a high-mileage engine, we suggest the use of new roller tappets with a new camshaft.

Flat tappets sit on the cam lobe like this. As the cam lobe spins, it spins the lifter in the bore to evenly distribute wear.

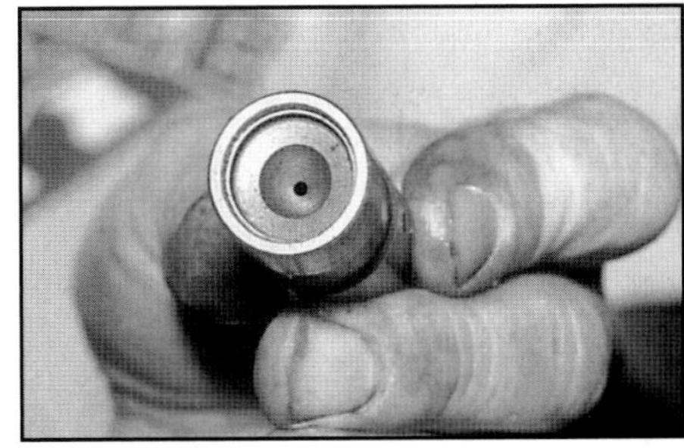

Mechanical (solid) tappets offer precise valve action events. These are solid, with no internal parts. Valve lash adjustment for these happens at the rocker arms.

Flat tappet mechanical camshafts are good for high revving engines where the inaccuracies of hydraulic camshafts (lifter collapse) are unacceptable. Mechanical camshafts give us accuracy because there's nothing left to chance. The lift moves with the cam lobe with solid precision. Given proper valve lash adjustment, mechanical lifters do their job very well. The thing is, mechanical flat and roller tappets have to be adjusted periodically, which can be annoying on a daily driven street engine. This is where you will need to do some soul searching before selecting a camshaft and valvetrain.

Rocker Arms & Pushrods

The pushrod and rocker arm transfer the cam lobe's energy to the valvestem. Think of the rocker arm as the camshaft's messenger, because the rocker arm multiplies lift, which makes the valve open further than the camshaft's lobe lift. Rocker arm types range from stock cast affairs all the way up to extruded and forged pieces with roller bearings and tips. Forged or extruded roller rocker arms are quite costly, which generally leaves them out of a budget engine program. However, this doesn't mean you have to settle for stock cast or stamped steel pieces either.

Stock cast or stamped steel rocker arms don't perform well under the heavy demands of radical camshaft profiles. An aggressive camshaft profile will break a stock rocker arm in short order. This is why it is always best to err on the side of heavy-duty whenever you're building an engine. Stamped steel, ball-stud, roller-tip rocker arms are a good first step toward valvetrain durability whenever you opt for a higher lift camshaft. The roller tip reduces the stress we experience with stock rocker arms. The thing is, when we increase lift and valve spring pressures, a stamped steel or cast roller tip rocker arm doesn't always stand up to the test, especially when spring pressures climb to over 350 pounds. Even the best stamped-steel, roller-tip rocker arm will fail when overstressed.

When lift and spring pressures go skyward, you're going to want a roller pivot, roller-tip forged rocker arm for your budget engine build. Going that extra mile with a super durable rocker arm ensure longer engine life, especially if you're going to drive it daily. For the weekend racer, stepping up to a better rocker arm is like writing a life insurance policy for your engine, because marginal rocker arms will not stand up to the high-revving task. Roller pivot, roller-tip rocker arms also ensure valvetrain precision and accuracy when the revs get high.

We suggest looking to Crane Cams, Comp Cams, or Crower for your Ford engine rocker arms and pushrods. These companies all have a lot of valuable experience with valvetrain components and offer wide selection. Good rule of thumb is to run the same brand of rocker arm and camshaft. See your favorite camshaft company or speed shop for more details.

When it comes to valvetrain adjustment, small-block Fords have flexibility in available aftermarket adjustable studs where adjustable studs were not originally used. The same is true for the 351C/351M/400M middle blocks. Early small-block Fords (1962-1967) had adjustable, ball/stud-mounted rocker arms. From 1968 to 1977, small blocks received no-adjust, positive-stop rocker-arm studs that are undesirable for the performance buff. From 1978 to present, the rocker arm stud was replaced with a new-design stamped-steel rocker arm, fulcrum, and bolt that mount atop a boss on the head.

Small-block Fords from May 8, 1966 and up have rail-style rocker arms, which eliminate the pushrod guide that was cast into the cylinder head. The rocker arm's side rails keep the rocker arm centered on the valvestem. The problem is, as the rocker-arm tip wears at the valvestem, the rails move closer to the valve spring retainer. As the rails push down on the retainer, the risk of valve keeper failure increases. When the keeper fails, the valve drops into the cylinder causing major engine failure. Excessively worn rail-style rocker arms cause a tell-tale clicking during engine operation. Close examination of the valve spring retainer will reveal wear marks from the rails if wear is excessive. Rail-style rocker arms don't perform well with high-lift camshaft profiles because the rails can contact the retainer. Sometimes these rocker arms pop off to one side or the other at high revs, pressing on the retainer and risking engine failure. During a rebuild, we suggest the use of 1962-1966-style conventional rocker arms with screw-in studs and

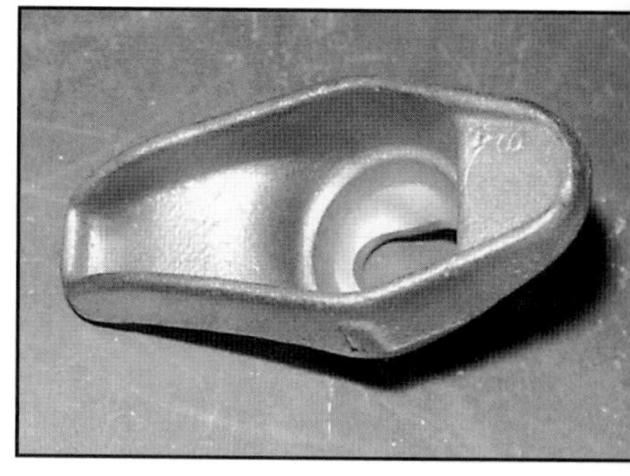

Small-block Ford rocker arms started out like this from 1962 through early 1966 (prior to May 8, 1966). This design employs pushrod guide holes cast into the cylinder head.

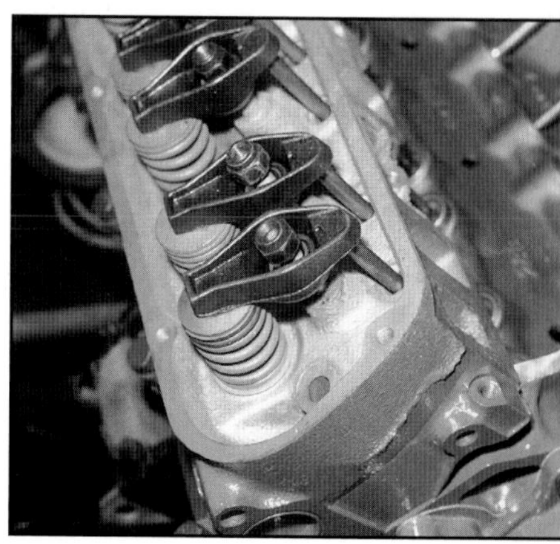

From May 8, 1966 through 1977, small-block Fords had rail-style rocker arms, which use rails cast into the rocker-arm tip to keep the rocker arm centered on the valve. Problems arise when the rocker-arm tip wears and the rails touch the valve spring retainer. This causes clicking and potential engine failure.

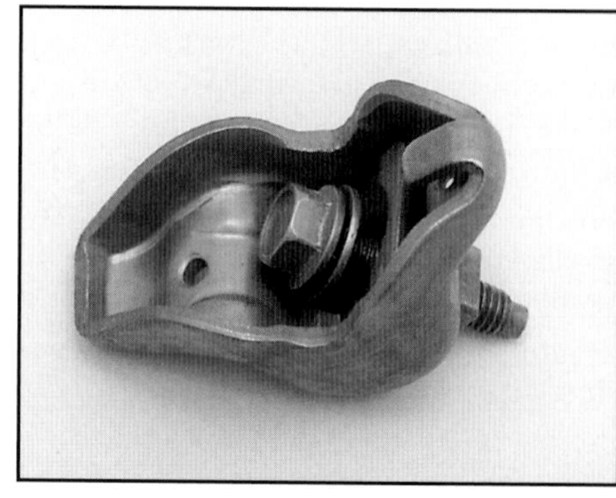

Beginning in 1978, small-block Fords were equipped with stamped steel rocker arms with a bolt/fulcrum arrangement. These are not adjustable.

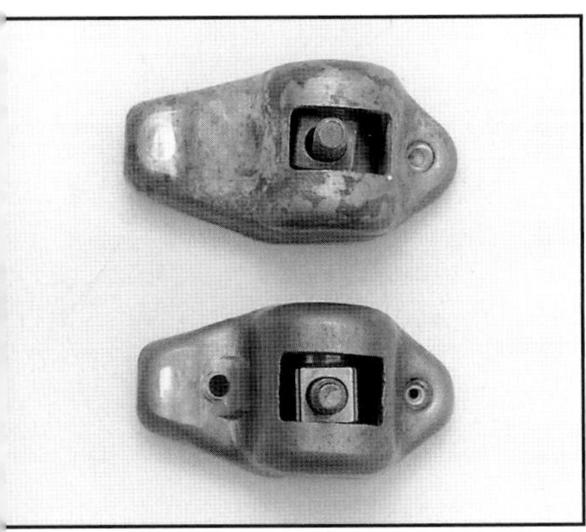

Cleveland (351) and Modified/Midland (351/400) engines have bolt-fulcrum style rocker arms that are not adjustable. The exception is 1971 Boss 351 and 1972 351 High Output, which have adjustable rocker arms mounted on screw-in studs (mechanical lifters).

This is a 351C head with screw-in rocker-arm studs, and adjustable, aftermarket roller-tip rocker arms.

pushrod guide plates for best results. For engine integrity, there really is no other choice.

The 335-series small-block engine family (351C, 351M, 400M) had two types of rocker arm arrangements from the factory. The Boss 351 (1971) and 351 High Output (1972) had adjustable, stud-mounted rocker arms. The rest had bolt/fulcrum style, no-adjust, stamped-steel rocker arms like we find on small-block Fords from 1978-up.

Rocker-Arm Adjustment

Small-block Fords sport an array of rocker-arm combinations depending on generation. We're going to walk you through how to do valve lash adjustment on each. Small-block Fords from 1962-1967 have adjustable ball-stud rocker arms. There are different theories on how these should be adjusted. Adjustment depends on how your engine will be used. For street engines, the best approach is to turn the rocker-arm stud nut clockwise (engine warm) until the rocker arm contacts the valvestem, then tighten the nut 1/2 to 3/4-turn.

Ford small blocks from 1968 to 1977 have no-adjust, positive-stop rocker arms, which makes adjustment impossible. However, modifying 1968-up heads with screw-in studs and pushrod guide plates makes adjustment possible. This is strongly suggested with your stroker project.

Beginning in 1978, small-block Fords were fitted with bolt/fulcrum, stamped-steel rocker arms, like the 335-series 351C, 351M, and 400M V-8s we're about to address. The 335-series engines also have no-adjust, bolt-fulcrum rocker arm set-up with the exception being the Boss 351C, which had mechanical lifters and adjustable ball/stud rocker arms.

When you're shopping for pushrods, we suggest a lightweight 5/16-inch ,welded-ball tip, chrome-moly piece for the best reliability. Regardless of budget, we must have components that will withstand the torture of valvetrain vibration and oscillation or the situation gets unpleasant quickly. A failed pushrod at high RPM can do extensive engine damage to a point where you will forget all about all that money you were trying to save.

Proper pushrod length is a very serious consideration for any engine builder. As we said earlier, it can mean the difference between long engine life and having to pull heads in a few thousand miles. A pushrod that's too long will push the rocker-arm tip under-center, causing excessive side loading to the valvestem and guide. Likewise, a pushrod that's too short will do the same thing on the opposite side. A pushrod checker will help you make the right decision for not much money. You can find one of these at your favorite speed shop and get right to work in your search for the correct length pushrod.

When you're checking pushrod length, you want the rocker-arm tip to be close to center on the valvestem tip. Remember, the rocker-arm tip is going to walk across the valvestem tip when we come up on the high side of the cam lobe. Take a black felt-tip marker and darken the valvestem tip. Then install the rocker arm and pushrod. Hand crank the engine and watch the valve pass through one full opening and closing. Get down along side the rocker arm and valvespring and watch how the rocker arm travels. Then inspect the black marking for a wear pattern. This will show you exactly where the rocker-arm tip has traveled across the valvestem tip. The pattern should be centered on the valvestem tip. If it runs too much toward the outside of the valvestem tip, the pushrod is too short. If it runs toward the inside of the valvestem tip, the pushrod is too long.

Pushrod length is checked by examining the rocker arm angle as it relates to the valve stem and pushrod.

Valves & Springs

Valves and springs play an important role in power and reliability. Weak spots in either area can rob you of power or lead to engine failure. This is why choosing the right valves and springs is so important. Most cam manufacturers offer a variety of valve spring combinations designed to work well with the camshaft you have chosen. In fact, the best way to shop and buy a cam is to purchase a camshaft kit, which includes valvesprings, retainers, and keepers matched to the camshaft profile chosen. We match a cam and springs because we want a compatible spring for the cam profile. More radical cams call for stiffer springs. Milder camshaft grinds need less valvespring pressure. Too much

Valvespring installed height looks like this. Always check your spring specs with the retainer installed.

This is a single valvespring arrangement like we see in stock applications. Some are equipped with dampeners as shown for spring stability.

Dual valvesprings are available for more aggressive camshaft profiles.

Triple valvesprings from Crane Cams ensure positive valve closure with the most aggressive cam profiles. Chances are you won't be using these in your budget application.

spring pressure can wipe the cam lobes. Too little can cause valve float (valve seating doesn't keep up with the revs) at high revs.

Choosing the right valvespring is strictly a matter of following a camshaft grinder's recommendations. Most springs are applicable to hydraulic or mechanical lifters. Some are specific only to roller camshafts. Crane Cams, for example, offers dozens of different valvespring types. The part number you select depends on camshaft profile. See your cam grinder for more details.

When you opt for a camshaft kit, there's comfort in knowing the manufacturer has matched the springs to the camshaft profile. Most of the homework has been done for you. There won't be concern about coil binding, or too much or too little spring pressure. The best time to check for coil bind is when you're degreeing in the camshaft. Do this before permanently bolting on the heads. Most cam grinders will tell you the recommended installed spring height and seat pressure. Correct installed height and spring pressure are achieved with the use of shims as necessary. Coil bind is checked by checking coil spacing with the valve at maximum lift. There should be no less than .040-inch between the coils at full valve lift. Retainer to valve guide clearance at full lift is the same – no less than .040-inch. This clearance is vital because coil bind or retainer contact with the head will cause valvetrain failure. The .040-inch we give it allows for thermal expansion of metal parts and any camshaft aggressiveness at high revs.

Another huge consideration whenever you're installing a camshaft with greater lift and duration is piston-to-valve clearance. The most common practice is to press modeling clay into the piston valve reliefs, temporarily install the head and valvetrain, then turn the crank two full revolutions. If you feel any resistance, back off and remove the head. Chances are you have piston-to-valve contact. Forcing the crank will bend the valve and/or damage the piston. If no resistance is felt in two turns of the crankshaft, remove the head and examine the clay. Slice the clay at the valve relief and check the thickness of the clay. This is your piston to valve clearance.

And finally, whenever you're rebuilding cylinder heads, always remember the valve guides and valve to guide clearances. Loose valve to guide clearance leads to loss of oil control. Clearances that are too tight can cause the valve to seize to the guide when the engine is hot. Precise valve-to-guide clearance and healthy seals make every difference.

Stroker Tuning & Operation

What we do with a stroker small block after assembly is complete is just as critical as the actual build-up. Improper performance tuning can damage an engine just as easily as dust and grit on bearing surfaces. Tuning begins with cylinder head, camshaft and induction selection, which determines how you will tune the engine in operating form. We presume you have already chosen the right camshaft, cylinder heads and induction system for your engine. This subject is covered earlier in Chapter 2. This leads us to what to do once the engine is safely nestled in your engine bay.

Before the engine is fired for the first time, it needs to be ready for a safe start-up. Fill the oil pan with the appropriate amount of SAE 30 weight engine oil. If you're going to use a synthetic engine oil, like Mobil 1 or Royal Purple, wait until the engine has 500 to 1,000 miles before switching over. Personally, we suggest the use of Castrol SAE 30 or 10w30 weight oil for your initial fire-up and break-in.

With the oil pan supplied and a Mobil 1 filter installed, the oiling system needs to be primed. When we prime the oiling system, we run the engine's oil pump to supply the bearings and cylinder walls with plenty of lubricating oil. This ensures that all lubricated surfaces have plenty of oil for the first fire-up. Oil system priming should happen within one hour of engine start.

We prime the engine's oiling system with a oil pump primer, which fits into the block in place of the distributor. The oil pump primer is propelled by an electric drill capable of turning the pump drive. Oil system priming should be done with the valve covers removed to check oil flow from the pushrods and rocker arms. Although it is physically impossible to check bearings for oil flow, oil flow at the rocker arms is a good indication that oil is flowing everywhere. Oil system priming is good not only for lubricated surfaces, but to fill the hydraulic lifters with oil prior to fire-up.

With oil pump priming out of the way, it is time to static tune the engine for fire-up. Crank the engine slowly, putting the #1 piston at top dead center on compression stroke (both valves closed). Installing a distributor in a small-block Ford can be very frustrating because the distributor doesn't always mate smoothly with the oil pump shaft. Slip the distributor into place, locating the rotor at #1 on the distributor cap. If the distributor does not seat, have someone jab the starter quickly, which will turn the camshaft and distributor, allow the distributor to find a smooth marriage with the oil pump shaft. Once the distributor is seated, crank the engine and determine correct location of the rotor. With the #1 cylinder at TDC on compression stroke, the distributor rotor should be at #1.

With static ignition timing out of the way, it is time to double check valve clearances. If you are running a hydraulic camshaft with adjustable rocker arms, crank the engine and follow the firing order to check valve adjustment. Most hydraulic roller camshafts have a 351W firing order, even if they're installed in a pre 1982 289/302ci engine. Determine your camshaft's firing order before getting started.

Begin with the #1 cylinder, with both valves closed. Loosen the rocker arm nut until the rocker feels loose. Slowly tighten the rocker arm nut until the rocker touches the valvestem. Tighten 1/2 to 3/4-turn. Move on to the next valve duo in the firing order, hand-cranking the engine until both valves are closed at compression stroke.

With the oiling system primed, the distributor installed and properly timed, and all 16 valves properly adjusted, it is time to set up the fuel system for a safe start. We're going to address the many types of carburetors in order to get you started on the right foot. Our objective is to get the air/fuel mixture adjusted in the middle of the road, and the idle-speed screw set where it should be for a slightly fast idle (around 1,000 rpm).

Because firing an engine for the first time can be nerve racking, we want to take the safest approach possible. Engines fitted with roller-tappet camshafts don't need the faster break-in speeds needed for flat-tappet camshafts. If you're running a roller-tappet camshaft, run the engine at 1,000 to 1,200 rpm for a good warm-up and piston ring seating.

When an engine is fitted with a flat tappet camshaft of any kind, we need to start the engine and allow it to run for 20-30 minutes at 2,500 rpm for proper camshaft lobe break-in. This allows the cam lobes to wear in and achieve a hardened surface. This is a process you don't want to fail with. If you skip this step, you can expect to wipe the cam lobes in short order. Then, you get to replace the new camshaft.

Before You Spin It

Before firing an engine, check two very important things – coolant and oil levels. Fill the radiator with straight water for that first firing, just in case there is a leak. We suggest running a coolant filter in the upper radiator hose to catch any iron or machining particles that would block new radiator tubes. Small-block Fords are notorious for stray iron particles that clog new radiators and heater cores.

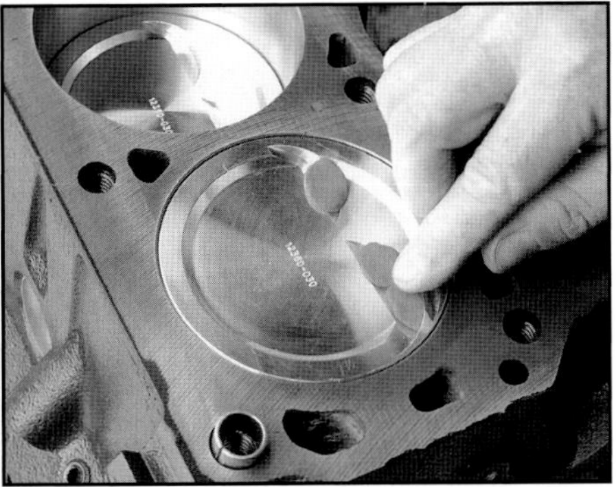

Piston to valve clearance is checked by molding clay into the valve reliefs as shown.

With the cylinder head, pushrod, and rocker arm installed, we hand crank the engine through two complete revolutions.

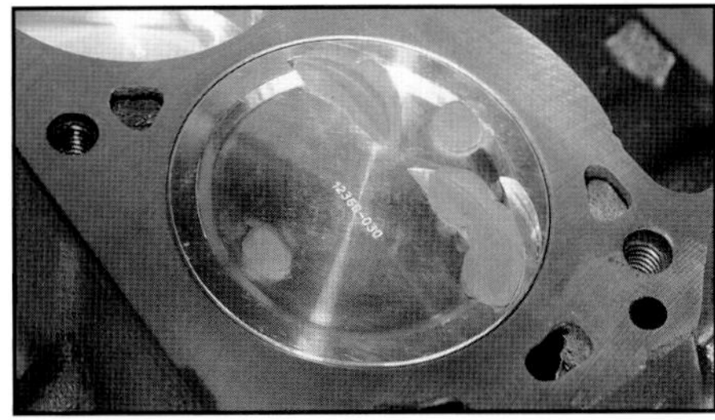

With the cylinder head removed, the clay is checked for valve impressions. If there is piston to valve interference, you will feel it with the resistance to crank rotation. Do not force it. Impressions in the clay also confirm interference.

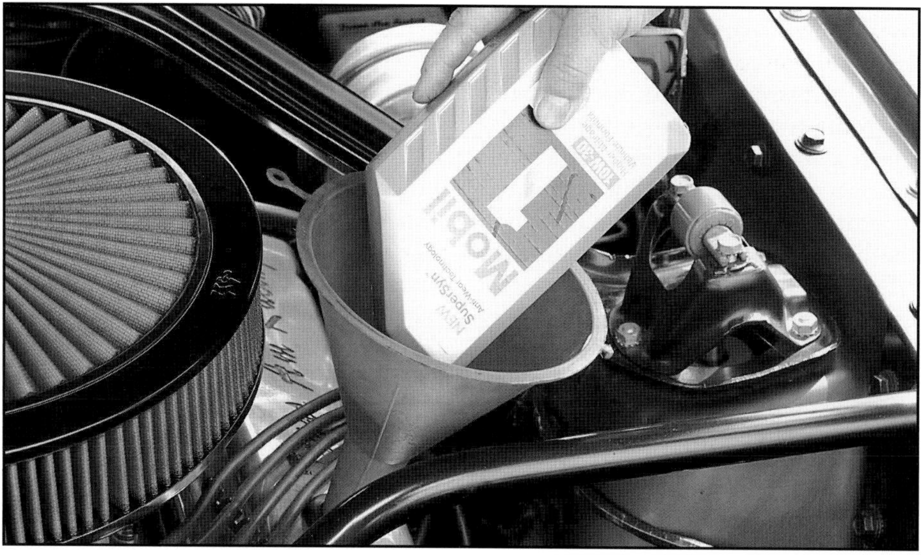

Fill your small-block's oil pan with regular SAE 30 weight engine oil. We suggest the use of Castrol SAE 30 or 10w30 weight oil for your break-in.

Note that we said "new" radiator tubes. Never put a new engine into service using an aging and dirty radiator. We see this sort of thing all the time. Performance enthusiasts, suffering from the sticker shock of an expensive engine build, just don't have the heart, or the money, to purchase a new radiator. But if you're going to build an engine, dial the cost of a good support system into the budget. That support system should include a radiator that is clean, serviceable, and ready to extract heat from a fresh engine. Fresh engines tend to run hot because break-in involves a certain amount of friction at the cylinder walls, bearings and journals, and valvestems.

When you're shopping for a radiator, always opt for a lot of cooling capacity. Classic Mustangs and other vintage Fords need four-row core radiators for maximum cooling effectiveness. And despite what you've heard about aluminum radiators, the old-fashioned tried and proven copper and brass radiator offer better cooling efficiency than aluminum. The only real disadvantage to copper and brass radiators is weight. They're heavier than aluminum radiators. Using a fan shroud around the cooling fan helps keep air velocity through the fins and tubes where it belongs. And one more thing about that fan-shroud. The fan blade tips should be half-exposed around the perimeter of the shroud. If the fan shroud completely covers the fan blade tips, you will lose cooling effectiveness. In fact, your engine will run considerable hotter with the fan blade tips covered. The reason we want the fan blade tips half exposed is airflow. Airflow needs to travel through and past the blade tips, which pulls more air through the radiator. When we completely shroud the fan, we greatly limit airflow through the fan.

The most efficient type of cooling fan, besides the electric fan, is an engine-driven thermostatic clutch fan. Thermostatic clutch fans free-wheel when they're not needed, engaging and turning with the water pump as needed. On a cool day, clutch fans do very little work. When it is hot, the clutch engages, moving critical air through the radiator.

Fill your radiator until the water level is 1-inch below the neck. Leave the cap off. In order to bleed any and all air bubbles out of the water jackets, remove the heater hose at the intake manifold and wait for water to rise to the nipple. This ensures most air has been displaced with water inside the block and heads. Fresh engines, especially, don't need hot spots in the block and heads, which can cause significant damage and ruin proper break-in.

With the engine at operating temperature, it is time for initial tuning. For initial tuning, you will need an intake manifold vacuum gauge and a timing light if you're working with a carbureted engine. For fuel-injected engines, you need a scan device to check for fault codes. Ideally, you will have an exhaust gas analyzer to examine mixture in either case.

Ignition timing should be checked first. Rev the engine to 3,500 rpm and hold it there, checking ignition timing with a timing light. This is where total spark advance should come into play. Depending on the camshaft you have chosen, total spark advance at 3,500 rpm should be 39-41 degrees BTDC (before top dead center). This allows your engine to take advantage of the air/fuel charge. Ignition timing at idle speed (roughly 600-800 rpm) should be around 12 degrees BTDC. Because vacuum advance units all must be calibrated for each specific application, you may have to make adjustments.

Aftermarket vacuum advance units are calibrated with an Allen wrench through the vacuum port. Turn the Allen wrench clockwise to slow the rate of spark advance. Turn it counter clockwise to increase the rate of spark advance. Slowing the rate of spark advance means the spark advance won't go to full advance as quickly. Speeding up the rate of advance means you will get full advance before the engine reaches 3,500 rpm. When this happens, you will likely hear detonation (pinging or spark knock) under acceleration. Pinging or spark knock is a bad thing. It means detonation is hammering the piston pin and rod bearings at the least. Worst case scenario, you will burn pistons. If there isn't enough spark advance, your engine will nose over and fall on its face. You won't get the power desired without enough spark advance.

With the engine at operating temperature and the ignition timing where it belongs, you're ready to adjust the fuel mixture and idle speed. Ideally, you will have adjusted your ignition timing at both normal idle speed and at 3,500 rpm. This leaves only the fuel/air mixture to check. In any case, hook up the vacuum gauge below the carburetor base plate where there is a constant vacuum and examine the vacuum reading. A normal, healthy idle should show 18-22 inches of vacuum. Of course, the more radical the camshaft, the lower the vacuum reading will be. With a streetable camshaft, vacuum should be healthy. Turn each mixture screw in one at a time until the idle begins to falter. Vacuum should falter as well. Slowly back the mixture screw out until the idle stabilizes. Seek the highest vacuum reading possible while adjusting the mixture screws. Do the same on the other side. Listen to the engine's idle. Is it smooth? What is your vacuum reading?

With all basic tuning out of the way, observe the way the engine idles. Listen to the valvetrain for noise. Lay under the vehicle and listen to the bottom end for unusual noises. Examine the oil pressure. Oil pressure should be 10 psi for every 1,000 rpm. This means your engine should be holding a solid 10-20 psi of oil pressure at idle speed. At 4,000 rpm, you should have at least 40 psi of oil pressure.

If you're dealing with a fuel-injected small block, it would be a good idea to check fuel pressure, which should be at least 40-45 psi. If it is low, suspect either the fuel pressure regulator or the electric fuel pump. Low fuel pressure can cause engine damage under hard acceleration and/or during the use of nitrous. Make sure your SEFI (sequential electronic fuel injection) small block is getting adequate fuel pressure.

After 500 to 1,000 miles of driving, do a spark plug reading on all eight cylinders. Your engine's spark plugs should have a light tan color with a minimum of deposits. If they are snow white, the mixture is too lean. If they are a sooty black, the mixture is too rich.

Stand at the tail pipes and listen to the engine at idle. Place your hand at the tailpipe and feel the pulsing. Is it consistent? Or is there a misfire? If there is any hint of suction at the pipe, this indicates exhaust valves that may not be seating properly. The exhaust pulse should be smooth and consistent. Have someone rev the engine and hold it at 3,000 rpm. Listen to the exhaust pulse. Again, it should be consistent. Any misfire or uneven pulsing is an indication of irregular fuel mixture or ignition timing that is too advanced. When the timing is too far away, an irregular misfire will occur. Back the timing off in slow increments until the misfire fades to a smooth pulsing at the tailpipe.

If all of this seems like a bit much, consider how important proper tuning will make a difference in longer, more reliable engine life. Good tuning not only makes a difference in engine life, it makes a big difference in performance. This is the time to give your engine the good start it deserves.

Preventive Stroker Maintenance

How do you keep a good healthy stroker small block alive? Most of it depends on you, your driving technique, and how often you take care of underhood maintenance. Throughout a lifetime of experience and significant changes in the world of internal combustion engines, we have learned there is no better life insurance policy for an engine than regular, preventative maintenance. Oil and filter should be changed every 3,000 miles. Once an engine has passed the 1,000-mile mark, we highly recommend the use of a quality synthetic engine oil like Mobil 1 in 10w30 weight. Of all of the filters we have used through the years, the two best ones are Mobil 1 and Purolator. If it boiled down to choosing between the two, we would choose Mobil 1. Mobil 1 oil filters employ an abundance of filtering material, making them a superior filter. The Mobil 1 oil and filter combination is unbeatable for safe engine lubrication.

Once you have confirmed the cooling system to be leak-free, completely drain the cooling system of all water. Remove the block drain plugs to ensure all coolant has escaped. Purge the heater core of all coolant.

When the cooling system is completely drained, fill it with a 50/50 mix of antifreeze and distilled water. Do not use tap water. Tap water often contains minerals and other contaminates that can be harmful to the engine's water jackets and radiator from a corrosion standpoint. The more pure you can keep your engine's coolant, the longer the cooling system will last.

Another option for performance buffs is Evans NPG+ non-aqueous propylene glycol coolant. This is a dream-come-true coolant designed to make dramatic improvements in heat transfer and viscosity. You can literally pour this no-water coolant into your radiator without any concern for coolant mix. This is because NPG+ is all the coolant your engine will need. All water must be purged from the cooling system when you use NPG+.

NPG+ pulls heat from your engine better than conventional antifreeze-water mixes. Whenever you run the antifreeze/water mix, boil-over can occur around 225 degrees F. sWith a closed radiator cap, the boiling point is raised to 259 degrees F, depending on where you are. NPG+ offers you even greater temperature limits because it doesn't boil until 375 degrees F, not that we would recommend running your engine at this temperature. NPG+ is a lifetime coolant that never has to be replaced (unless contaminated).

This is an oiling system primer for the small-block Ford. As you can see, it fits into the distributor opening in the block and splines over the oil pump shaft below. You will need a powerful reversible drill for this task.

289/302 STROKER KITS & PROJECTS

The marketplace is filled with a wealth of great stroker kits for your 289/302ci engine building project. Which kit you choose depends on your expectations, budget, and needs. This means you have to examine the contents of each kit to determine which kit works for your engine-building project.

Stroker selection depends on your planned mission for the engine. Despite everything you have likely been told in bench racing circles, street engines do not need steel or billet crankshafts. High-nodular iron crankshafts (also known as cast steel) work quite well for street use in applications up to 500 horsepower. If you're going to supercharge or throw high concentrations of nitrous at your engine, a steel crankshaft becomes mandatory in the interest of engine survival. If you do weekend road racing with your driver, a steel crank is good life insurance for your engine. Weekend drag racers don't always need a steel crankshaft because the high-stress experience is brief, unless you are using nitrous or supercharging.

Choosing a connecting rod is right in there with choosing a crankshaft. If you're going to go with H-beam rods, then you will likely go with a steel or billet crank. For cast steel or nodular iron cranks, sportsman level I-beam

302ci

Speed-O-Motive
131 North Lang Ave.
West Covina, CA 91760
626/869-0270 • 626/869-0278 FAX
www.speedomotive.com

Bore:	4.000"
Stroke:	3.000"
Crankshaft:	Nodular Iron Ford 302
Rod Type:	Stage 1 with ARP Wave-Loc Bolts
Rod Length:	5.565"
Rod Ratio:	1.85:1
Pistons:	Keith Black Hypereutectic
Rings:	Speed Pro Cast Iron
Bearings:	Clevite Tri-Metal
Max. RPM:	6,500
Max. HP:	400
Approx. Price:	$1,000.00
Comments:	The Speed-O-Motive Long Rod 302 kit doesn't increase stroke or displacement. But, it increases piston dwell time at the top and bottom of the bore to make the most of your fuel/air mixture. The Long Rod 302 kit gives you more torque.

317ci

Coast High Performance
2555 W. 237th St.
Torrance, CA
310/784-2977 • 310/784-2970 FAX
www.coasthigh.com

Bore:	4.060"
Stroke:	3.100"
Crankshaft:	Nodular Iron 302
Rod Type:	Eagle H-Beam
Rod Length:	5.400"
Rod Ratio:	1.60:1
Pistons:	Probe Forged Aluminum
Rings:	Childs & Albert
Bearings:	Clevite 77
Max. RPM:	7,800
Max. HP:	550
Approx. Price:	$1,700.00
Comments:	This kit provides a solid foundation on which to build. You can grow into this kit with a supercharger, nitrous, a more radical camshaft, you name it. This is a kit you can spin tight without worry, assuming proper assembly technique.

rods will work just fine. Each kit listing is specific about the type of connecting rod and crankshaft used. Most stroker-kit manufacturers have this packaging process down to a science. Connecting rods and crankshafts tend to be quite compatible in most of these kits.

Piston selection boils down to the type of driving you're going to do. Warmed up street engines really don't need forged pistons. If seat-of-the-pants torque is what you are seeking from your street small block, you can get away with using hypereutectic pistons. Opt for forged pistons if you are going to supercharge or use nitrous. Forged pistons for powerful street engines don't make much sense in terms of cost and engine noise. Forged pistons have more unforgiving expansion properties. It takes a forged piston more time to expand as the engine warms. Forged pistons also expand more than cast or hypereutectic pistons, which means they need greater clearances. This is why forged pistons tend to rattle in cold engines.

Most of the following stroker kits are available as published. But most manufacturers will allow you to custom tailor your stroker kit. Coast High Performance, for example, will package a stroker kit any way you desire as long as it makes good sense. Plus, they will advise you along the way.

The following stroker kits are listed how they were available at the time of printing. Not all of these kits will forever remain the same. Kits are developed and kits are dropped from time to time, depending on availability and consumer demand. In our description of each of these kits, we are completely frank about the kit described. We are not at the mercy of advertising dollars and will tell it just like it is.

319ci

Propower
4750 N. Dixie Highway, No. 9
Fort Lauderdale, FL 33334
954/491-6988 • 954/491-2874 FAX
www.propowerparts.com

Bore:	4.030"
Stroke:	3.120"
Crankshaft:	Nodular Iron 302
Rod Type:	Eagle
Rod Length:	5.400"
Rod Ratio:	1.73:1
Pistons:	JE Pistons
Rings:	JE Plasma Moly
Bearings:	King High Performance
Max. RPM:	7,500
Max. HP:	500
Approx. Price:	$2,000.00
Comments:	A good improvement over stock. Better reliability.

317ci

Ford Performance Solutions
1004 Orangefair Lane
Anaheim, CA 92801
714/773-9027 • 714/773-4178 FAX
www.f-p-s.com

Bore:	4.060"
Stroke:	3.100"
Crankshaft:	Nodular Iron 302
Rod Type:	Eagle H-Beam
Rod Length:	5.400"
Rod Ratio:	1.74:1
Pistons:	Ross Ultra-Lite
Rings:	Childs & Albert
Bearings:	Clevite 77
Max. RPM:	8,000
Maxx. HP:	650
Approx. Price:	$1,700.00
Comments:	This kit provides a solid foundation on which to build. You can grow into this kit with big horsepower adders. Very similar to the Coast High Performance kit just mentioned.

317ci

Speed-O-Motive
131 North Lang Ave.
West Covina, CA 91760
626/869-0270 • 626/869-0278 FAX
www.speedomotive.com

Bore:	4.030"
Stroke:	3.100"
Crankshaft:	Race Prepped Nodular Iron 302 Crank
Rod Type:	Forged I-Beam
Rod Length:	5.565"
Rod Ratio:	1.85:1
Pistons:	Keith Black Hypereutectic
Rings:	Speed Pro Cast Iron
Bearings:	Clevite Tri-Metal
Max. RPM:	6,500
Max. HPr:	400
Approx. Price:	$1,000.00
Comments:	This mild increase in stroke will net you increases in power. Properly assembled, your 317ci Speed-O-Motive stroker can spin to 6,500 rpm.

320ci

D.S.S. Competition Products
960 Ridge Avenue
Lombard, IL 60148
630/268-1630 • 630/268-1649 FAX
www.dssracing.com

Bore:	4.030"
Stroke:	3.125"
Crankshaft:	Nodular Iron 302
Rod Type:	Eagle
Rod Length:	5.400"
Rod Ratio:	1.72:1
Pistons:	Venolia
Rings:	Speed-Pro
Bearings:	Federal-Mogul
Max. RPM:	6,500
Max. HP:	500
Approx. Price:	$2,000.00
Comments:	This kit has a good rod ratio and is good for a few extra horses. But this is not a kit you want to use with nitrous or supercharging. This kit is good for a strong, naturally-aspirated street engine.

326ci

Ford Performance Solutions
1004 Orangefair Lane
Anaheim, CA 92801
714/773-9027 • 714/773-4178 FAX
www.f-p-s.com

Bore:	4.030"
Stroke:	3.190"
Crankshaft:	Australian 302C
Rod Type:	Eagle (Oliver or Pro-Billet aluminum rods available)
Rod Length:	5.400"
Rod Ratio:	1.69:1
Pistons:	Ross Ultra-Lite
Rings:	Childs & Albert
Bearings:	Clevite 77
Max. RPM:	8,500
Max. HP:	750
Approx. Price:	$2,500.00
Comments:	This is one of Ford Performance Solution's best kits for the money. It is a kit you can spin extremely tight without the need for a catcher's mitt. This is called the Aussie Saturday Night Special. You can throw nitrous and/or supercharging at this one with caution.

331ci

Coast High Performance
2555 W. 237th St.
Torrance, CA
310/784-2977 • 310/784-2970 FAX
www.coasthigh.com

BUDGET KIT

Bore:	4.030"
Stroke:	3.235"
Crankshaft:	High Nodular Iron 302
Rod Type:	Ford 1600cc I-Beam
Rod Length:	5.200"
Rod Ratio:	1.60:1
Pistons:	Probe Industries Forged
Rings:	Childs & Albert
Bearings:	Clevite 77
Max. RPM:	6,000
Max. HP:	400
Approx. Price:	$1,500.00
Comments:	A good street kit. Naturally aspirated only. No superchargers or nitrous.

331ci

D.S.S. Competition Products
960 Ridge Avenue
Lombard, IL 60148
630/268-1630 • 630/268-1649 FAX
www.dssracing.com

Bore:	4.030"
Stroke:	3.250"
Crankshaft:	Billet Steel
Rod Type:	Crower Sportsman
Rod Length:	5.400"
Rod Ratio:	1.66:1
Pistons:	Venolia
Rings:	Speed-Pro
Bearings:	Federal-Mogul
Max. RPM:	8,200
Max. HP:	600
Approx. Price:	$4,000.00
Comments:	This is an excellent street/strip (mostly strip!) kit.

327ci

Nowak Racing Engines
249 E. Emerson Avenue
Orange, CA 92665
714/282-7996 • 714/637-0425 FAX

Bore:	4.030"
Stroke:	3.200"
Crankshaft:	Australian 302 Cleveland
Rod Type:	Eagle
Rod Length:	5.400"
Rod Ratio:	1.69:1
Pistons:	Nowak
Rings:	Childs & Albert or Speed-Pro
Bearings:	Clevite 77
Max. RPM:	7,500
Max. HP:	550
Approx. Price:	$2,500.00
Comments:	Good street/strip kit that can take nitrous and supercharging.

331ci

Coast High Performance
2555 W. 237th St.
Torrance, CA
310/784-2977 • 310/784-2970 FAX
www.coasthigh.com

PREMIUM KIT

Bore:	4.030"
Stroke:	3.235"
Crankshaft:	High Nodular Iron 302
Rod Type:	Crower
Rod Length:	5.200"
Rod Ratio:	1.60:1
Pistons:	Probe Industries Forged
Rings:	Childs & Albert
Bearings:	Clevite 77
Max. RPM:	6,500
Max. HP:	500
Approx. Price:	$2,500.00
Comments:	Similar to the above CHP kit. Equipped with stronger Crower rod.

331ci

Ford Performance Solutions
1004 Orangefair Lane
Anaheim, CA 92801
714/773-9027 • 714/773-4178 FAX
www.f-p-s.com

Bore:	4.030"
Stroke:	3.250"
Crankshaft:	Cola 4340 Steel
Rod Type:	Eagle
Rod Length:	5.400"
Rod Ratio:	1.66:1
Pistons:	Ross Ultra-Lite
Rings:	Childs & Albert
Bearings:	Clevite 77
Max. RPM:	9,000
Max. HP:	850
Approx. Price:	$3,200.00
Comments:	If you haven't figured it out by now, this is a full-race kit. Throw everything and anything at this kit, including nitrous and blowers.

331ci

Speed-O-Motive
131 North Lang Ave.
West Covina, CA 91760
626/869-0270 • 626/869-0278 FAX
www.speedomotive.com

Bore:	4.000"
Stroke:	3.250"
Crankshaft:	High Nodular Iron
Rod Type:	4340 Forged I-Beam
Rod Length:	5.400"
Rod Ratio:	1.66:1
Pistons:	Keith Black Hypereutectic
Rings:	Sealed Power Iron
Bearings:	Clevite Tri-Metal
Max. RPM:	6,500
Max. HP:	400
Approx. Price:	$1,200.00
Comments:	This is a good budget kit, able to rev freely to six grand. Make the most of the Speed-O-Motive 331ci kit with the right engine packaging including a good cam and cylinder heads.

331ci

Scat Crankshafts
1400 Kingsdale Ave.
Redondo Beach, CA 90278
310/370-5501 • 310/214-2285 FAX
www.scatcrankshafts.com

BUDGET KIT

Bore:	4.030"
Stroke:	3.250"
Crankshaft:	Series 9000 Cast Crankshaft
Rod Type:	Forged I-Beam
Rod Length:	5.400"
Rod Ratio:	1.66:1
Pistons:	Forged
Rings:	Unknown
Bearings:	Unknown
Max. RPM:	6,500
Max. HP:	500
Approx. Price:	$1,500.00
Comments:	Good combination of parts that allow you to make power at high revs.

337ci

Ford Performance Solutions
1004 Orangefair Lane
Anaheim, CA 92801
714/773-9027 • 714/773-4178 FAX
www.f-p-s.com

Bore:	4.030"
Stroke:	3.300"
Crankshaft:	High Nodular Iron 351C
Rod Type:	Eagle H-Beam
Rod Length:	5.400"
Rod Ratio:	1.64:1
Pistons:	Ross Ultra-Lite
Rings:	Childs & Albert
Bearings:	Clevite 77
Max. RPM:	6,800
Max. HP:	550
Approx. Price:	$2,000.00
Comments:	A good bang for the buck kit that will accept nitrous and boost. Some options available for this kit to make it stronger – rods, pistons, crank heat-treating.

331ci

Nowak Racing Engines
249 E. Emerson Avenue, Unit F
Orange, CA 92665
714/282-7996 • 714/637-0425 FAX

Bore:	4.030"
Stroke:	3.250"
Crankshaft:	Steel Forged/Billet
Rod Type:	Crower Sportsman
Rod Length:	5.400"
Rod Ratio:	1.66:1
Pistons:	Nowak Forged
Rings:	Childs & Albert or Speed-Pro
Bearings:	Clevite 77
Max. RPM:	7,500
Max. HP:	550
Approx. Price:	$3,200.00
Comments:	Good combination of parts that allow you to make power at high revs.

331ci

Scat Crankshafts
1400 Kingsdale Ave.
Redondo Beach, CA 90278
310/370-5501 • 310/214-2285 FAX
www.scatcrankshafts.com

PREMIUM KIT

Bore:	4.030"
Stroke:	3.250"
Crankshaft:	Forged Steel
Rod Type:	Scat H-Beam
Rod Length:	5.400"
Rod Ratio:	1.66:1
Pistons:	Forged
Rings:	Unknown
Bearings:	Unknown
Max. RPM:	8,000
Max. HP:	600
Approx. Price:	$3,000.00
Comments:	This is a high-revving, full-race kit.

347ci

Coast High Performance
2555 W. 237th Street
Torrance, CA 90505
310/784-2977 • 310/784-2970 FAX
www.coasthigh.com

Bore:	4.030"
Stroke:	3.400"
Crankshaft:	Cast Steel
Rod Type:	Blue Thunder
Rod Length:	5.315"
Rod Ratio:	1.56:1
Pistons:	Probe Industries Forged
Rings:	Childs & Albert
Bearings:	Clevite 77
Max. RPM:	7,000
Max. HP:	600
Approx. Price:	$2,000.00
Comments:	This is Coast High Performance's most popular kit – the 347 Street Fighter.

347ci

Bennett Racing
P.O. Box 593
Highway 5 South
Haleyville, AL 35565
205/486-8441 • 205/486-5520 FAX
www.bennettracing.com

PREMIUM KIT

Bore:	4.030"
Stroke:	3.400"
Crankshaft:	Forged Steel
Rod Type:	Eagle
Rod Length:	5.400"
Rod Ratio:	1.58:1
Pistons:	Ross Ultra-Lite
Rings:	Speed-Pro
Bearings:	Clevite 77
Max. RPM:	7,200
Max. HP:	600
Approx. Price:	$2,100.00
Comments:	This is a good street/strip kit with a variety of piston options.

347ci

D.S.S. Competition Products
960 Ridge Avenue
Lombard, IL 60148
630/268-1630 • 630/268-1649 FAX
www.dssracing.com

Bore:	4.030"
Stroke:	3.400"
Crankshaft:	Cast Steel
Rod Type:	Eagle
Rod Length:	5.400"
Rod Ratio:	1.58:1
Pistons:	Venolia
Rings:	Speed-Pro
Bearings:	Federal-Mogul
Max. RPM:	6,250
Max. HP:	550
Approx. Price:	$2,300.00
Comments:	This is a good kit for low to mid-range torque applications. Because this kit has a poor rod ratio and high piston pin height, we suggest staying away from nitrous and supercharging. Excellent for good, naturally-aspirated torque.

347ci

Ford Performance Solutions
1004 Orangefair Lane
Anaheim, CA 92801
714/773-9027 • 714/773-4178 FAX
www.f-p-s.com

BUDGET KIT

Bore:	4.030"
Stroke:	3.400"
Crankshaft:	Cast Steel
Rod Type:	4340 Steel
Rod Length:	5.400"
Rod Ratio:	1.59:1
Pistons:	Ross Ultra-Lite
Rings:	Childs & Albert
Bearings:	Clevite 77
Max. RPM:	6,800
Max. HP:	550
Approx. Price:	$2,000.00
Comments:	A good, affordable street stroker kit. We do not recommend nitrous or boost with this kit.

347ci

Bennett Racing
P.O. Box 593
Highway 5 South
Haleyville, AL 35565
205/486-8441 • 205/486-5520 FAX
www.bennettracing.com

SUPER PREMIUM KIT

Bore:	4.030"
Stroke:	3.400"
Crankshaft:	Cola Forged Steel
Rod Type:	Eagle
Rod Length:	5.400"
Rod Ratio:	1.59:1
Pistons:	Ross Ultra-Lite
Rings:	Speed-Pro
Bearings:	Clevite 77
Max. RPM:	8,500
Max. HP:	850
Approx. Price:	$2,500.00
Comments:	This is a good kit, well thought out. Piston options are many.

347ci

Ford Racing Performance Parts
44050 N. Groesbeck Highway
Clinton Township, MI 48036
586/468-1356
www.fordracing.com

Bore:	4.030"
Stroke:	3.400"
Crankshaft:	Nodular Iron M-6303-B340
Rod Type:	Forged I-Beam
Rod Length:	5.400"
Rod Ratio:	1.56:1
Pistons:	KB Flat-Tops
Rings:	Grant
Bearings:	Speed-Pro
Max. RPM:	6,500
Max. HP:	500
Approx. Price:	$2,000.00
Comments:	This kit is priced right. Ask for the M-6013-A342 for a standard bore or the M-6013-A347 for a 4.030" bore.

347ci

Ford Performance Solutions
1004 Orangefair Lane
Anaheim, CA 92801
714/773-9027 • 714/773-4178 FAX
www.f-p-s.com

BUDGET KIT/UPGRADE

Bore:	4.030"
Stroke:	3.400"
Crankshaft:	High Nodular Iron 351C
Rod Type:	Eagle
Rod Length:	5.400"
Rod Ratio:	1.59:1
Pistons:	Ross Ultra-Lite
Rings:	Childs & Albert
Bearings:	Clevite 77
Max. RPM:	6,500
Max. HP:	500
Approx. Price:	$2,500.00
Comments:	Again, a good street kit designed for weekend racing. No nitrous or boost. Some upgrades available.

347ci

Lunati Cams
4770 Lamar Avenue
Memphis, TN 38118-7403
901/365-0950 • 901/795-9411 FAX
www.holley.com

BUDGET KIT

Bore:	4.030"
Stroke:	3.425"
Crankshaft:	Nodular Iron
Rod Type:	Street/Race
Rod Length:	5.400"
Rod Ratio:	1.58:1
Pistons:	Venolia
Rings:	Speed-Pro
Bearings:	Federal-Mogul
Max. RPM:	7,000
Max. HP:	500
Approx. Price:	$2,500.00
Comments:	This is a good street/strip kit designed for regular use and weekend racing.

347ci

Nowak Racing Engines
249 E. Emerson Avenue, Unit F
Orange, CA 92665
714/282-7996 • 714/637-0425 FAX

Bore:	4.030"
Stroke:	3.400"
Crankshaft:	Forged Steel
Rod Type:	Eagle
Rod Length:	5.400"
Rod Ratio:	1.69:1
Pistons:	Nowak Forged
Rings:	Childs & Albert or Speed-Pro
Bearings:	Clevite 77
Max. RPM:	7,500
Max. HP:	550
Approx. Price:	$2,600.00
Comments:	An outstanding kit for the money with a lightweight steel crankshaft. It provides quick throttle response when the accelerator is pressed.

347ci

Scat Crankshafts
1400 Kingsdale Ave.
Redondo Beach, CA 90278
310/370-5501
310/214-2285 FAX
www.scatcrankshafts.com

BUDGET KIT

Bore:	4.030"
Stroke:	3.400"
Crankshaft:	High Nodular Cast Iron Crank
Rod Type:	Forged I-Beam
Rod Length:	5.400"
Rod Ratio:	1.59:1
Pistons:	Forged Pistons
Rings:	Unknown
Bearings:	Unknown
Max. RPM:	6,500
Max. HP:	500
Approx. Price:	$1,500.00
Comments:	A good street/strip kit. Plenty of nice options to make it better. The beauty of a Scat stroker kit is the custom services available.

347ci

Lunati Cams
4770 Lamar Avenue
Memphis, TN 38118-7403
901/365-0950 • 901/795-9411 FAX
www.holley.com

PREMIUM KIT

Bore:	4.030"
Stroke:	3.425"
Crankshaft:	4340 Forged Steel
Rod Type:	Billet
Rod Length:	5.400"
Rod Ratio:	1.58:1
Pistons:	Venolia
Rings:	Speed-Pro
Bearings:	Federal-Mogul
Max. RPM:	8,000
Max. HP:	600
Approx. Price:	N/A
Comments:	This one is more a full-race stroker kit.

347ci

Powered By Ford
1516 S. Division Avenue
Orlando, FL 32805
407/843-3673 • 407/841-7223 FAX
www.poweredbyford.com

Bore:	4.030"
Stroke:	3.400"
Crankshaft:	Powered By Ford 6415 Forged Steel
Rod Type:	Crower Billet
Rod Length:	5.400"
Rod Ratio:	1.58:1
Pistons:	JE Pistons
Rings:	Speed-Pro
Bearings:	Vandervell
Max. RPM:	8,000
Max. HP:	800
Approx. Price:	$3,500.00
Comments:	Powered By Ford needs no introduction. This company produces outstanding stroker kits. This is one of their best for street and strip.

347ci

Scat Crankshafts
1400 Kingsdale Ave.
Redondo Beach, CA 90278
310/370-5501
310/214-2285 FAX
www.scatcrankshafts.com

PREMIUM KIT

Bore:	4.030"
Stroke:	3.400"
Crankshaft:	Forged Steel
Rod Type:	H-Beam
Rod Length:	5.400"
Rod Ratio:	1.59:1
Pistons:	SRP Forged
Rings:	Unknown
Bearings:	Unknown
Max. RPM:	8,000
Max. HP:	600
Approx. Price:	$2,000.00
Comments:	This is a great go-racing kit. Again, Scat gives you many options.

347ci

Speed-O-Motive
131 North Lang Ave.
West Covina, CA 91760
626/869-0270 • 626/869-0278 FAX
www.speedomotive.com

FORGED H-BEAM ROD KIT

Bore: 4.000"
Stroke: 3.400"
Crankshaft: High Nodular Iron
Rod Type: 4340 Forged H-Beam
Rod Length: 5.400"
Rod Ratio: 1.58:1
Pistons: Keith Black Hypereutectic
Rings: Speed Pro Cast Iron
Bearings: Clevite Tri-Metal
Max. RPM: 6,500
Maxi. HP: 450-500
Approx. Price: $1,300.00
Comments: Get into horsepower and torque without having to sell your best china. The Speed-O-Motive 347 Forged H-Beam Rod Kit allows you to spin the 347 higher without concern. The custom high-nodular crankshaft will take punishment. Stronger rods are the life insurance. Nitrous, used responsibly, won't hurt it. For about $500.00 more, you can upgrade to a forged steel crank. There are plenty of upgrades available for your Speed-O-Motive 347 kit.

347ci

Speed-O-Motive
131 North Lang Ave.
West Covina, CA 91760
626/869-0270 • 626/869-0278 FAX
www.speedomotive.com

FORGED PISTON KIT

Bore: 4.000"
Stroke: 3.400"
Crankshaft: High Nodular Iron
Rod Type: 4340 Forged H-Beam
Rod Length: 5.315"
Rod Ratio: 1.56:1
Pistons: Forged Flattops
Rings: Speed Pro Moly
Bearings: Clevite Tri-Metal
Max. RPM: 6,500
Max. HP: 450-500
Approx. Price: $1,400.00
Comments: The main difference in this kit is piston type. Because Speed-O-Motive allows you to custom package your kit with nice options, there isn't much difference here. Pistons may be custom ordered, depending on your needs.

355ci

Performance Automotive Warehouse
21001 Nordhoff Street
Chatsworth, CA 91311
818/678-3000 • 818/678-3001 FAX
www.pawinc.com

Bore: 4.030"
Stroke: 3.480"
Crankshaft: High Nodular Iron
Rod Type: Forged I-Beam
Rod Length: 5.500"
Rod Ratio: 1.50:1
Pistons: Forged Federal-Mogul
Rings: Sealed Power Moly
Bearings: Clevite 77
Max. RPM: 6,000
Max. HP: 500
Approx. Price: $2,900.00, including a 302 block.
Comments: This is a good street kit with a wide variety of options available. Nitrous and supercharging are not recommended.

347ci

ProPower
4750 N. Dixie Highway, No. 9
Fort Lauderdale, FL 33334
954/491-6988 • 954/491-2874 FAX
www.propowerparts.com

Bore: 4.030"
Stroke: 3.400"
Crankshaft: Forged Steel
Rod Type: Eagle
Rod Length: 5.400"
Rod Ratio: 1.59:1
Pistons: JE Pistons
Rings: JE Plasma Moly
Bearings: King High Performance
Max. RPM: 7,500
Max. HP: 600
Approx. Price: $2,600.00
Comments: A good street/strip kit. Plenty of nice options to make it better.

355ci

Coast High Performance
2555 W. 237th Street
Torrance, CA 90505
310/784-2977 • 310/784-2970 FAX
www.coasthigh.com

Bore: 4.030"
Stroke: 3.480"
Crankshaft: High Nodular Iron 351C
Rod Type: Eagle
Rod Length: 5.500"
Rod Ratio: 1.58:1
Pistons: Probe Industries Forged
Rings: Childs & Albert
Bearings: Clevite 77
Max. RPM: 7,000
Max. HP: 670
Approx. Price: $2,500.00
Comments: Good street/race kit. Makes a lot of torque. This kit is pushing the limits of the 302 block.

357ci

Speed-O-Motive
131 North Lang Ave.
West Covina, CA 91760
626/869-0270 • 626/869-0278 FAX
www.speedomotive.com

Bore: 4.060"
Stroke: 3.500"
Crankshaft: High Nodular Iron 351C
Rod Type: Eagle
Rod Length: 5.500"
Rod Ratio: 1.54:1
Pistons: Ross Ultra-Lites
Rings: Speed-Pro
Bearings: Clevite 77
Max. RPM: 7,000
Max. HP: 500
Approx. Price: $2,500.00
Comments: At the limits of the 302 block. Plenty of torque available.

Building A JMC Motorsports 331 Stroker

We're going to show you the ropes on the Scat budget 331ci stroker kit from JMC Motorsports in San Diego, California. The Scat kit includes a new nodular-iron, hardened crankshaft, forged I-beam connecting rods with 3/8 inch rod bolts, forged Ross pistons, Total Seal piston rings, Clevite 77 bearings, and more. John Da Luz of JMC Motorsports is building this 331ci stroker for a 1965-1966 Mustang with a front sump oil pan, ARP 185 heads, Edelbrock Performer Air Gap intake manifold, and a 600cfm Holley carburetor.

JMC Motorsports is also able to build this engine with Edelbrock Performer RPM heads and induction for late-model 5.0L Mustangs. The nice part about the Edelbrock Performer 331ci stroker from JMC Motorsports is its emissions-legal status. You can pump displacement into your 1986-95 Mustang GT or LX with ease thanks to this engine package from JMC Motorsports. Lets get started.

This is the Scat 331ci stroker kit from JMC Motorsports. Included, depending on your budget, is a high-nodular iron crankshaft, forged I-beam rods, forged Ross pistons, Total Seal piston rings, and Clevite 77 bearings.

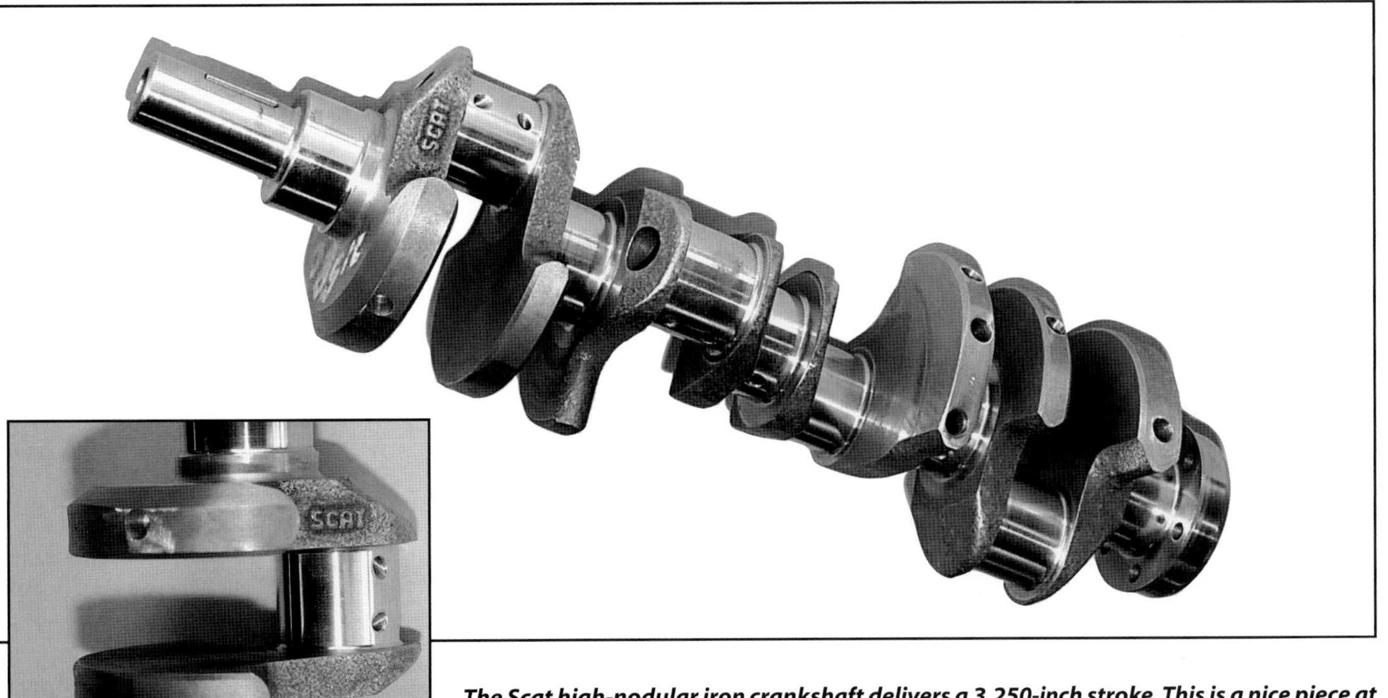

The Scat high-nodular iron crankshaft delivers a 3.250-inch stroke. This is a nice piece at a budget price. Because Scat pays such strict attention to quality and workmanship, it is easy to feel comfortable with this kit.

Building A JMC Motorsports 331 Stroker (continued)

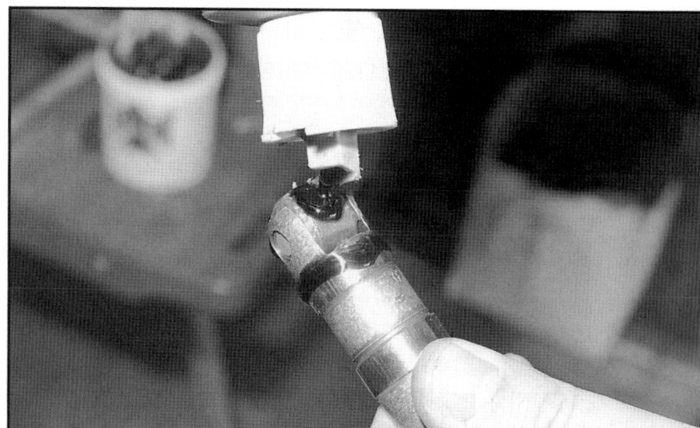

John lubes up (above) the Crane roller hydraulic camshaft bound for his 331 stroker. Assembly lube is used for extra measure. Hydraulic roller tappets get the same treatment once the camshaft is installed.

The cam plate is installed, with the oil passage toward the camshaft. Two bolts get Loc-Tite for security.

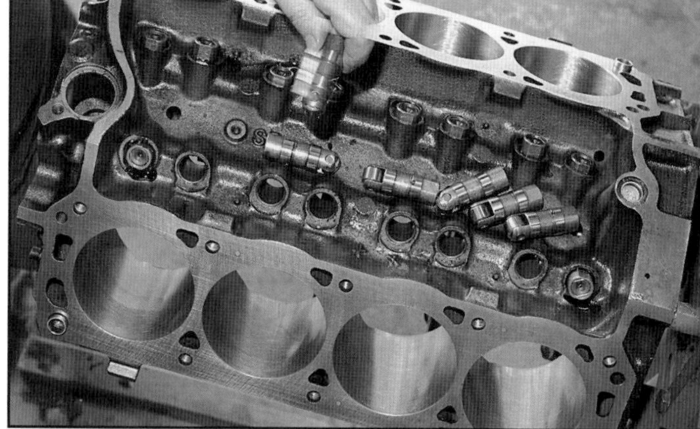

Each lifter slips into place with ease.

Before John rolls the block over, dumping all 16 lifters onto the floor, he installs the dog bones and spider to keep the lifters in place.

Building A JMC Motorsports 331 Stroker (continued)

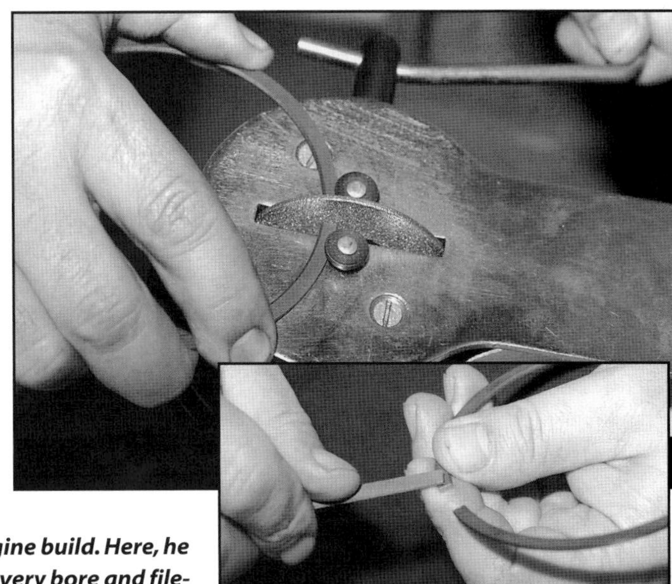

John Da Luz stresses the application of strict tolerances in your engine build. Here, he checks the ring gap, which should be around .010-inch. He checks every bore and file-fits every ring set.

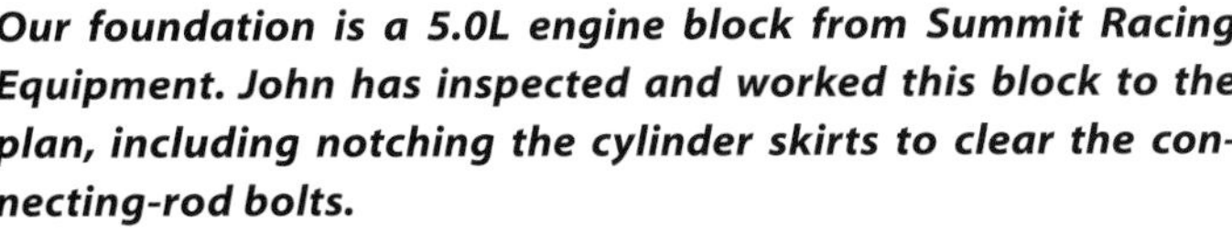

Our foundation is a 5.0L engine block from Summit Racing Equipment. John has inspected and worked this block to the plan, including notching the cylinder skirts to clear the connecting-rod bolts.

John uses plenty of assembly lube on main and connecting-rod bearings. This gives the journals something slippery to ride on for that first firing. If the engine sits for any length of time, assembly lube gives bearings and journals a fighting chance at life.

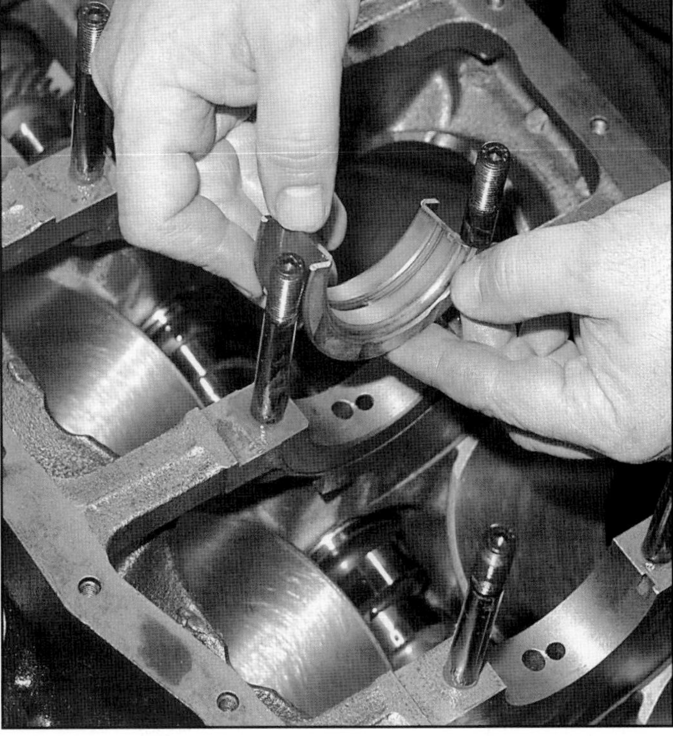

Clevite 77 street main bearings are used here. John says super hard race bearings have their place, but not on a street engine with a nodular cast-iron crankshaft. He stresses that he would rather see a stray piece of dirt damage a soft bearing than the crankshaft journal. Hard bearings will force the dirt into the crank journal, doing damage to the crank instead of the bearing.

Building A JMC Motorsports 331 Stroker (continued)

The Scat 331 stroker crank is carefully installed. End play must be checked with a dial indicator at the front of the crankshaft. When we check end play, we are checking side clearances at the thrust bearing shown here. End play should be .0004 to .0008-inch.

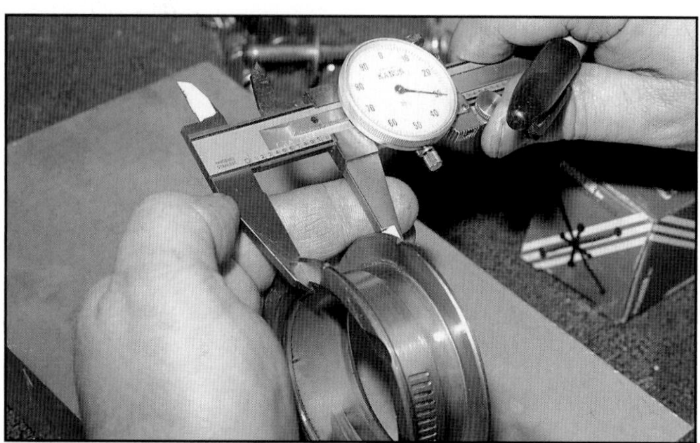

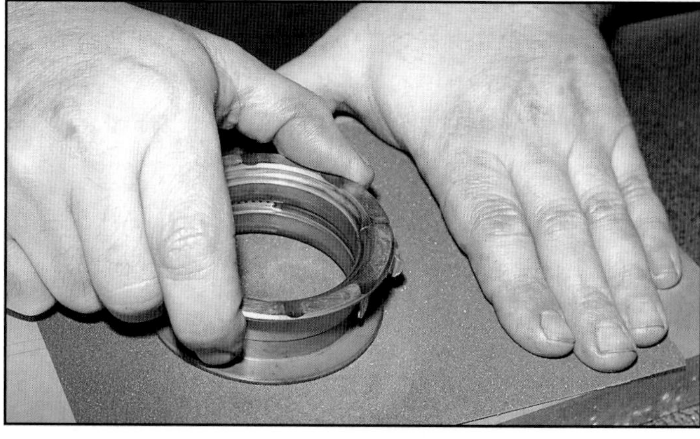

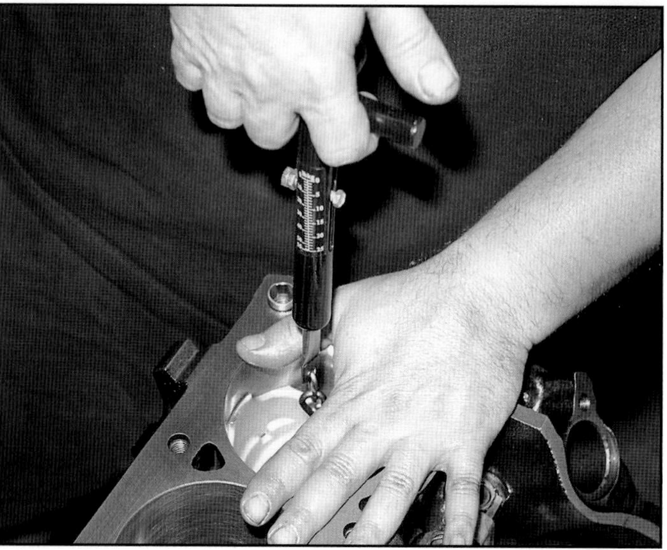

Above left and above right: When thrust bearings and crankshafts don't measure up, modifications must be made. Never ever assume a stroker kit is dead-on accurate out of the box. Few are. John has checked crankshaft end play and isn't happy with the numbers. Too tight. So, he will measure the thrust bearing as shown, then sand the sides on 220-grit paper on a hard surface to shave some of the bearing material. Then, he will clean up the bearing and check again. Would you believe John had to do this three times before proper end play was achieved?

Left: Here's something John showed us that will tell us something about friction. Part of John's clearance checking plan is piston-ring tension. He uses a fish scale to check piston friction, which comes from oil ring tension. He installs the piston upside down with only the oil rings installed. Then, he uses a fish scale to pull the piston out of the bore. If drag is any more than eight pounds, a change must be made in oil rings.

Building A JMC Motorsports 331 Stroker (continued)

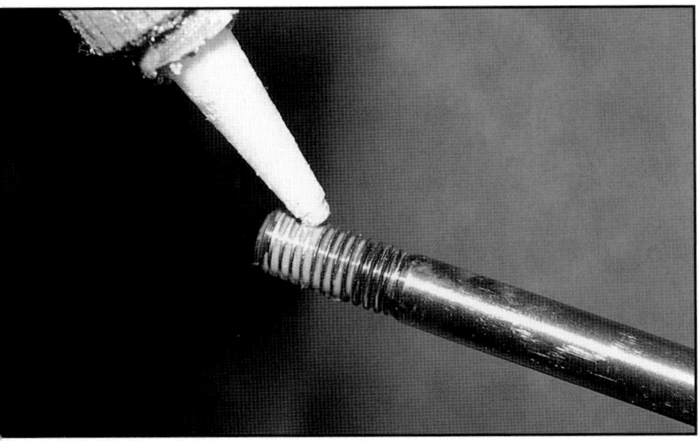

ARP main studs are being used on this 331 engine because John is employing a stud girdle from Coast High Performance. Loc-Tite is used on the threads.

The Coast High Performance stud girdle is designed to stiffen the block. Some modifications had to be made to the main caps to clear the girdle. Main stud nuts are torqued from the #3 main cap outward. John does this in three steps. First, 1/3 of the full torque value. Then 1/2. Then the full amount. He then checks the torque again on all main caps, just to be safe. Crankshaft end play is checked again.

Left: John mates the pistons to the rods. If you're used to the old C-clip approach, times have changed. John rolls in this new-fangled clip that won't come out. It offers a fail-safe design that keeps your cylinder walls out of harm's way.

Right: Oil rings are installed next. John stresses making sure the oil rings have good freedom of movement. Ring gaps should be 180 degrees opposite each other.

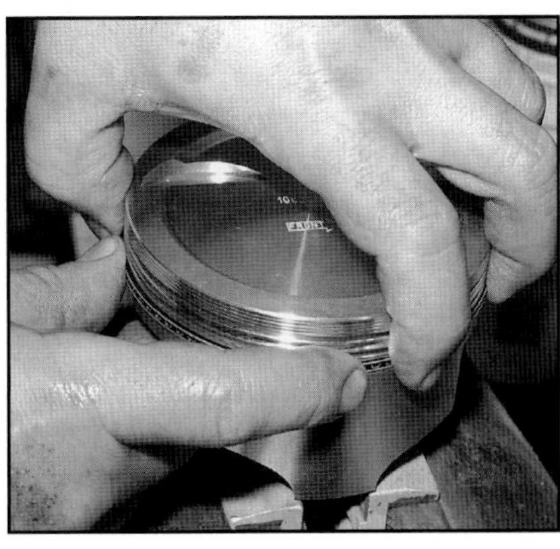

Building A JMC Motorsports 331 Stroker (continued)

Compression rings are rolled onto the piston like this. Take extra care not to scratch the piston with the ring. Compression ring end gaps should be 180 degrees opposite as well, but not in alignment with the oil-ring gaps. Gaps should be at 9, 12, 3, and 6 o'clock.

Billet piston-ring compressors like this are nice, but expensive. An adjustable ring compressor will work for your home shop. John bathes the piston rings and cylinder walls in engine oil. With two thumbs, he pushes the slug in the bore, taking extra care to protect the cylinder wall and crankshaft journal below.

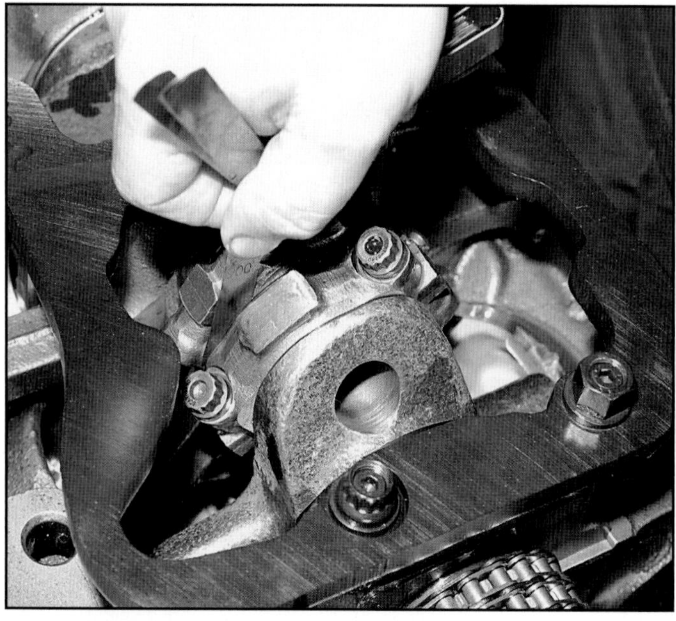

With all eight pistons installed, John checks connecting rod side clearances. Clearances should be .010 to .020-inch.

Cap-screw rod bolts are torqued to specs. Then, John checks the torque again.

Building A JMC Motorsports 331 Stroker (continued)

A Melling high-volume oil pump is installed and clearanced. The pump has to clear the girdle and the crankshaft counterweight. This is where you need the expertise of a good machine shop. Expect the oil pump to interfere with the girdle, which will involve milling in places. Sometimes, the pump has to be carefully milled to clear the crankshaft counterweight.

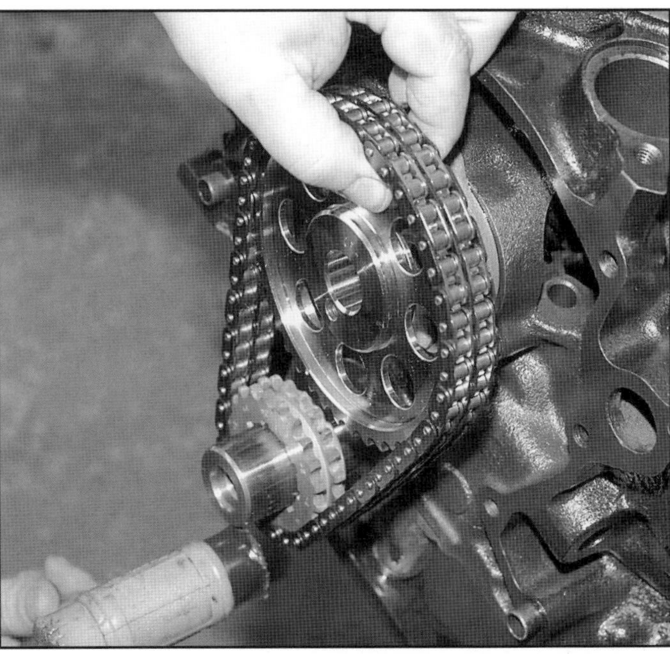

Next, the Crane dual-roller timing set is installed to tie things together. Take note of the proper location of the timing marks.

John checks two things with a Comp Cams degree wheel. Using a TDC indicator, John determines true top dead center. Then, using a dial-indicator tied to the #1 cylinder lifters, he checks cam-timing events. Would you believe he discovered we had the wrong camshaft? Valve timing events did not match the cam card. This is why you must always check cam-timing events with a degree wheel.

Building A JMC Motorsports 331 Stroker (continued)

Because we are using a new 5.0L block from Summit Racing Equipment, our block employs dowel pins that are not compatible with a vintage 289/302 timing cover. We can do one of two things. The vintage reproduction timing cover from California Pony Cars can be drilled to accept the dowel pins, or the dowel pins may removed. Guess what John decided to do, using Channel Locks?

Above and Below: John drives in a new crankshaft seal. Remember, the lip and spring always go toward the inside. After installing the gasket from SCE, John positions the timing cover in place. We suggest the use of a thin film of silicone sealer around the coolant passages.

Before you install the timing cover, make sure the dipstick tube hole has been drilled.

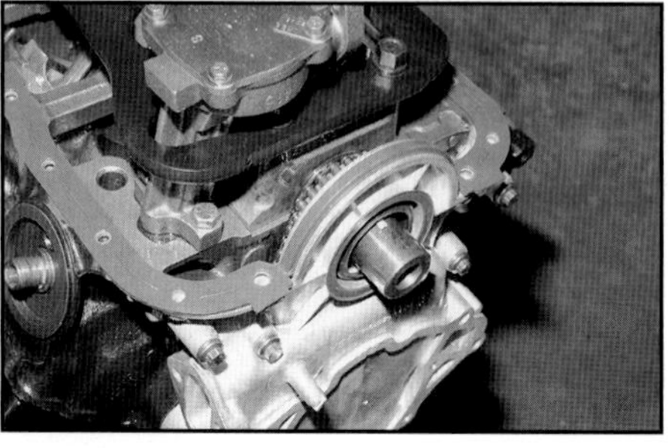

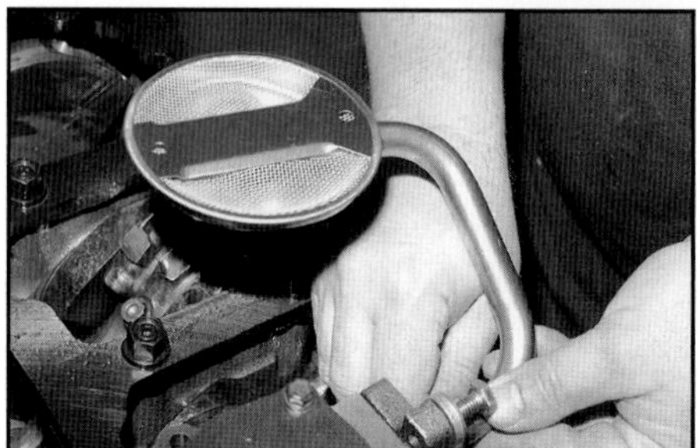

John is using a one-piece rubber oil pan gasket/seal combo from SCE to make short work of oil pan installation. It is also designed not to leak. Lay it in place, using silicone sealer at the trouble spots in the corners of the pan rails. Because this is a front-sump arrangement for older Mustangs, Falcons, and Fairlanes, it gets the short pick-up shown. A new front-sump pan from JMC Motorsports is installed next. John snugs the corners first, then snugs all of the bolts in a crisscross fashion and does not over tighten them.

Building A JMC Motorsports 331 Stroker (continued)

John is opting for the AFR 185 cylinder head for his 331 stroker build-up. This is a great street/strip cylinder head, with its 2.02/1.60-inch valves. D-shaped exhaust ports provide a smoother exit for hot gasses. Good bang for the buck going on here.

ARP head studs have been installed. John opted for studs because he wants to supercharge this engine eventually. SCE has provided the gaskets for this build-up. After checking the deck and cylinder head surfaces for scoring or debris, John is ready for the AFR-185 heads.

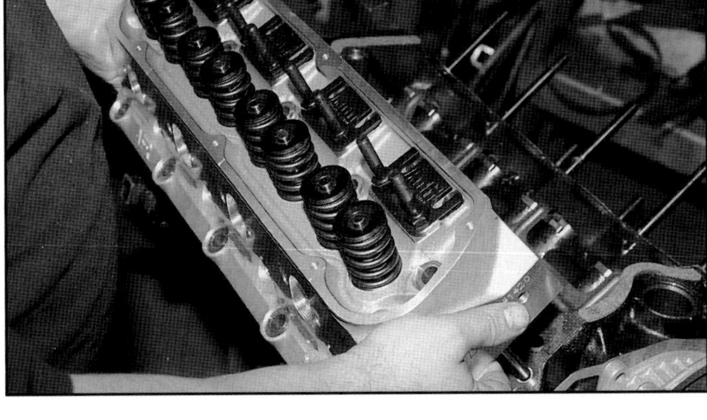

John lays down the AFR-185 cylinder head. When John received these heads from Air Flow Research, he tore them down and did some port and bowl work. We will be interested to see what this does for power.

Valve adjustment is straightforward with hydraulic roller tappets. John runs the nut down until there is full contact, then gives the nut 1/2-turn. This allows for lifter float at high revs while keeping things friendly.

Building A JMC Motorsports 331 Stroker (continued)

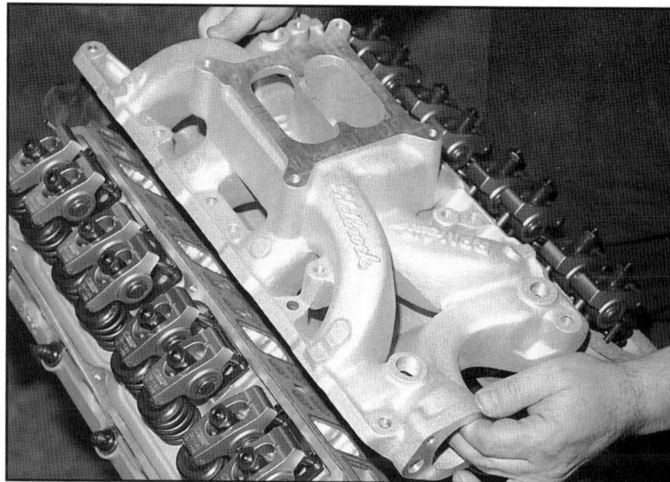

SCE intake manifold gaskets are employed here. In this instance, John decided to try those cork gaskets at the end rails. A large bead of silicon works quite well if you don't trust these gaskets. John sets the Edelbrock Air Gap in place. This is a new dual-plane manifold from Edelbrock that provides a cooler air charge.

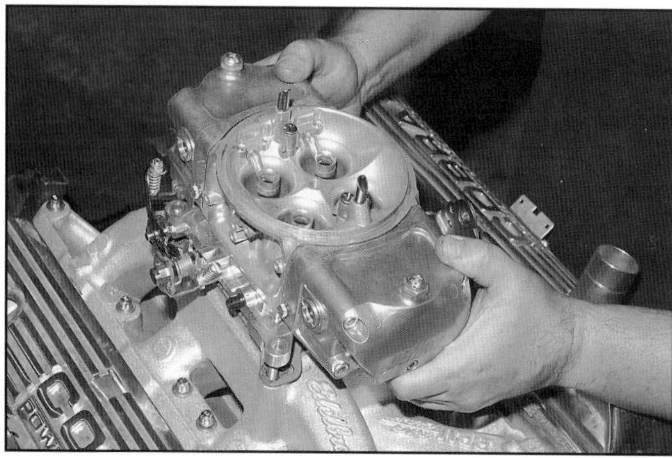

John likes the Race Demon 650cfm carburetor, although it is unclear whether or not he will actually use this one. The 600-600cfm Holley is an alternative.

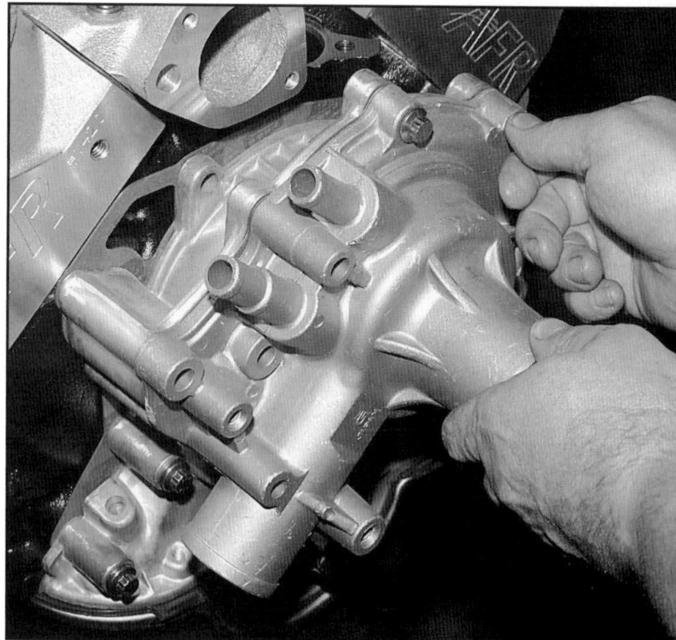

You have choices when it comes to water pumps. This is a high-flow water pump from JMC Motorsports. You may also use an Edelbrock water pump.

The crowning touch is a harmonic balancer from Ford Racing Performance Parts. One issue with this balancer, and some others, is its weight. Excessive weight with some aftermarket balancers can actually break the crankshaft. Do your homework before purchasing an aftermarket balancer.

Building A JMC Motorsports 331 Stroker (concluded)

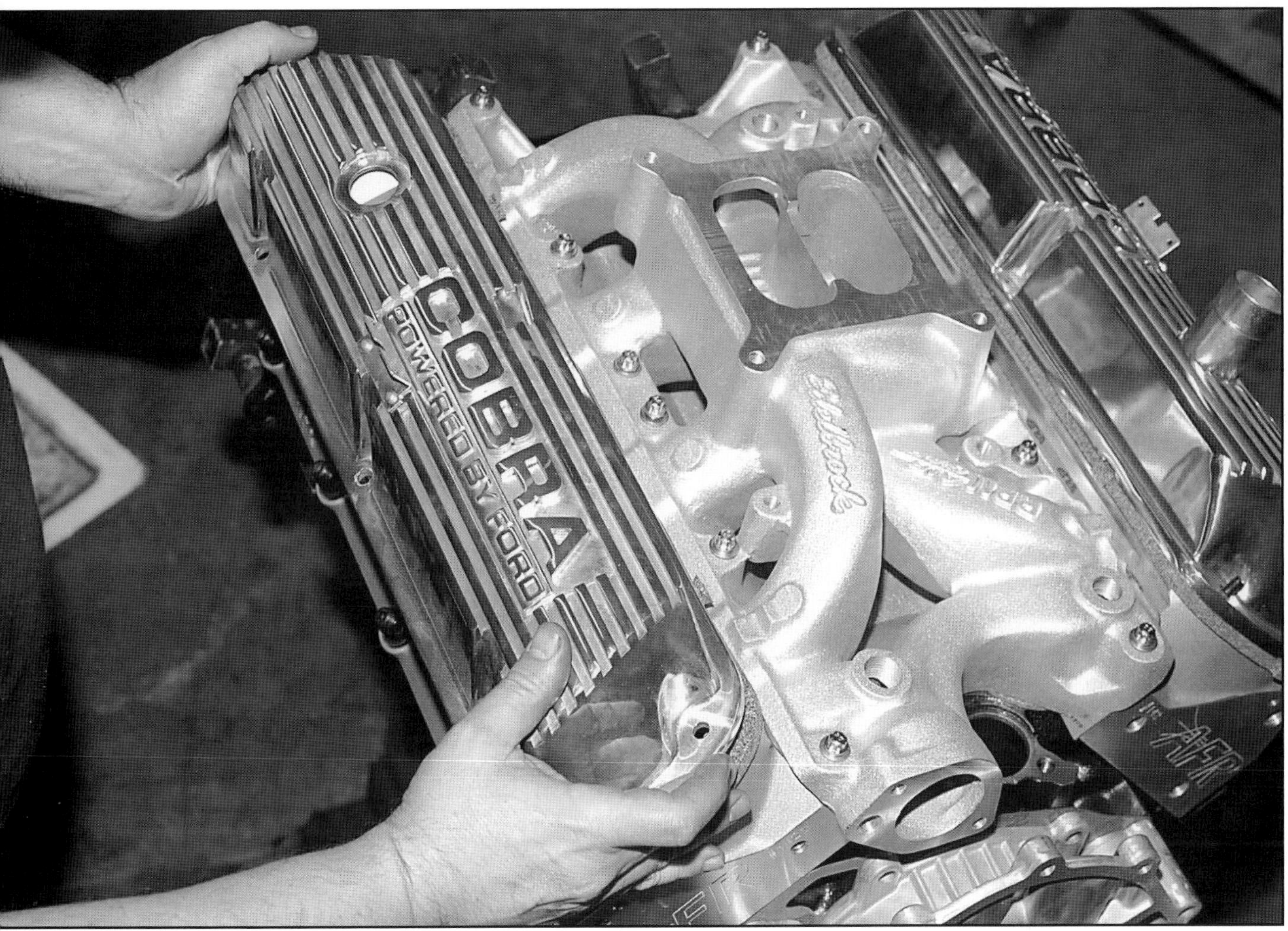

Cobra valve covers from Scott Drake Reproductions are a nice touch for a vintage Ford. Unfortunately, at press time, Ford has ordered Scott Drake Reproductions to halt production of these striking valve covers. Availability is unknown.

JMC Motorsports
2277 National Ave.
San Diego, CA 92113
619/230-8866
619/230-8824 FAX
www.jmcmotorsports.com

JMC Motorsports 331 Dyno Test

What Will This Thing Do?

RPM	Horsepower	Torque	VE%
2000	134	332	69.9
2500	174	342	73.3
3000	220	365	76.9
3500	270	384	81.8
4000	320	391	86.2
4500	367	**398**	89.0
5000	401	387	90.0
5500	422	373	89.7
6000	**425**	362	87.2

Building a 347 Street Fighter

One of the most well-known names in the stroker business is Coast High Performance. Coast High Performance's area of expertise is the small-block Ford. We're pretty convinced Coast has probably built more 347ci stroker small blocks than anyone else in the industry. This is why we decided to look in on the assembly of one of Coast's 347ci Street Fighter small blocks. The Street Fighter is a great bang-for-the-buck engine kit because you get a whole lot of kit for the money. For a few extra bucks, Coast High Performance will assemble your engine kit into a completed, ready-to-fire engine package. Think of the 347 Street Fighter as a crate engine without the stigma of a crate engine. These folks build solid reliability into each of their engines. This makes the Street Fighter an excellent value.

This time, our focus is late-model, Fox-body small-block power. Our platform is a 1993 Mustang GT hatchback with an AOD transmission. Because we're building a lot of power into our 302ci small-block foundation, the rest of the vehicle will have to be up to the task. More on that later. Meanwhile, we need to build a powerful 347ci Street Fighter from Coast High Performance.

Assembly of the short-block begins at Coast High Performance, with completion happening at JMC Motorsports in San Diego, California, where Trick Flow cylinder heads and induction will be installed. Our hydraulic roller camshaft and valvetrain have been provided by Comp Cams. Underneath, there's a Canton double-sump road-race pan.

We have a stock 5.0L block from Summit Racing Equipment. Priced under $300.00, the Summit block is an unbeatable deal for stroker builders. The cylinder bores have been notched at the bottoms to clear the connecting rods and journals. Coast High Performance has done a nice job of block prep.

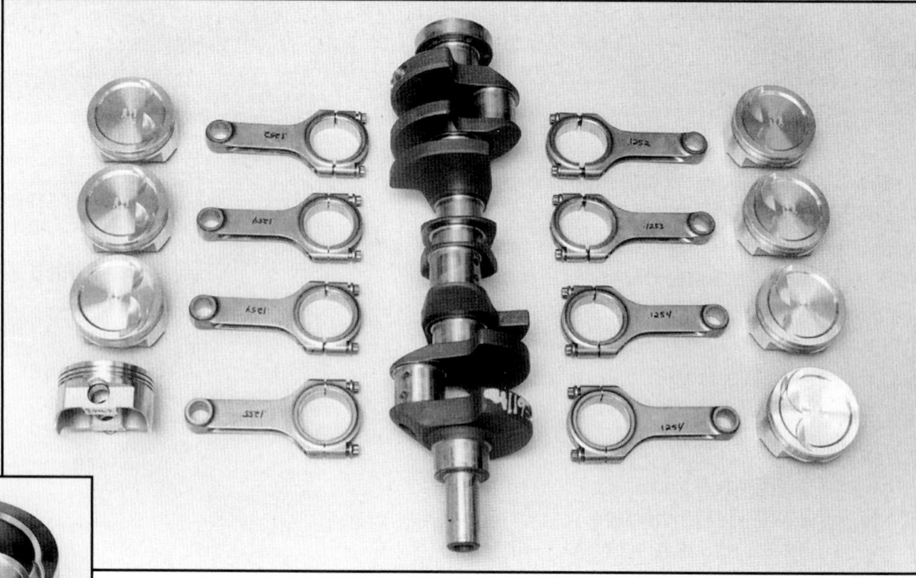

This is the 347ci Street Fighter stroker kit from Coast High Performance. Included is a cast steel crankshaft with a 3.400-inch stroke, 5.315-inch H-beam connecting rods, and Probe Industries 4.030-inch forged pistons. These pistons (shown at left) are dished to control compression.

Building a 347 Street Fighter (continued)

Stock, press-in oil galley plugs have been replaced with screw-in plugs for oiling system security.

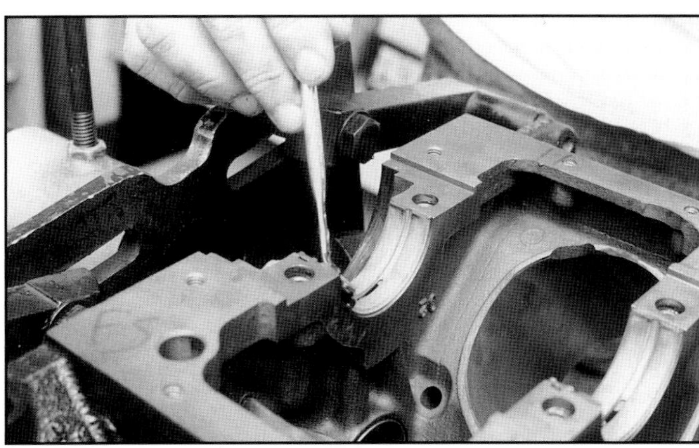

The Clevite main bearings have been installed. We're lubricating them with engine assembly lube.

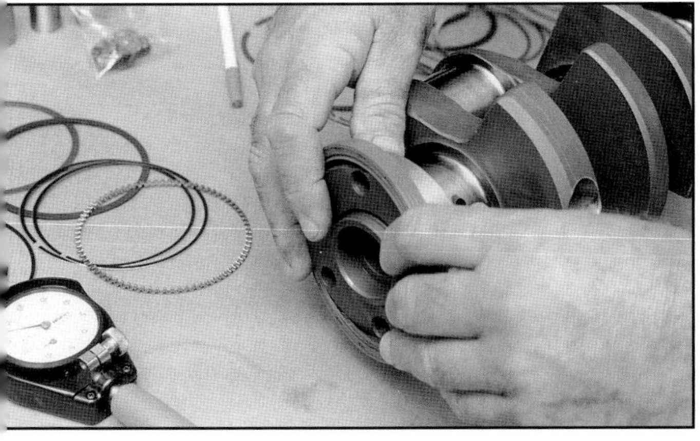

The nice thing about a late-model 5.0L block is the one-piece crankshaft rear-main seal shown here. The one-piece seal provides solid security compared to those old two-piece seals in the 289/302/351W prior to 1982.

The crankshaft is installed as shown. Mains have been lubricated.

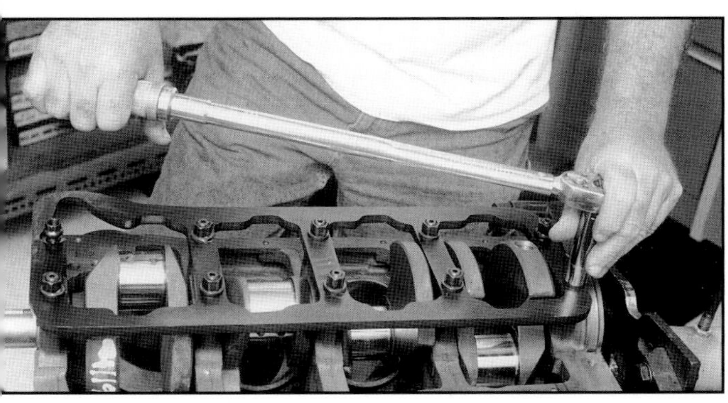

The mains are torqued to specs as shown. Crankshaft end play will be checked next.

Because we're going to throw nitrous at this one, we're studding the mains. Main bearing studs and a girdle will stiffen up the bottom end and provide stability.

Building a 347 Street Fighter (continued)

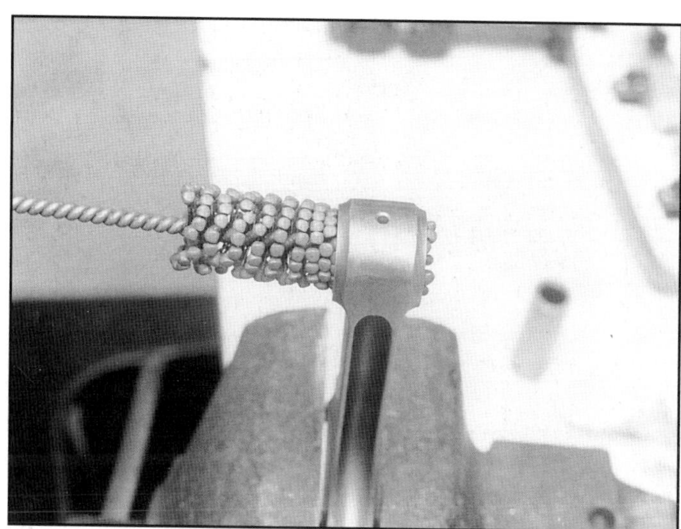

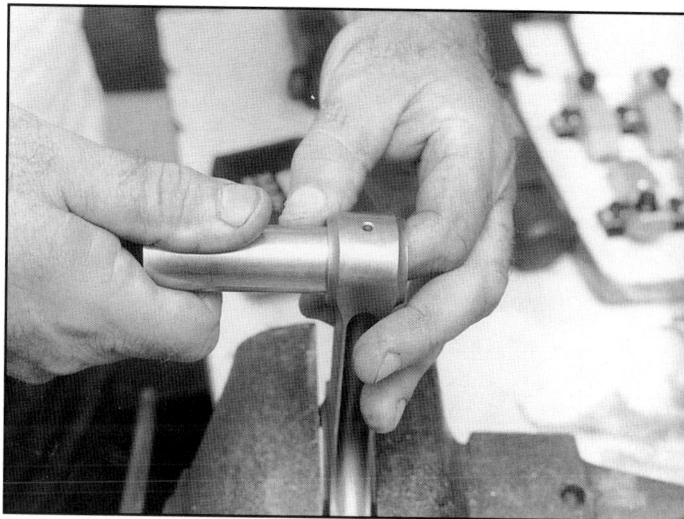

Fitting the piston pins proves challenging. To achieve a perfect fit, we are honing the small end of the connecting rods. Bushings aren't always sized right from the factory. This is where you have to be something of a machinist to get the job done.

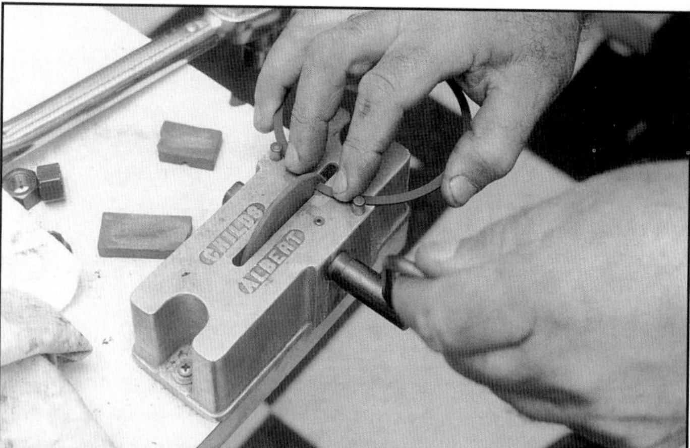

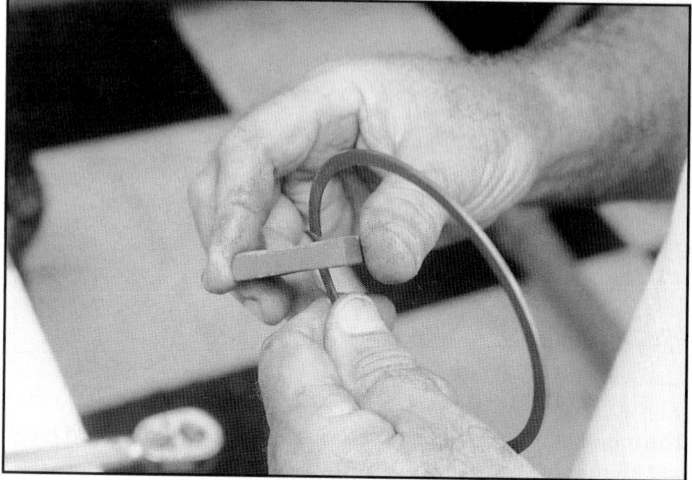

Piston rings aren't pre-gapped, which means we have to do this task. Ring gaps are checked first at each bore, then ground to fit, then their rough edges filed smooth.

Building a 347 Street Fighter (continued)

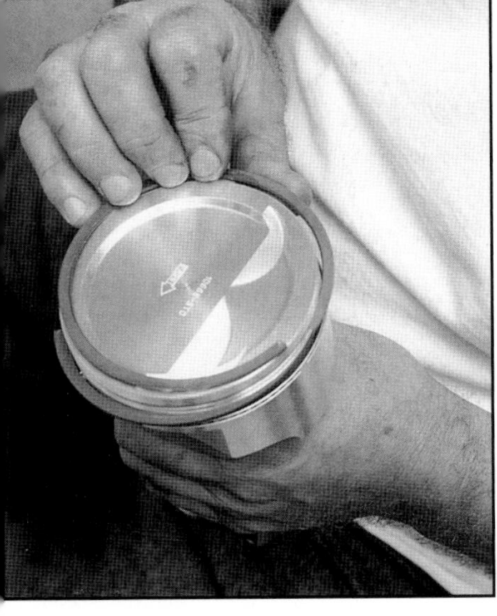

Piston rings are walked onto the pistons as shown. Ring end gaps should be positioned at 12, 3, 6, and 9 o'clock. Never should any of the gaps be aligned with one another.

Our Trick Flow roller hydraulic camshaft is lubed and installed. Valve overlap makes this camshaft nitrous-friendly.

Probe pistons and 4340 H-beam rods are installed next. Each is torqued to specs, one at a time, then double-checked again for proper torque.

Building a 347 Street Fighter (continued)

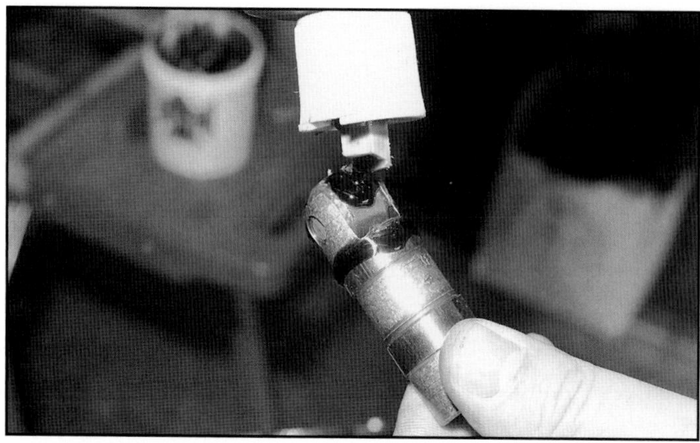

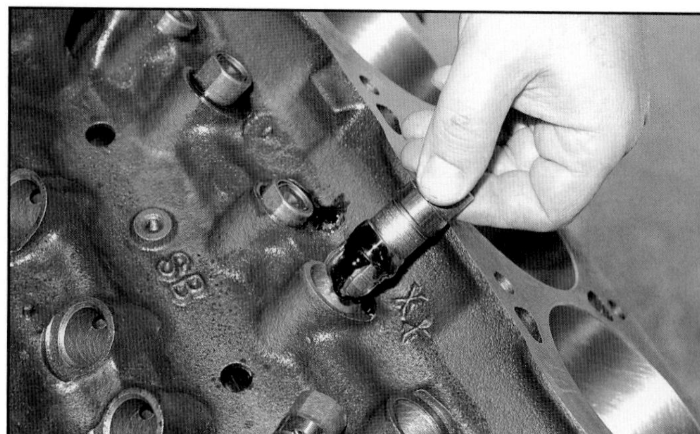

Roller hydraulic tappets are lubricated with engine assembly lube, then installed in the block as shown.

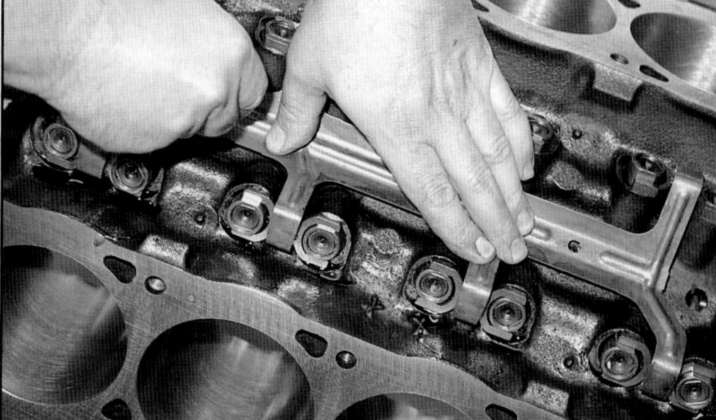

Because this is a roller block, installation is easy. Lifters are seated. Dog bones are installed. And the spider is secured using two bolts screwed into the valley.

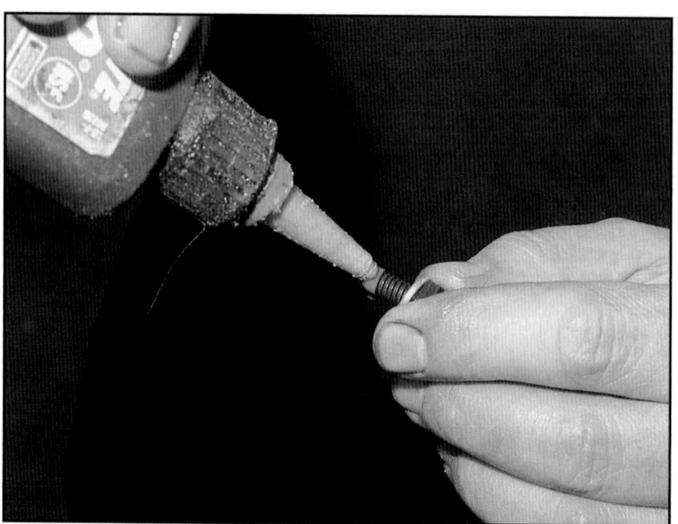

Loc-Tite is used on the spider bolts as shown.

JMC Motorsports is continuing assembly with a dual-roller timing set. Timing marks are aligned at 12 and 6 o'clock.

Building a 347 Street Fighter (continued)

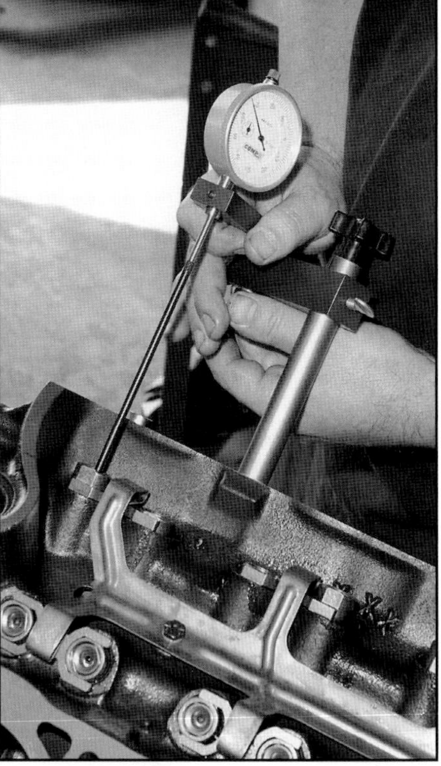

John Da Luz of JMC Motorsports degrees the camshaft and checks crankshaft indexing at the same time. This determines proper camshaft specifications and piston deck height.

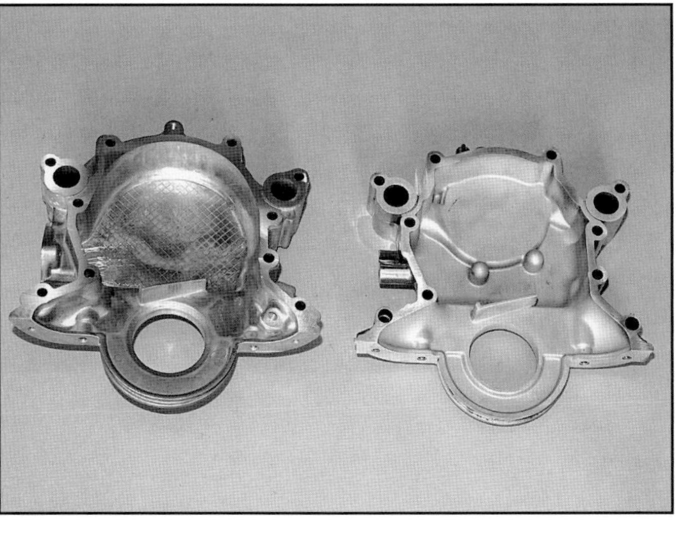

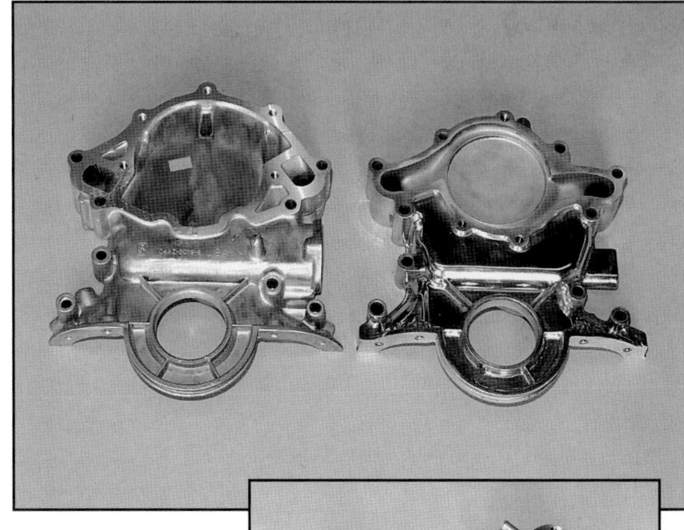

Before we install the timing cover, it is important for us to explain the differences. Shown here are two small-block timing covers. On the left is a vintage timing cover designed for conventional water pumps and mechanical fuel pumps. On the right is a late-model 5.0L timing cover designed for a reverse-rotation water pump and an electric fuel pump. Note the different water pump design and shape (right). The small, monkey-ear water pump is the reverse-rotation design. None of this interchanges.

Building a 347 Street Fighter (continued)

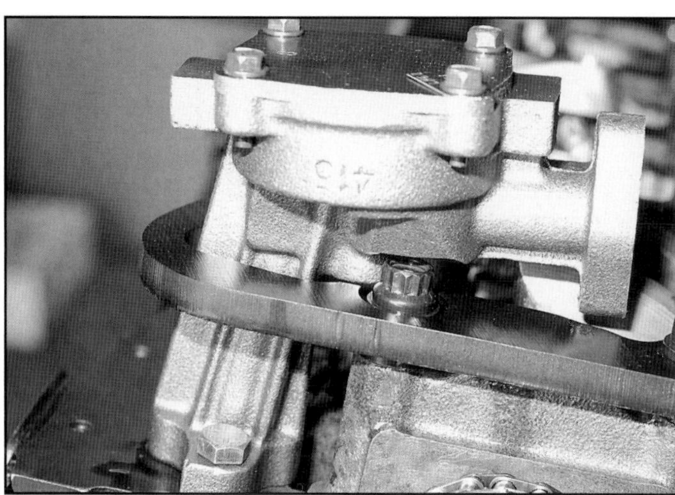

The oil pump is clearanced to clear the stud girdle. Ascertain this clearance during your build-up. The pump housing cannot touch the girdle. Crankshaft counterweights must also clear the girdle.

John installs the oil pump pick-up, taking extra care to ensure proper fit. This is the Fox-body, double-sump design, with the pick-up at the rear.

Above and right: Late-model 5.0L blocks use a one-piece oil pan gasket that is easy to install and remove. Enthusiasts like the one-piece, no-leak design. John lays this revolutionary gasket in place, checks fit, and installs the Canton pan. Bolts are tightened in a crisscross fashion, which secures the gasket and the pan.

Building a 347 Street Fighter (continued)

We're using a SCE composition head gasket on our 347 Street Fighter. This gasket, coupled with a studded block, ensures cylinder leakage security.

Trick Flow heads top our 347 Street Fighter. These are the Twisted Wedge units with 2.02/1.60-inch valves, born for a small-block Ford.

Because the Twisted Wedge head is designed for both the 302 and the 351W, the bolt holes are sized for the larger 351W head bolt. Spacers are installed to take up the difference between the 351W hole size and the smaller 302 head bolt/stud.

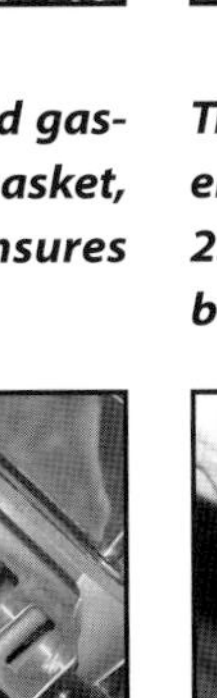

Pushrod guide plates and screw-in rocker studs are installed and adjusted next. The plates are adjusted to where the pushrods are centered properly. The rocker arm studs get Teflon sealer on their threads before being screwed into the heads.

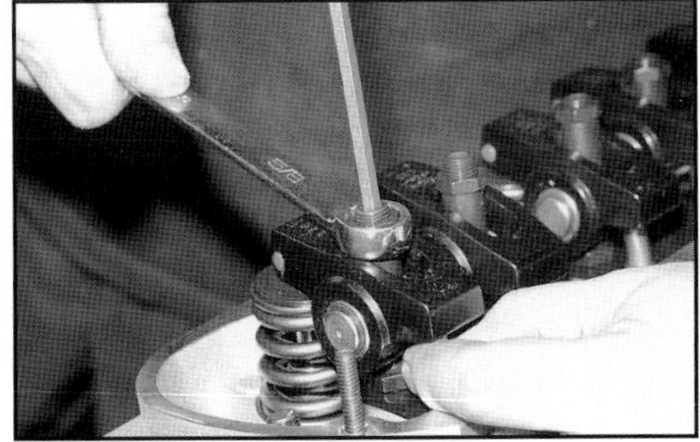

Roller-tip rocker arms are installed and adjusted to specs. Because this is a roller hydraulic camshaft, adjustment is straightforward. With each cam lobe at base circle (valve closed), the adjustment is tightened 1/2-turn.

Cast aluminum valve covers from JME Motorsports are installed next.

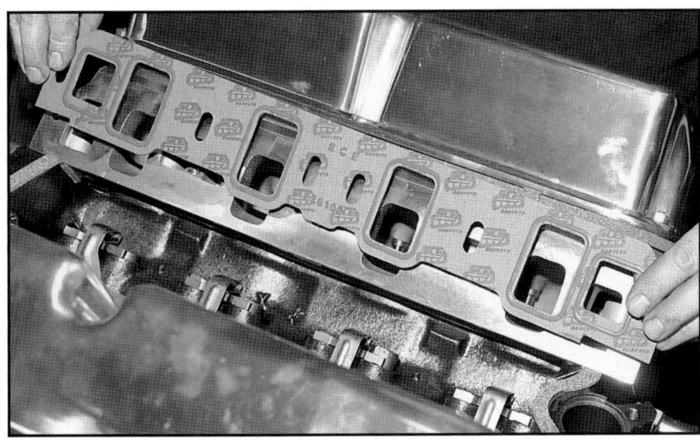

Intake manifold gaskets from SCE are next. John has run a bead of silicone sealer along the block rails. We're ready for manifold installation.

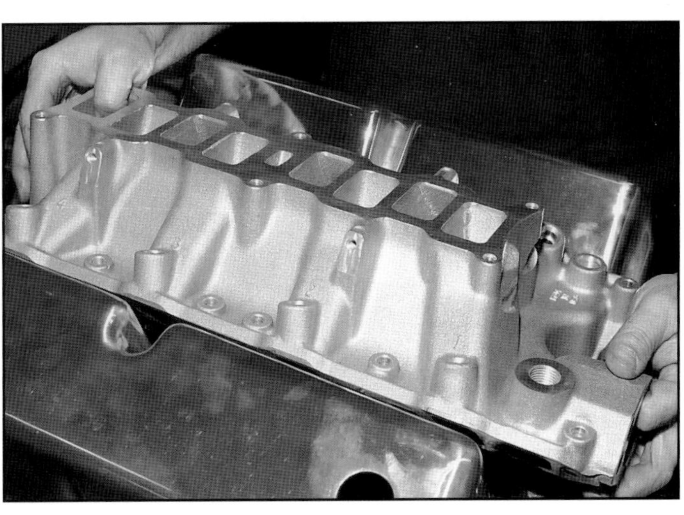

The Trick Flow lower intake is installed next.

Building a 347 Street Fighter (concluded)

A gasket is placed between the upper and lower intake manifolds.

John lowers the Trick Flow upper intake manifold in place.

JMC Motorsports opts for an MSD ignition system to fire the mixture here.

CHP/JMC Motorsport 347 Street Fighter Dyno Test

What Will This Thing Do?

RPM	Horsepower	Torque	VE%
2000	124	305	71.5
2500	165	320	75.7
3000	209	345	79.6
3500	264	377	86.5
4000	312	389	90.4
4500	355	**398**	92.9
5000	387	389	93.8
5500	400	377	93.5
6000	**405**	342	91.0

Coast High Performance
2555 W. 237th Street
Torrance, CA 90505
310/784-2977
310/784-2970 FAX
www.coasthigh.com

JMC Motorsports
2277 National Ave.
San Diego, CA 92113
619/230-8866
619/230-8824 FAX
www.jmcmotorsports.com

No Brainer MCE Custom Engines

It isn't very often we find fiercely committed professionals dedicated to customer service in the engine building business. MCE Engines in Los Angeles, California is a solid exception to this rule. MCE stands for "Marvin's Custom Engines." As the name implies, you can order a complete, custom-built crate engine, that will be ready to fire in a matter of weeks. And if you're on a tight clock, MCE can make it happen even faster. On top of that, these guys will bring tech support to your home garage or racetrack, that is, as long as you live in Southern California. If you don't live in Southern California, they will give you personalized service right over the telephone or on the internet. This means you can order an MCE custom engine anywhere in the world and get solid, experienced tech support that results from their more than 45 years of experience. We're willing to bet you won't get that from your local machine shop.

So, what do we mean by "no brainer" custom engines? MCE Engines has three basic engine formulas that work very well for a variety of budgets and needs. Think of MCE Engines as a user friendly engine builder. Marvin McAfee, who owns MCE Engines, has developed a successful formula cultivated over a lifetime of engine building. He has a hand picked team that includes Ken Van Fleet, Benton Jackson, and Fred Christian.

All of this aside, MCE Engines offers three basic levels of engines. Each level can be customized to your specifications. Level 1 is your basic street engine, with a flat tappet hydraulic camshaft, cast or forged pistons, forged I-beam factory rods with ARP bolts, standard three-angle valve job, pushrod guide plates with screw-in studs, and more.

Level 2 is a more-powerful, more-durable engine with roller hydraulic lifters, more extensive head work, and the like. Think of Level 2 as a 400-horse small block, good for street and weekend strip.

Level 3 is an all-out racing engine, ready for road racing or drag racing. Each of these engines is detailed below. And for more details, you need to call MCE Engines and speak with Marvin. He and his team can help you make the right decisions. On top of that, they can build you a solid, reliable engine. Always bear in mind that a quality engine build does not come cheaply. If your goal is low buck, then remember something important. You get what you pay for.

Here, Benton Jackson works a 302 block, getting it ready for a made-to-order stroker package. Benton's area of expertise is induction systems. Each engine is hand-built. No mass-production thinking here.

This is Marvin McAfee of MCE Engines. What makes this man shine is enthusiasm for internal combustion. His background, and that of his partners, encompasses more than 45 years of experience, including aircraft engines. Each custom-built crate engine is something of a signature-series special. Each gets Marvin's close attention.

Here is where man and ignition become one. Ken Van Fleet curves an MSD distributor for a customer engine. To curve a distributor, you have to know something about the engine it serves. Each MCE engine gets this kind of attention.

No Brainer MCE Custom Engines (concluded)

Fred Christian of MCE Engines degrees a small-block Ford. Like the distributor curving just mentioned, degreeing in a camshaft does the same thing. It determines accuracy. Degreeing in a camshaft gets everything in synch. Fred's area of expertise is fabrication and hydraulics. He is an aircraft maintenance technician with Continental Airlines.

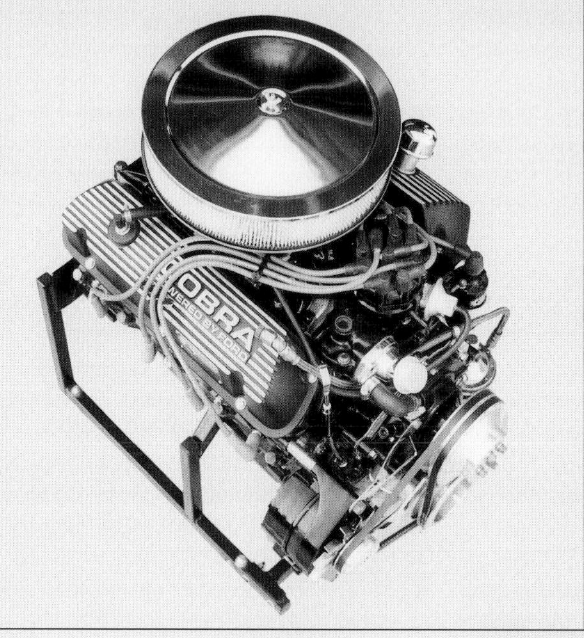

If you want a warmed up street small-block from Marvin's Custom Engines, these gentlemen can dial one in for you. This particular 302ci engine is a cut above the one just mentioned. The nice thing about MCE Engines, is never having to concern yourself with choosing the wrong combination of parts. Marvin will guide you through the order, playing devil's advocate every step of the way. He will ask you why. Then, he will tell you what's best for your mission.

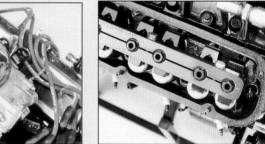

MCE Engines
323/731-0462
mceengines@aol.com

From budget to high-end is what MCE Engines is all about. This is MCE's road-race small block displacing 302ci. If you look closely, it is high-end, built for the rigors of road racing. It incorporates a thoroughly machined block, 4340 steel crankshaft with large radius journals, 4340 H-beam rods with 7/16-inch ARP bolts, SRP forged pistons, Speed-Pro moly rings, Clevite 77 bearings, Milodon high-volume oil pump, screw-in freeze plugs, stainless steel valves (1.94/1.60-inch), titanium retainers, stud girdle, screw-in studs and guideplates, and more. Large chamber, ported 302 heads are standard with this engine. Aftermarket heads are optional and certainly available.

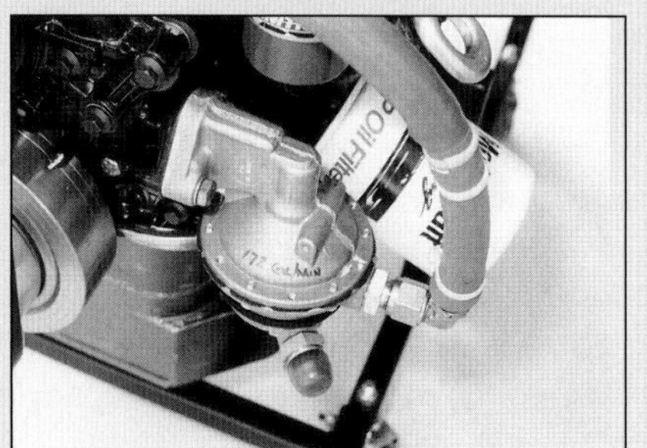

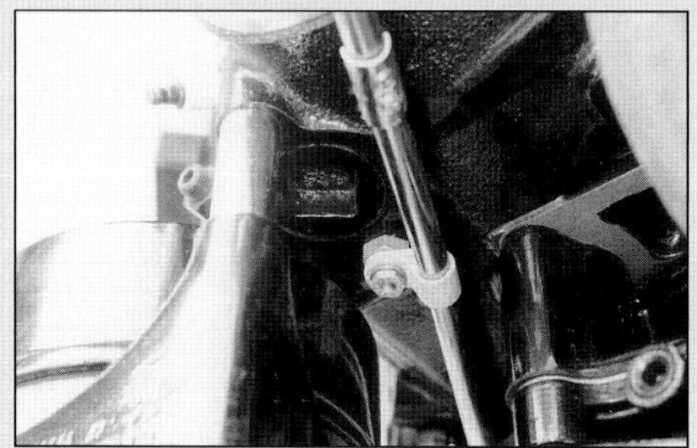

CHAPTER 5

351W STROKER KITS & PROJECTS

What a great playground the middle-block world has become. Just imagine being able to stuff as much as 429ci into your 351W-based block. This gives you big-inch power in a lightweight small block. How far should you go with your 351W? Displacement depends on the amount of power desired and how you're going to get there. You can pump big-inch displacement into a mild-mannered 351W if your main objective is torque. For example, you might be building a big-inch small block displacing 427ci for your F-150 truck. We're not talking a high-revving screamer here, but a solid, dependable, big-twist powerhouse designed to pull heavy loads like a trailer. This is where the long arm of torque comes into play. A lightweight 427ci middle block will make as much power as an FE-series 428ci big-block without the weight penalty. We do this by expanding the stroke out to 4.170-inches and using a 4.030-inch bore. That's less iron, with the 428's bore and stroke dimensions.

Hauling may be the last thing on your mind. Maybe you're building a big-inch middle block for your '68 Mustang fastback where handling is desired, and you wants the intense, persistent power of a big block. The beauty of the 351W-based mill is the weight advantage for your Mustang. Mustang's fitted with FE-series or 385-series big blocks suffer from poor weight distribution (they're nose heavy). With the stroked 351W small block, the Mustang gains aggressive displacement without putting on weight.

In the Mustang, your 427ci stroker can be a mild-mannered mill for week-end cruising, or a screamer with a nasty attitude for the drag strip. That's the beauty of a stroker. It can be anything you want it to be without the weight penalty.

351ci

Speed-O-Motive
131 North Lang Ave.
West Covina, CA 91790
626/869-0270 • 626/869-0278 FAX
www.speedomotive.com

LONG ARM KIT

Bore:	4.030"
Stroke:	3.500"
Crankshaft:	Modified Nodular Iron 351W
Rod Type:	Stage 1 with ARP Wave-Loc Bolts
Rod Length:	6.580"
Rod Ratio:	1.88:1
Pistons:	Hypereutectic Flattops
Rings:	Speed-Pro Cast Iron
Bearings:	Clevite Tri-Metal
Max. RPM:	6,500
Max. HP:	400-450
Approx. Price:	$1,000.00

Comments: Like the Long-Rod 302 mentioned earlier in this book, the 351 Long-Arm kit uses a longer than stock connecting rod, which allows the piston to dwell longer at the top and bottom of the bore. This allows us to make the most of the fuel/air charge. The result is greater torque.

351ci

Speed-O-Motive
131 North Lang Ave.
West Covina, CA 91790
626/869-0270 • 626/869-0278 FAX
www.speedomotive.com

ALL FORGED KIT

Bore:	4.030"
Stroke:	3.500"
Crankshaft:	4340 Forged Steel Crank
Rod Type:	4340 Forged Steel H-Beam Rods
Rod Length:	5.956"
Rod Ratio:	1.70:1
Pistons:	Forged Flattops
Rings:	Plasma Moly File Fit
Bearings:	Federal-Mogul Race Bearings
Max. RPM:	8,000
Max. HP:	600-700
Approx. Price:	$1,650.00
Comments:	This is a 351ci kit designed to take high revs, including nitrous and supercharging. You may go racing with this one.

377ci

Coast High Performance
2555 W. 237th Street
Torrance, CA 90505
310/784-2977
310/784-2970 FAX
www.coasthigh.com

Bore:	4.030"
Stroke:	3.680"
Crankshaft:	Nodular Iron 351W
Rod Type:	Mopar I-Beam Forged
Rod Length:	6.125"
Rod Ratio:	1.66:1
Pistons:	Probe Forged Aluminum
Rings:	Childs & Albert
Bearings:	Clevite 77
Max. RPM:	6,500
Max. HP:	500
Approx. Price:	$1,500.00
Comments:	Called the Street Fighter, this engine is good for street or racing applications. Options, like Eagle rods, are available.

377ci

Nowak Racing Engines
249 E. Emerson Avenue, Unit F
Orange, CA 92665
714/282-7996 • 714/637-0425 FAX

Bore:	4.030"
Stroke:	3.680"
Crankshaft:	High Nodular 351W
Rod Type:	Mopar I-Beam
Rod Length:	6.125"
Rod Ratio:	1.66:1
Pistons:	Nowak Forged
Rings:	Childs & Albert or Speed-Pro
Bearings:	Clevite 77
Max. RPM:	6,500
Max. HP:	500
Approx. Price:	$1,600.00
Comments:	Affordable way to displacement and power. You may upgrade to Crower Sportsman or Eagle H-beam rods. Plenty of room for improvement in this kit from Nowak Racing Engines.

383ci

Bennett Racing
P.O. Box 593
Highway 5 South
Haleyville, AL 35565
205/486-5520 • 205/486-8441 FAX
www.bennettracing.com

Bore:	4.030"
Stroke:	3.750"
Crankshaft:	Billet Steel
Rod Type:	Lunati Pro Mod
Rod Length:	6.200"
Rod Ratio:	1.64:1
Pistons:	Ross Ultra-Lite
Rings:	Speed-Pro
Bearings:	Clevite 77
Ma. RPM:	8,000
Max. HP:	850
Approx. Price:	$3,500.00
Comments:	This is a serious racing stroker kit, designed for high RPM and those power adders like nitrous and boost.

377ci

Ford Performance Solutions
1004 Orangefair Lane
Anaheim, CA 92801
714/773-9027 • 714/773-4178 FAX
www.f-p-s.com

Bore:	4.030"
Stroke:	3.700"
Crankshaft:	High Nodular 351W
Rod Type:	Pro H-Beam
Rod Length:	6.125"
Rod Ratio:	1.66:1
Pistons:	Ross Ultra-Lite
Rings:	Childs & Albert
Bearings:	Clevite 77
Max. RPM:	7,500
Max. HP:	600
Approx. Price:	$1,700.00
Comments:	You may upgrade to a heat-treated or billet crankshaft, H-beam rods, etc.

377ci

Performance Automotive Warehouse
21001 Nordhoff Street
Chatsworth, CA 91311
818/678-3000 • 818/678-3001 FAX
www.pawinc.com

Bore:	4.030"
Stroke:	3.700"
Crankshaft:	High Nodular 351W
Rod Type:	Eagle
Rod Length:	6.200"
Rod Ratio:	1.68:1
Pistons:	JE Pistons
Rings:	JE Plasma Moly
Bearings:	King High Performance
Max. RPM:	7,000
Max. HP:	600
Approx. Price:	$2,000.00
Comments:	A good street/strip kit.

393ci

Coast High Performance
2555 W. 237th Street
Torrance, CA 90505
310/784-2977 • 310/784-2970 FAX
www.coasthigh.com

Bore:	4.030"
Stroke:	3.850"
Crankshaft:	High Nodular 351W
Rod Type:	Mopar I-Beam
Rod Length:	6.125"
Rod Ratio:	1.66:1
Pistons:	Probe Forged Aluminum
Rings:	Childs & Albert
Bearings:	Clevite 77
Max. RPM:	6,300
Max. HP:	500
Approx. Price:	$1,600.00
Comments:	Good, affordable street power that will make boatloads of torque. Doesn't need to spin at 7,000 rpm to make torque either. Optional Eagle rods available.

393ci

Bennett Racing
P.O. Box 593
Highway 5 South
Haleyville, AL 35565
205/486-5520 • 205/486-8441 FAX
www.bennettracing.com

Bore:	4.030"
Stroke:	3.850"
Crankshaft:	Cast Steel
Rod Type:	Eagle
Rod Length:	6.250"
Rod Ratio:	1.63:1
Pistons:	Ross Ultra-Lite
Rings:	Speed-Pro
Bearings:	Clevite 77
Max. RPM:	7,000
Max. HP:	650
Approx. Price:	$2,500.00
Comments:	This is a great street/strip kit because it does both so well. It is a kit you can grow into as your power needs develop.

393ci

Speed-O-Motive
131 North Lang Ave.
West Covina, CA 91790
626/869-0270 • 626/869-0278 FAX
www.speedomotive.com

Bore:	4.030"
Stroke:	3.850"
Crankshaft:	High Nodular Iron
Rod Type:	Stage 1 with ARP Wave-Loc Bolts
Rod Length:	5.956"
Rod Ratio:	1.54:1
Pistons:	Federal Mogul Hyper-eutectic
Rings:	Sealed Power Cast Iron
Bearings:	Clevite Tri-Metal
Max. RPM:	6,500
Max. HP:	500
Approx.e Price:	$1,200.00
Comments:	This is a good budget kit with enough stroke to make lots of power. Stay away from nitrous and heavy boost.

398ci

Bennett Racing
P.O. Box 593
Highway 5 South
Haleyville, AL 35565
205/486-5520 • 205/486-8441 FAX
www.bennettracing.com

Bore:	4.030"
Stroke:	3.900"
Crankshaft:	Billet Steel
Rod Type:	Lunati Pro Mod
Rod Length:	6.200"
Rod Ratio:	1.59:1
Pistons:	Ross Ultra-Lite
Rings:	Speed-Pro
Bearings:	Clevite 77
Max. RPM:	8,000
Max. HoP:	850
Approx. Price:	$3,500.00
Comments:	This is a good kit for racing, capable of high revs and power adders like nitrous and super-charging. Here, you need large-port heads and intake.

393ci

ProPower
4750 N. Dixie Highway, No. 9
Fort Lauderdale, FL 33334
954/491-6988 • 954/491-2874 FAX
www.propowerparts.com

Bore:	4.030"
Stroke:	3.700"
Crankshaft:	High Nodular Iron 351W
Rod Type:	Eagle
Rod Length:	6.200"
Rod Ratio:	1.68:1
Pistons:	JE Pistons
Rings:	JE Plasma Moly
Bearings:	King High Performance
Max. RPM:	7,000
Max. HP:	600
Approx. Price:	$2,000.00
Comments:	Pump displacement into your 351W at an affordable price. This is free power because it doesn't cost any more than a stock rebuild.

396ci

D.S.S. Competition Products
960 Ridge Avenue
Lombard, IL 60148
630/268-1630 • 630/268-1649 FAX
www.dssracing.com

Bore:	4.030"
Stroke:	3.850"
Crankshaft:	Cast Steel
Rod Type:	Eagle
Rod Length:	6.200"
Rod Ratio:	1.56:1
Pistons:	Pro Series Forged
Rings:	Sealed Power or Speed Pro
Bearings:	Federal-Mogul
Max. RPM:	6,500
Max. HP:	600
Approx.e Price:	$2,200.00
Comments:	Figure on roughly 50 more horsepower just by building this kit into your 351W block.

398ci

Nowak Racing Engines
249 E. Emerson Avenue, Unit F
Orange, CA 92665
714/282-7996 • 714/637-0245 FAX

Bore:	4.030"
Stroke:	3.900"
Crankshaft:	Cast Steel
Rod Type:	Eagle
Rod Length:	6.200"
Rod Ratio:	1.59:1
Pistons:	Nowak Forged
Rings:	Childs & Albert or Speed-Pro
Bearings:	Clevite 77
Max. RPM:	6,500
Max. HP:	700
Approx. Price:	$2,100.00
Comments:	This is a good street/strip kit. Power adders like nitrous and supercharger okay. Watch the amount of power adding.

408ci

Bennett Racing
P.O. Box 593
Highway 5 South
Haleyville, AL 35565
205/486-5520 • 205/486-8441 FAX
www.bennettracing.com

Bore: 4.030"
Stroke: 4.000"
Crankshaft: Cast Steel
Rod Type: Eagle
Rod Length: 6.250"
Rod Ratio: 1.56:1
Pistons: Ross Ultra-Lite
Rings: Speed-Pro File Fit
Bearings: Clevite 77
Max. RPM: 7,200
Max. HP: 650
Approx. Price: $2,500.00
Comments: This is a great street/strip kit. The message here is lots of torque from a 351W based engine. This is a kit designed for high revs, which calls for deep breathing heads and a single-plane intake. If you desire good street torque, opt for a dual-plane intake manifold that serves both low and high-RPM use well.

408ci

Ford Performance Solutions
1004 Orangefair Lane
Anaheim, CA 92801
714/773-9027 • 714/773-4178 FAX
www.f-p-s.com

Bore: 4.030"
Stroke: 4.000"
Crankshaft: High Nodular 400M
Rod Type: Pro H-Beam
Rod Length: 6.125"
Rod Ratio: 1.53:1
Pistons: Ross Ultra-Lite
Rings: Childs & Albert
Bearings: Clevite 77
Max. RPM: 6,000
Max. HP: 600
Approx. Price: $1,700.00
Comments: Optional heat-treated or steel crankshaft available. Also Eagle 6.200" or 6.250" H-beam rods available. Pro-Lite aluminum rods also available.

408ci

Speed-O-Motive
131 North Lang Ave.
West Covina, CA 91790
626/869-0270 • 626/869-0278 FAX
www.speedomotive.com

Bore: 4.030"
Stroke: 4.000"
Crankshaft: High Nodular Iron
Rod Type: 4340 Forged I-Beam
Rod Length: 6.200"
Rod Ratio: 1.55:1
Pistons: Keith Black Hypereutectic
Rings: Sealed Power Cast Iron
Bearings: Clevite Tri-Metal
Max. RPM: 6,500
Max. HP: 500
Approx. Price: $1,400.00
Comments: Good, high-torque budget kit for street and weekend strip. Nitrous and supercharging not recommended.

408ci

Coast High Performance
2555 W. 237th Street
Torrance, CA 90505
310/784-2977 • 310/784-2970 FAX
www.coasthigh.com

Bore: 4.030"
Stroke: 4.000"
Crankshaft: High Nodular 400M
Rod Type: Eagle
Rod Length: 6.200"
Rod Ratio: 1.55:1
Pistons: Probe Forged Aluminum
Rings: Childs & Albert
Bearings: Clevite 77
Max. RPM: 6,500
Max. HP: 650
Approx. Price: $2,000.00
Comments: Powerful street/strip stroker kit. Will handle nitrous and boost. Optional forged steel crankshaft available.

408ci

Nowak Racing Engines
249 E. Emerson Avenue, Unit F
Orange, CA 92665
714/282-7996 • 714/637-0425 FAX

Bore: 4.030"
Stroke: 4.000"
Crankshaft: Billet
Rod Type: Crower Billet
Rod Length: 6.250"
Rod Ratio: 1.56:1
Pistons: Nowak Forged
Rings: Childs & Albert or Speed-Pro
Bearings: Clevite 77
Max. RPM: 7,500
Max. HP: 700
Approx.e Price: $3,600.00
Comments: This kit makes a great foundation for your big-cube building project. Nowak's four-bolt main conversion kit (optional) gives this bulletproof bottom end strength. A 6.400" rod is available.

410ci

D.S.S. Competition Products
960 Ridge Avenue
Lombard, IL 60148
630/268-1630 • 630/268-1649 FAX
www.dssracing.com

Bore: 4.030"
Stroke: 4.000"
Crankshaft: Billet Steel
Rod Type: Eagle
Rod Length: 6.250"
Rod Ratio: 1.56:1
Pistons: Venolia
Rings: Speed-Pro
Bearings: Federal-Mogul
Max. RPM: 6,500
Max. HP: 650
Approx. Price: $4,500.00
Comments: With proper prep and assembly, this is a race-ready kit.

426ci

Coast High Performance
2555 W. 237th Street
Torrance, CA 90505
310/784-2977 • 310/784-2970 FAX
www.coasthigh.com

Bore:	4.030"
Stroke:	4.170"
Crankshaft:	Nodular Iron 400M
Rod Type:	Eagle
Rod Length:	6.200"
Rod Ratio:	1.48:1
Pistons:	Probe Forged Aluminum
Rings:	Childs & Albert
Bearings:	Clevite 77
Max. RPM:	6,200
Max. HP:	650
Approx. Price:	$2,000.00
Comments:	Good for the street or strip. Big-block torque from a small-block V-8. You will need large port/valve heads for this one. Nitrous and boost will work with this one.

426ci

Nowak Racing Engines
249 E. Emerson Avenue, Unit F
Orange, CA 92665
714/282-7996 • 714/637-0425 FAX

Bore:	4.030"
Stroke:	4.100"
Crankshaft:	Billet
Rod Type:	Crower Billet
Rod Length:	6.250"
Rod Ratio:	1.56:1
Pistons:	Nowak Forged
Rings:	Childs & Albert or Speed-Pro
Bearings:	Clevite 77
Max. RPM:	7,500
Max. HP:	700
Approx. Price:	$3,600.00
Comments:	A strong foundation for your big-inch stroker project. This kit has special considerations. It calls for the Nowak four-bolt main conversion in a two-bolt 351W block. An optional 6.400" rod is available.

427ci

Coast High Performance
2555 W. 237th Street
Torrance, CA 90505
310/784-2977 • 310/784-2970 FAX
www.coasthigh.com

Bore:	4.030"
Stroke:	4.170"
Crankshaft:	Nodular Iron
Rod Type:	Forged Steel
Rod Length:	Unknown
Rod Ratio:	Unknown
Pistons:	Probe Forged Aluminum
Rings:	Childs & Albert
Bearings:	Clevite 77
Max. RPM:	6,500
Max. HP:	500
Approx. Price:	$1,400.00
Comments:	This is a great value because it yields plenty of torque, along with the quality and reliability you expect from Coast High Performance and Probe products.

426ci

Ford Performance Solutions
1004 Orangefair Lane
Anaheim, CA 92801
714/773-9027 • 714/773-4178 FAX
www.f-p-s.com

Bore:	4.030"
Stroke:	4.170"
Crankshaft:	High Nodular 400M
Rod Type:	Pro H-Beam
Rod Length:	6.125"
Rod Ratio:	1.47:1
Pistons:	Ross Ultra-Lite
Rings:	Childs & Albert
Bearings:	Clevite 77
Max. RPM:	6,000
Max. HP:	600
Approx. Price:	$1,800.00
Comments:	Heat-treated or billet crank available. Nice upgrades, like the Eagle 6.200" H-beam, Oliver billet, or Pro-Lite aluminum rods available.

426ci

Speed-O-Motive
131 North Lang Ave.
West Covina, CA 91790
626/869-0270 • 626/869-0278 FAX
www.speedomotive.com

Bore:	4.030"
Stroke:	4.170"
Crankshaft:	High Nodular 400M
Rod Type:	Eagle
Rod Length:	6.125"
Rod Ratio:	1.47:1
Pistons:	Ross Ultra-Lites
Rings:	Speed-Pro
Bearings:	Clevite 77 H
Max. RPM:	6,200
Max. HP:	500
Approx. Price:	$1,900.00
Comments:	This is a torque powerhouse. A lot of bang for the buck.

482ci

D&D Motorsports
25845 San Fernando Rd., Unit 4
Saugus, CA 91350
661/260-2226 • 661/260-2225 FAX

Bore:	4.030"
Stroke:	4.375"
Crankshaft:	Velasco Steel Billet
Rod Type:	Childs & Albert Billet
Rod Length:	7.100"
Rod Ratio:	1.62:1
Pistons:	Ross Ultra-Lite
Rings:	Childs & Albert
Bearings:	Childs & Albert
Max. RPM:	9,000
Max. HP:	1,400
Approx. Price:	$10,000.00
Comments:	This kit mandates an aftermarket block with four-bolt mains. Strictly a racing stroker kit where a deck spacer plate is used. A lot of custom work involved.

Building The CHP/TA Racing 408

Most of us who live in Southern California know Mark Jeffrey of Trans Am Racing out of Gardena, 15 miles south of downtown Los Angeles. Mark's business is about Fords, mostly. He does business in the company of a lot of familiar names in the Ford realm, including Carroll Shelby. Last we looked in on Mark, he was building a 408ci stroker for *Mustang Monthly* magazine. Luckily, we were allowed photograph the buildup alongside the magazine staffers.

Mark was building a 408 Street Fighter package from Coast High Performance. This 408 stroker is more a budget project with a nodular iron custom crankshaft, I-beam rods, forged pistons, Edelbrock Performer RPM heads and induction, and a 1980s-vintage 351W block fitted with a Comp Cams roller hydraulic camshaft. We're building a budget 351W stroker because its mission will be towing and hauling in a Ford E-150 van. Low and mid-range pulling torque is the goal here.

Our foundation for the Trans Am Racing 408ci stroker is a 1980s-vintage 351W block that has been properly modified. It has been bored .030-inch oversize and line-bore checked. It had its decks milled, its cylinder skirts notched, and it has also been thoroughly cleaned. Now we're ready for assembly. This is not a roller block.

Building The CHP/TA Racing 408 (continued)

This is the 408ci Street Fighter stroker kit from Coast High Performance, available from Trans Am Racing. The kit includes a custom nodular iron crankshaft, forged I-beam connecting rods, and custom forged pistons. Because having a greater stroke means more compression, the pistons are dished to keep compression under control at 10.0:1.

Our valvetrain package comes from Comp Cams in Memphis, Tennessee. Mark is going with a roller hydraulic camshaft that will yield good low and mid-range torque. Remember, this engine is designed for towing and hauling. We're not seeking a 6,500 rpm screamer, but a V-8 that pulls strongly from a stop and under a load. Note that this is a small base circle camshaft to clear the non-roller block.

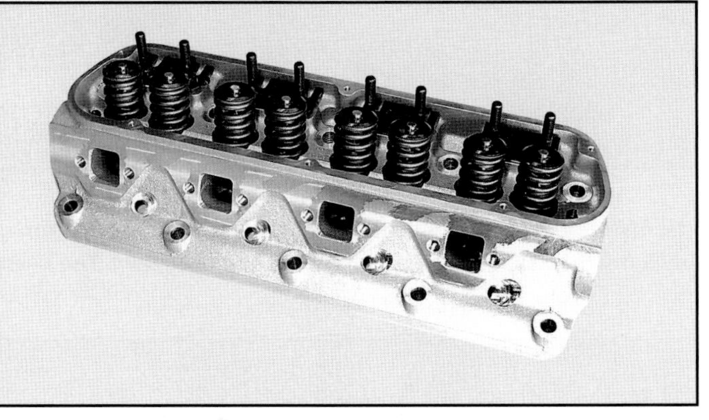

We're going to top this engine with Edelbrock Performer RPM heads with 2.02-inch intake and 1.60-inch exhaust valves. Chambers are 64cc. Valve springs have been changed to work well with the roller hydraulic camshaft from Comp Cams.

Above right and right: Mark Jeffrey of Trans Am Racing stresses measuring twice. Here, he checks the main bearing diameters, then crank journal dimensions. Rod bearings will be checked later on. This tells Mark the fit between bearings and journals.

Building The CHP/TA Racing 408 (continued)

The one-piece rear-main seal groove gets a light application of gasket sealer where the seal will seat.

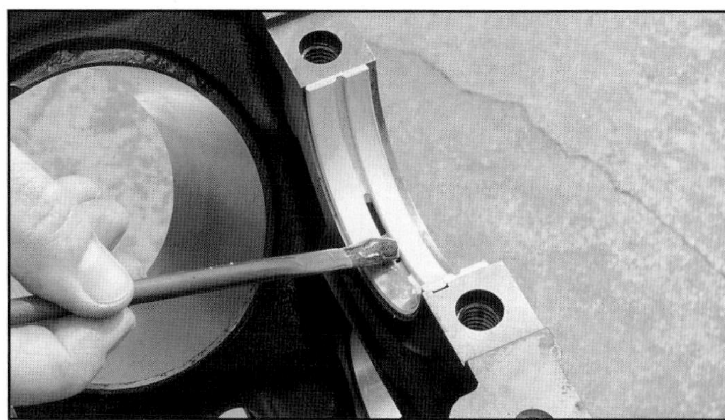

Main bearings receive a dressing of engine assembly lube before the crank goes in.

The desirable one-piece rear-main seal has been improved with a plastic installation sleeve, which prevents seal damage or distortion during installation. Mark dresses the crankshaft surface with assembly lube, then slips the seal onto the crank as shown. The plastic sleeve gets tossed.

The high-nodular iron custom crankshaft from Trans Am Racing is laid in the block as shown. Mark will check the crank for freedom of rotation.

With the main caps properly torqued to 95-105 ft-lbs, Mark checks crankshaft end play, which should be between 0.004 and 0.008-inch.

Building The CHP/TA Racing 408 (continued)

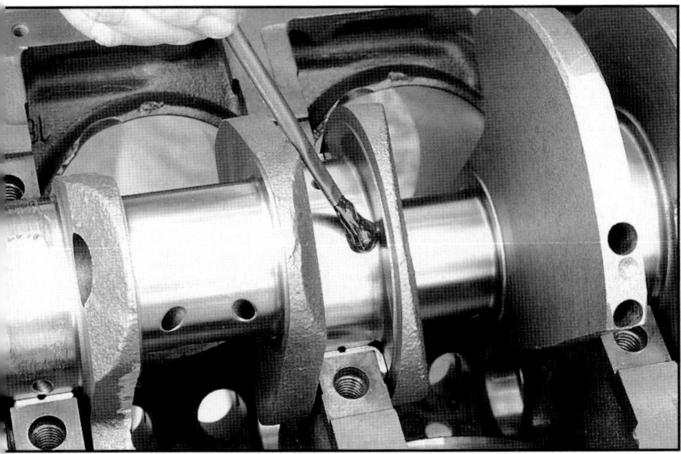

Above, below, and bottom: Main bearing journals get liberal doses of engine assembly lube to protect them during start-up. Main caps are installed and torqued next.

The one-piece rear-main seal has been a nice upgrade for small-block Fords since the mid-1980s. It is less prone to leakage and is easy to install. Mark went the extra mile by applying sealer between the seal and block to further prevent leakage.

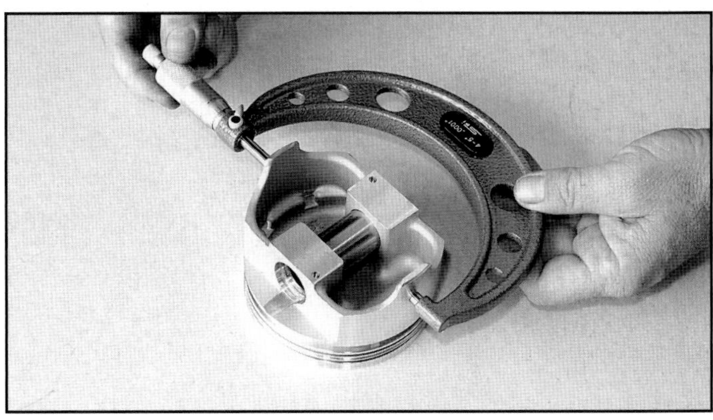

Mark is double-checking piston-to-cylinder wall clearances by mic'ing each piston and cylinder wall. Cast pistons don't experience the expansion of forged pistons as the engine warms.

Building The CHP/TA Racing 408 (continued)

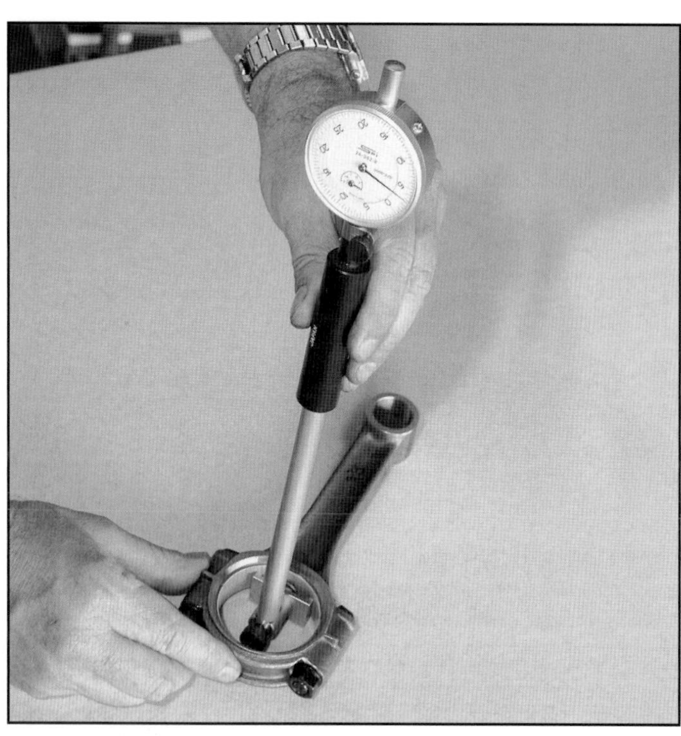

Rod bearing dimensions are checked, as are the crankshaft journals mentioned earlier.

When you build your stroker, expect to see a new kind of piston-pin retaining clip. Instead of the conventional C-clip used for many years, this is a roll-in clip that is easy to install and difficult to remove. The humble C-clip was replaced because they tended to pop out and damage cylinder walls.

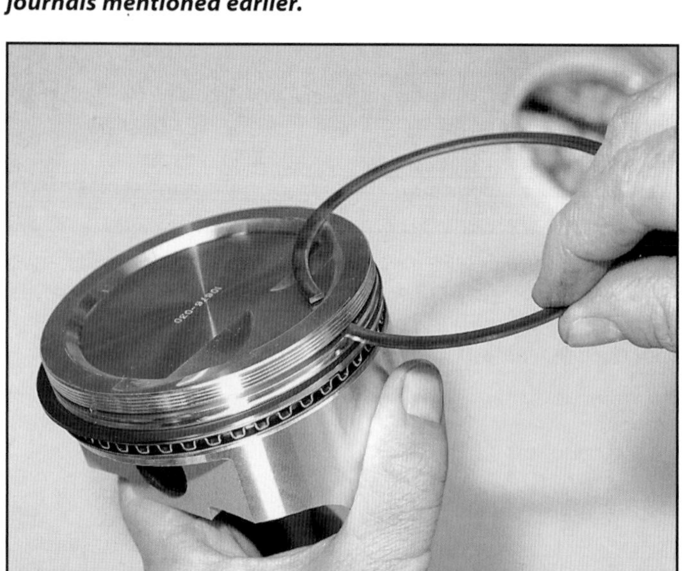

Mark Jeffrey makes piston ring installation look easy. He rolls the compression ring on, doing the second ring first, then the top ring. He stresses always clearing the piston ring lands, making sure you don't nick or scar these critical areas with the ring. Ring gaps must be positioned around the piston in a 9, 12, 3, and 6 o'clock pattern. None of the gaps should be close to one another.

Piston-ring end gaps are checked in the interest of integrity. This isn't even an option. Do it with every compression ring on every bore. Top ring gap is .010-inch. The second compression ring gap is .020-inch.

Building The CHP/TA Racing 408 (continued)

Each piston and rod assembly is guided into the bore carefully. Mark tells us to keep the large end of the connecting rod away from the cylinder wall and crankshaft journal. The ARP rod bolts can nick the cylinder wall and journal, making it necessary for you to tear down the block and repair these surfaces.

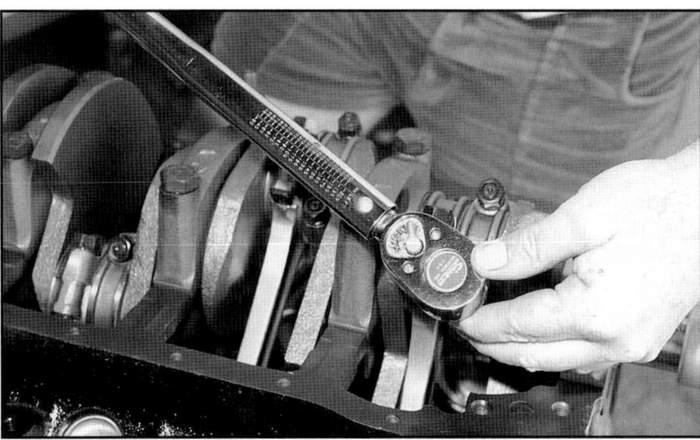

Rod bolts are torqued to 40-45 ft-lbs. Check connecting rod side clearance when all rods are torqued. Check your work twice.

With our Comp Cams roller hydraulic camshaft lubed up and ready to go, Mark slips the bumpstick into the block, taking care not to mar the bearings and journals in the process.

The cam retainer plate is installed next. Mark uses Loc-Tite on the bolt threads for insurance.

Building The CHP/TA Racing 408 (continued)

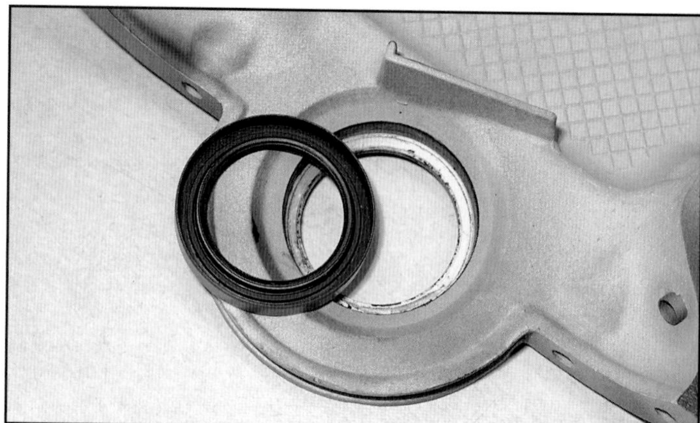

Small-block Ford timing covers can be confusing. When it comes to front seals, there are two designs. Early timing covers have oil seals installed from the inside where they seat against a pocket. Newer and reproduction timing covers have seals with a lip that install from the outside in. Whenever you are in doubt, remember that the tiny spring that retains the rubber lip always goes toward the inside.

The dual-roller timing set is installed next, getting the timing marks at 12 and 6 o'clock. This one gets a fuel pump eccentric, which actuates the fuel pump.

Mark applies gasket sealer to the block mating surfaces as shown. Then, he installs the timing cover as shown. He uses a special tool to center the timing cover on the crankshaft. But, you may use your harmonic balancer to center your timing cover. Don't forget the oil slinger shown here. The oil slinger keeps oil away from the crankshaft seal. Don't make the mistake of using a 351C oil slinger on a 351W. It will tear up the timing cover when the engine is fired.

Building The CHP/TA Racing 408 (continued)

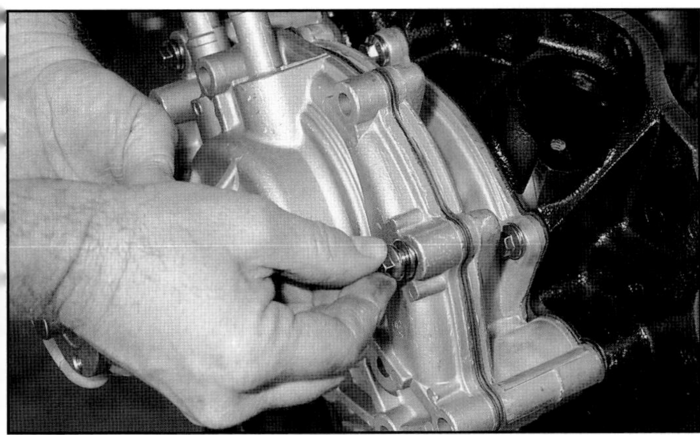

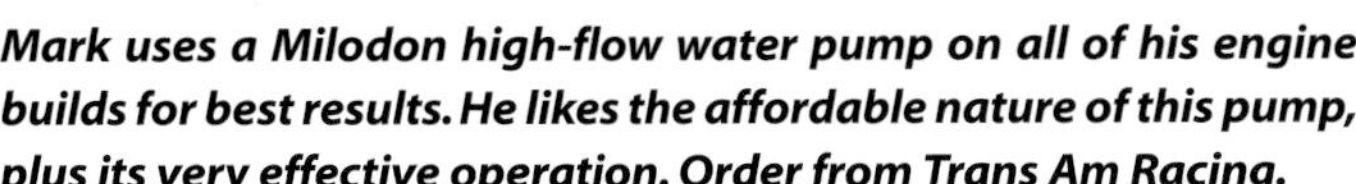

Mark uses a Milodon high-flow water pump on all of his engine builds for best results. He likes the affordable nature of this pump, plus its very effective operation. Order from Trans Am Racing.

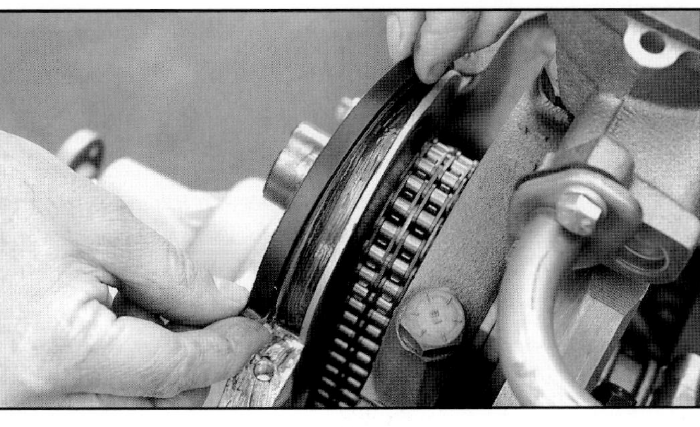

Above middle, above, and right: Oil pan installation begins with the right preparation. Mark dresses the end seal areas with gasket sealer. He does the same thing between the side rail gaskets and the block. Silicone sealer is applied where the end seals join the block.

Above and below: We're using a Speed-Pro high-volume oil pump from Federal-Mogul. Whenever you're building an engine using a stroker kit, check oil pump to crankshaft counterweight clearances. You need at least .050-inch of clearance. Things get even tighter whenever we use a Trans Am Racing main stud girdle. Expect a tight fit there. You will have to carefully grind away iron where interference with the oil pump occurs.

Building The CHP/TA Racing 408 (continued)

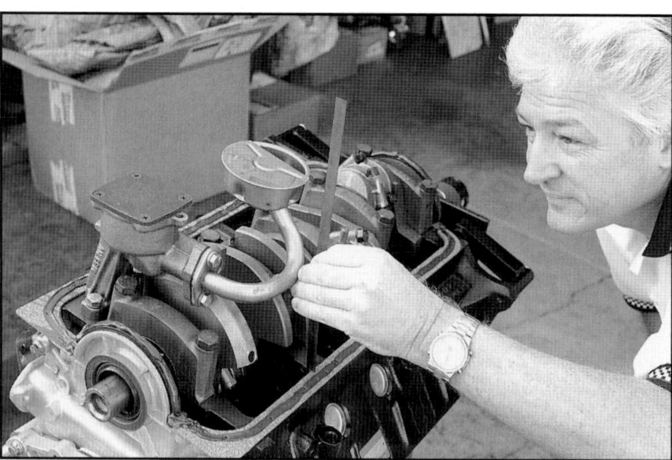

Mark checks oil pick-up to pan clearance at least two ways. He measures the distance between the pick-up and block, then he measures the depth of the oil pan. The pick-up should not touch the oil pan. Touching the pan could wear a hole in the steel, not to mention creating metal particles that would be ingested into the oil pump and circulated into the engine.

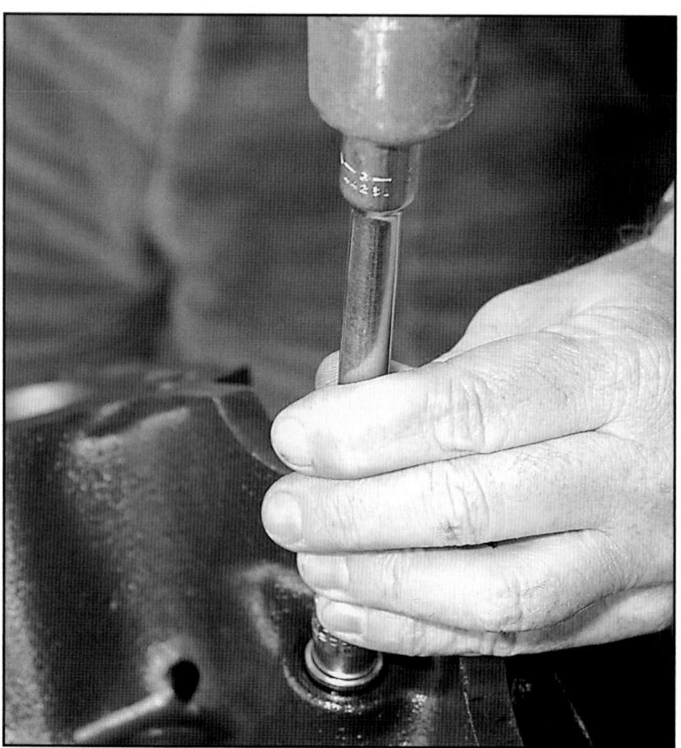

Topside, Mark installs the oil galley plug at the rear of the block at the manifold rail. Too many builders forget to install this important plug, which results in zero oil pressure when it's time to fire the engine.

Mark installs the new oil pan from Trans Am Racing. Although this is a chrome oil pan, per the customer's request, Mark discourages the use of chrome oil pans. They retain heat. They also rust because the plating quality is generally poor.

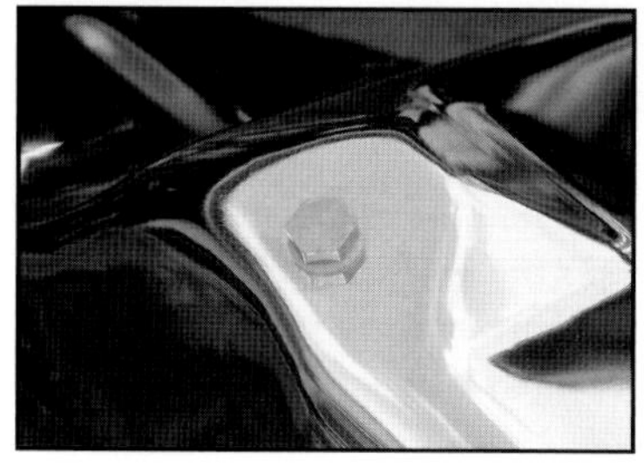

All engine builds from Trans Am Racing receive magnetic oil drain plugs. The magnetic drain plug catches any metal particles that could do engine damage. They also tell us a story whenever it's time to change the oil.

Building The CHP/TA Racing 408 (continued)

Trans Am Racing uses Ferrea cylinder head gaskets, which are the same head gaskets used by NASCAR racers.

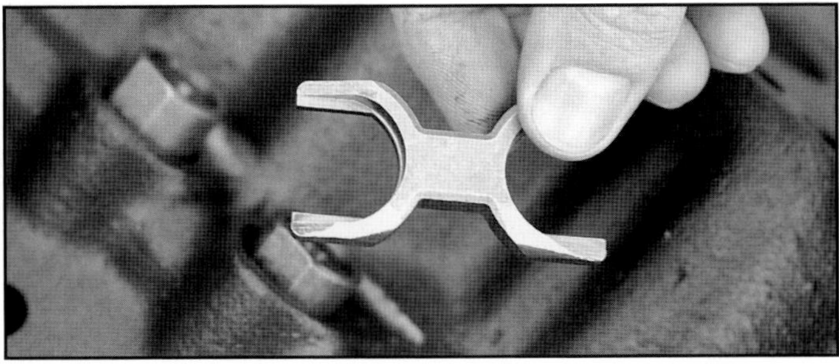

Above and right: Whenever you are converting a flat-tappet block to roller tappets, some modification may be required. Mark shows us where he had to modify this block for roller tappets. The area around the lifter bores had to be ground to clear the dog bones. The dog bones themselves had to be ground to clear the block in these areas. This happens when the block is being machined, not during assembly. Mark lays in the spider as shown.

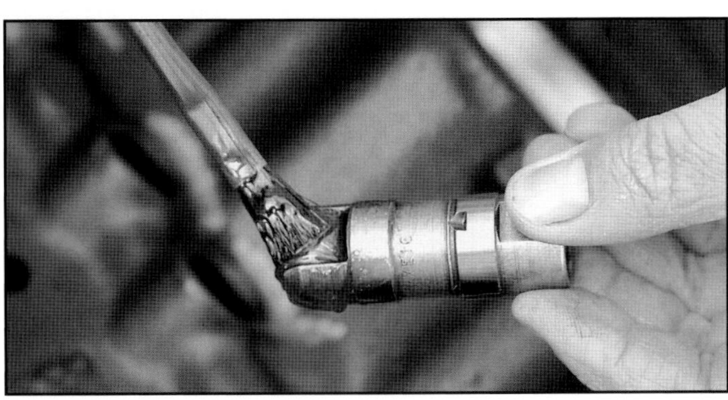

Before we lay the heads on this block, we want you to see what a difference 4.000-inches of stroke makes. As a 351W, this engine had 3.50-inches of stroke. Here, with the Coast High Performance kit from Trans Am Racing, we have a full 1/2-inch of additional stroke. What it means for you is mucho torque.

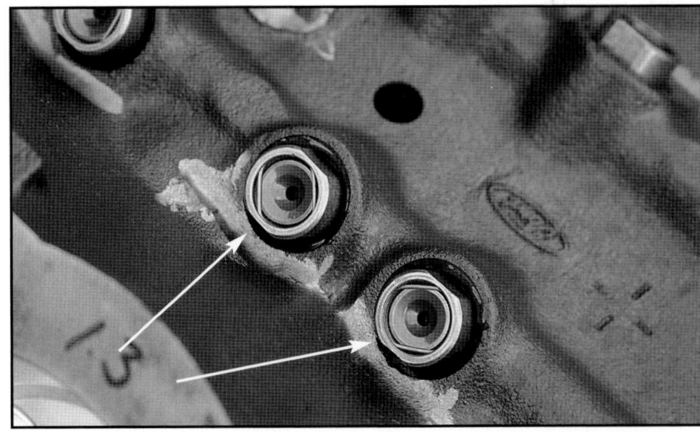

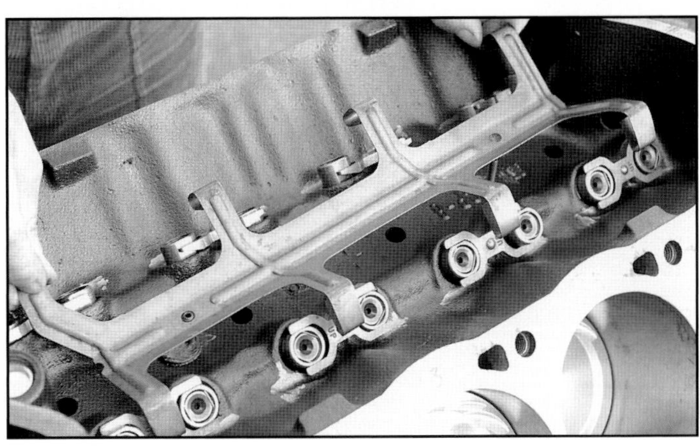

Building The CHP/TA Racing 408 (concluded)

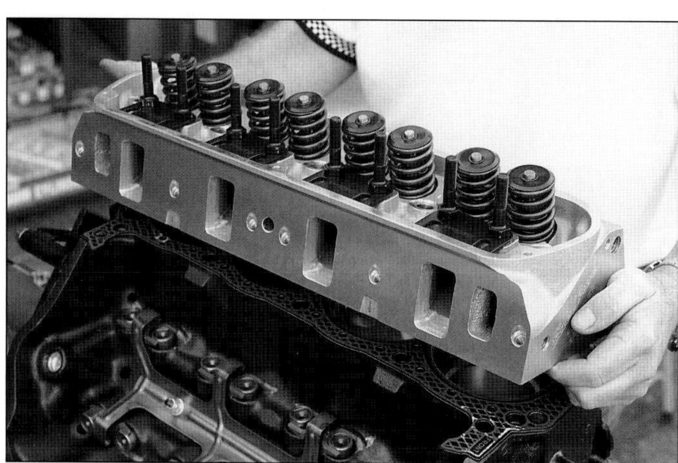

Mark installs the Edelbrock Performer RPM heads, which will allow our 408 to breathe nicely in the RPM ranges it will be operating. Were we building a 408 for street/strip performance or all-out racing, we would opt for Edelbrock Victor Jr. heads instead.

Heads are torqued next, per the instructions provided by Edelbrock. ARP bolts are being used in this application.

Comp Cams billet roller rockers seem like overkill for an engine like this one, but they are what the customer asked for. Forged steel roller-tip rockers are plenty enough for this application. Rocker ratio is 1.6:1.

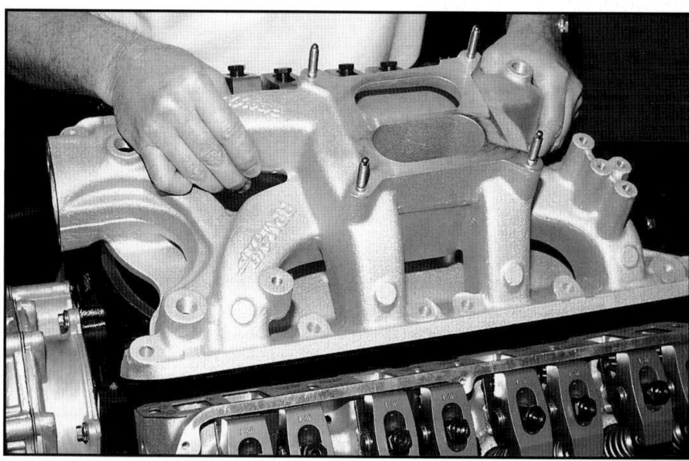

Mark applies silicone sealer along the manifold rails. He does this instead of a cork gasket because it is proven more reliable. Using sealer around the coolant passages is also a good idea to keep coolant out of the oil. We're topping this puppy with Edelbrock's new Performer RPM Air Gap manifold and a Holley 650cfm atomizer with vacuum secondaries.

CHP / TA Racing 408ci Stroker Dyno Test

What Will This Thing Do?

RPM	Horsepower	Torque
2000	154	404
2500	201	421
3000	245	429
3500	295	443
4000	343	**450**
4500	384	448
5000	409	430
5500	**414**	395
6000	399	349

Trans Am Racing
13307 S. Manhattan Place
Gardena, CA 90249
310/323-5417
www.taracing.com

CHAPTER 6

351C Stroker Kits & Projects

Ford's 351ci Cleveland middle block entered production more than three decades ago in the fall of 1969. Its production and service life was all too brief, unfortunately, lasting through the 1974 model year. Ford's decision to terminate 351C production was rooted in scaling down production costs. After the 351C was introduced in 1970, Ford was already at work on an FE Series big-block replacement called the 400M – the tall-deck Cleveland block displacing 400ci that was introduced for 1972. The 400M looks a lot like its smaller 351C counterpart except for the taller deck and wider profile that come from the 4.00-inch stroke inside. Instead of the 351C's small-block bellhousing bolt pattern, the 400M has the 429/460's big-block pattern, which makes it compatible only with 385-series big-block transmissions, such as the C6 automatic.

The 400M replaced the FE Series 390ci big block, which was common in full-sized Fords and Mercurys. Later on in 1977, the 400M design would find its way into F-Series trucks as well. In 1975, Ford took the 400M and destroked it to 3.50-inches to achieve the 351M, an underpowered, overweight version of the 351C it replaced. This means the 351M isn't just a 351C with a new designation. It means the 351M is 351ci inside a 400M block, which is considerably heavier than the 351C block. The 351M and 400M have the 351C-2V head, with open chambers and smaller ports.

If you're going to build an M block, bore and stroke this block to more than 400ci for a wealth of good torque. Top the block with 351C Aussie heads, with wedge chambers and the 351C-2V ports for optimum torque. A stroked 400M isn't for performance use, but more for good power in a tow vehicle. It is not an engine you would want to spin to 7,500 rpm in a road-race vehicle or drag car.

Our focus here isn't the 351/400M, but the 351C and what can be done with this short-lived Ford powerhouse. Most of us will never know what Ford engineers were thinking when the 351C was developed. Its huge ports mirror the 429/460ci big-block's. Yet, there isn't the displacement in the 351C witnessed with the high-displacement fat-blocks. The 351C-4V head is long on potential if you're planning a 7,500-rpm engine. Those huge intake ports allow an abun-

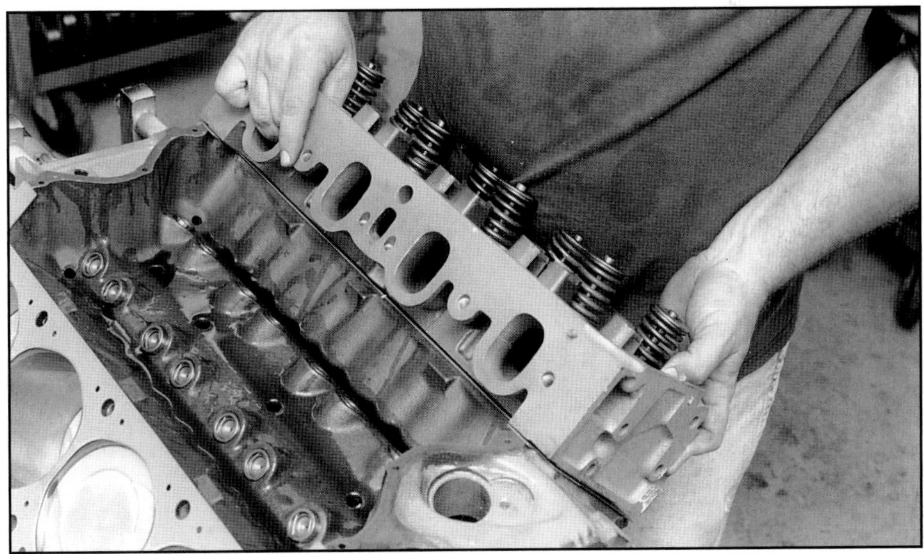

The 351 Cleveland has huge ports. Yet, the factory displacement never takes advantage of the size. When we huff displacement through these extra-large ports, we get raw power. This is exactly what the 351C is famous for when we spin it to 7,000 rpm. A stroker kit enables us to get the same amount of power at lower revs.

dance of air and fuel to pass. But these ports are useful only at high revs, where enough velocity can be developed to feed the bores and provide cylinder pressure.

The 351C-4V is virtually the same head casting used on top of the BOSS 302 small block produced in 1969 and 1970. Ford engineers borrowed this head for the BOSS 302 to make the most of the high-revving 302ci small-block's potential. This approach worked with great success in SCCA Trans Am competition. The 351C-4V head has huge 2.50 x 1.75-inch intake ports. On the exhaust side, 2.00 x 1.74-inch. Valve sizing runs 2.19-inch intake and 1.71-inch exhaust. These dimensions are overwhelming in a street engine. What they mean for you is poor low-end torque, short on the grunt factor. Large ports like these don't give you the hole-shot advantage on the street. On the drag strip, they come on strong at high revs. Ditto for the race course.

Poor low-end torque has an unpleasant feel. Lean on the throttle coming out of the hole and the large-port Cleveland or BOSS 302 falls right on its face. It doesn't make torque down there. Carry the revs skyward and these ports begin to go to work. But even in the most powerful of 351C engines, the potential of these ports is never realized. They need 7,000 rpm and higher to be working at all with a displacement of 351ci.

The best way to make the most of the 351C-4V head is to stroke your 351C to utilize this engine's displacement potential. Both Coast High Performance and Speed-O-Motive offer stroker kits for the 351C middle block. These stroker kits are available in price ranges to meet all budgets. If you want a high-revving screamer, there are high-end kits available for the 351C that will allow you to make the most of this legendary performer. If you are limited by budget, you don't have to be limited on power. You can pump as much as 408ci into the 351C for under $2,000. Because the 351C makes a lot of power in stock displacement form, it only gets better with more displacement. With 377ci inside, the 351C makes even more power. But with 408ci, the displacement of a big block, the 351C comes on very strong. You may also bore the 351C to 4.040-inches for a pinch more power. We discourage taking the Cleveland block to 4.060-inches.

The key to making real stroker power with the 351C is to stroke as much displacement as possible into its bores in order to make the most of its large-port heads. This means you need a stroker kit that will allow you to spin it to at least 6,000 rpm for best results. If you want to spin the Cleveland even higher, we suggest a 377ci stroker kit with H-beam rods and a steel crankshaft in the interest of staying well within the limits of the Cleveland's design. Based on what we've been told by seasoned engine builders, the 408ci Cleveland stroker approach pushes this engine to the limits of its intended design, which puts the package more at risk if we try spin it to 7,500 rpm. Closely examine each engine kit to determine limits and approach your build-up from there.

While you are planning your 351C stroker build, close attention to camshaft selection must be practiced, which is where the folks at Comp Cams come in. Comp Cams is customer friendly, and eager to help you with your camshaft and valvetrain selection. Comp Cams will sit down with you on the telephone and get you pointed in the right direction on your camshaft and valvetrain. Always order your cam and valvetrain as a cohesive package from the same manufacturer.

Comp Cams, for example, tests the daylights out of its products with real dyno and road testing. The great talent within these companies discovers what works on the street, just like the rest of us. Comp Cams, for example, refines its product this way. When you stuff a Comp Cams bumpstick inside your block, you're getting the result of extensive testing and refinement, making it an excellent value for your hard-earned dollars.

Camshaft selection for a 351C stroker depends on how you plan on using the engine. For one thing, we suggest a good roller hydraulic camshaft just for starters. Then, you need to look at valve timing events closely. Cam-timing events need to make the most of the displacement, bore, and stroke that you have selected. These elements also have to capitalize on the cylinder head design as well. Because we're dealing with two cylinder head designs with the 351C, this becomes easier.

We've addressed the 351C-4V head at length. Because the 4V head has such huge ports, we have to spin the 351C high to make the most of these woefully over-engineered castings. The thing is, not all 351C projects need to spin to 6,500 rpm. You may be building a 351C for a pick-up or a van where you need pulling power. This means you need only rev to 5,500 rpm to get the job done.

So what do you do when cylinder heads yield way more potential than your 351C will ever realize? There are two answers for this one. One is the 351C-2V head with smaller sized ports and open chambers. The other is Australian 302C and 351C heads, which have the smaller wedge chambers we find with the U.S. 351C-4V head, coupled with the smaller 351C-2V ports. The 351C-2V head has 2.02 x 1.65-inch intake ports, followed by 1.84 x 1.38-inch exhaust ports. Stopcocks are sized at 2.04-inch intake and 1.67-inch exhaust.

The Aussie 351C head is your best choice because it employs the Cleveland's best features – adequately sized ports and valves, coupled with the wedge chambers. We like the Aussie head because its wedge chamber gives us the best result. The open, lower compression chamber we find with U.S. 351C-2V heads tends to cause detonation, regardless of how you tune the engine. One theory is that the 351C-2V head sets up two flame fronts that collide, causing the detonation we hear as pinging under acceleration. We don't experience this with 351C-4V heads or the 351C Aussie head. This tells us something positive about this cozy wedge chamber.

Regardless of what type of 351C/351M/400M cylinder head type you're going to use, you need to fit yours with pushrod guide plates and screw-in, adjustable studs. This enables you to adjust your valvetrain accordingly.

The aftermarket offers us very few types of intake manifolds for the 351C.

393ci

StrokerKits.com
700 First Capitol Dr
St. Charles, MO 63301
636/946-4747 • 636/946-5757 FAX
www.StrokerKits.com

Bore:	4.030"
Stroke:	3.850"
Crankshaft:	Forged Steel
Rod Type:	Forged I-Beam (optional H-beam)
Rod Length:	6.000"
Rod Ratio:	1.54:1
Pistons:	Custom Forged
Rings:	Unknown
Bearings:	Unknown
Max. RPM:	7,000 rpm
Max. HP:	550
Approx. Price:	$1,750.00 ($1,900.00 with H-beam rods)
Comments:	If you'd like a displacement increase in your 351C that will rev to seven grand and make all kinds of power, this is the affordable stroker kit for you. You can spin this one to 7,000 because it has a forged steel crank with optional H-beam rods. The truth is, you don't have to spin this one to seven grand because it will make its greatest torque around 6,000 rpm with the right cam, heads, and induction system. But, it's nice to know it will go higher if needed.

393ci

Coast High Performance
2555 W. 237th Street
Torrance, CA 90505
310/784-2977
310/784-2970 FAX
www.coasthigh.com

Bore:	4.030"
Stroke:	3.850"
Crankshaft:	Nodular Iron
Rod Type:	Forged I-Beam
Rod Length:	5.956"
Rod Ratio:	1.54:1
Pistons:	Probe SRS Forged
Rings:	Unknown
Bearings:	Unknown
Max. RPM:	6,500 rpm
Max. HP:	450
Approx. Price:	$2,000.00
Comments:	This is a good, affordable budget powerhouse. Your objective with this kit should be low-end torque and an engine that will rev to a maximum of 6,000 rpm.

426ci

Speed-O-Motive
131 North Lang Ave.
West Covina, CA 91790
626/869-0270 • 626/869-0278 FAX
www.speed-o-motive.com

Bore:	4.030"
Stroke:	4.170"
Crankshaft:	4340 Forged Steel
Rod Type:	4340 H-Beam
Rod Length:	6.000"
Rod Ratio:	1.44:1
Pistons:	Ross Custom Forged Flat Tops
Rings:	Total Seal
Bearings:	Clevite H-Series
Max. RPM:	7,000 rpm
Max. HP:	600
Approx. Price:	$2,225.00 (Base Kit)

Comments: This is a severe-duty racing kit designed for motorsports activities. A good value, this is a stroker kit you can whirl to 7,000 rpm. Because it delivers a 4.170-inch stroke, you can count on a lot of torque without having to spin it very high. This is a whole lot of stroker kit for under $2,500.00. Price does not include the block.

408ci

Speed-O-Motive
131 North Lang Ave.
West Covina, CA 91790
626/869-0270 • 626/869-0278 FAX
www.speed-o-motive.com

Bore:	4.030"
Stroke:	4.000"
Crankshaft:	High Nodular Iron
Rod Type:	5140 I-Beam
Rod Length:	6.000"
Rod Ratio:	1.50:1
Pistons:	Ross Custom Forged
Rings:	Speed Pro Cast Rings
Bearings:	Clevite Tri-Metal
Max. RPM:	6,500 rpm
Max. HP:	500
Approx. Price:	$1,495.00 (Base Kit)

Comments: This is a great budget kit long on torque. A lot of bang for the buck. You can take this one to 6,500 rpm, but it will make torque all day at 5,000 rpm depending on cam, heads, and induction selection.

434ci

StrokerKits.com
700 First Capitol Dr
St. Charles, MO 63301
636/946-4747 • 636/946-5757 FAX
www.StrokerKits.com

Bore:	4.060"
Stroke:	4.200"
Crankshaft:	Nodular Iron 400M
Rod Type:	Scat H-Beam
Rod Length:	6.250"
Rod Ratio:	1.48:1
Pistons:	Cast Pistons
Rings:	Unknown
Bearings:	Unknown
Max. RPM:	6,000 rpm
Maxi. HP:	500
Approx. Price:	$1,495.00 ($1,970.00 with forged pistons)

Comments: This is a sure-fire way to pump a lot of cubes into your 351C engine. Be advised this is not a high-revving kit, but designed more with brute torque in mind between 5,000 and 6,000 rpm. We suggest the forged pistons for best results. The .060-inch overbore pushes the limits of the Cleveland.

Edelbrock brings us the Perfomer series manifolds for the 2V and 4V engines. The Performer manifolds are two-plane pieces designed to deliver good low-end torque. These manifolds also work quite well at high RPM. There is also the Edelbrock Torker single-plane manifold, which is more appropriate for drag and road racing applications where the engine does its best work at high revs only.

Swap meets offer us a wealth of older 351C aftermarket manifold designs from Offenhauser, Edelbrock, Weiand, Holman/Moody, Ford, and others. Good rule of thumb is to opt for the dual-plane types for street use and single-plane for racing.

Building the Speed-O-Motive 408ci Cleveland

Seems we've forgotten the legendary 351 Cleveland middle block in the 30 years since production ended in 1974. But, this engine stood the drag racing world on its ear three decades ago with its blistering, coyote-nasty performance. Jack Roush understood this with the *Tijuana Taxi* Maverick sedan that could crack a solid 8-second quarter mile pass. Ford fans loved the *Tijuana Taxi* for its extraordinary power and speed. That speed was achieved with the 351C.

What has hurt the 351C in performance circles has been casting availability. This engine was produced for the four years spanning 1970 through 1974, which greatly limits available parts for project engines. But all is not lost for the 351C. There are still cores laying around, waiting to be discovered. There is also talk of the aftermarket getting involved on 351C block and heads for those who still believe in this engine's legendary performance.

Few manufacturers believe in the 351C more than Speed-O-Motive, which has been producing stroker kits for Fords since 1946. Speed-O-Motive has a couple of stroker kits for the 351C middle weight, displacing 377 and 408ci. Because the 351C-4V head has huge ports that don't really serve us very well on the street at low revs, the greatest favor we can do these tunnels is huff more air and fuel through them. Speed-O-Motive's very affordable 408ci stroker kit will get the job done with room to spare.

We're going to show you the Speed-O-Motive 408ci stroker kit and stuff it inside a 1970 351C block. Then, we're going to tell you what kind of power you can expect from this torque-making powerhouse.

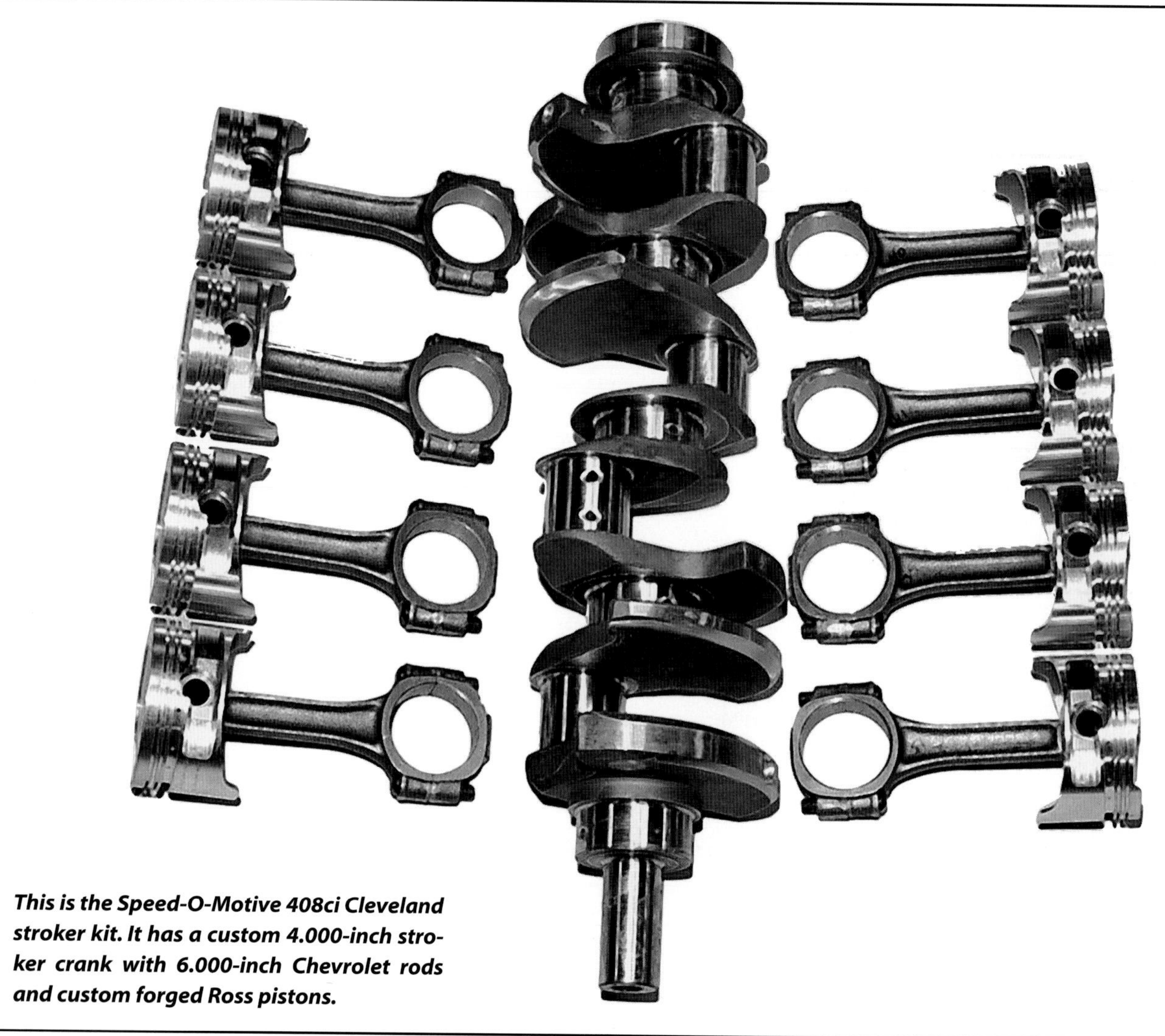

This is the Speed-O-Motive 408ci Cleveland stroker kit. It has a custom 4.000-inch stroker crank with 6.000-inch Chevrolet rods and custom forged Ross pistons.

Building the Speed-O-Matic 408ci Cleveland (continued)

Our foundation is a 1970-vintage 351C block pulled from a '70 Mercury Cougar. It is a virgin two-bolt main block that has never been rebuilt. Speed-O-Motive has bored this block .030-inch oversize. The line bore looks good, and the decks are straight.

With the block completely machined, we're going to wash it thoroughly. Speed-O-Motive's environmentally-responsible parts washer gets the Cleveland block and custom crankshaft clean for assembly.

Comp Cams cam to the rescue with a 260H High Energy flat-tappet hydraulic camshaft and a dual-roller timing set. This cam is perfect for our streetable 351C stroker. An improvement would be a hydraulic roller camshaft with a more aggressive breathing profile. The 260H is what the customer wanted, but we could make more power with this 408C with the right camshaft.

These are 351C-4V cylinder heads with the large ports and small wedge chambers with canted valves. Each casting has been fitted with new valves and guides. Valve springs are from Comp Cams, designed for an aggressive flat tappet hydraulic camshaft. Budget prohibits the use of a roller camshaft.

Building the Speed-O-Motive 408ci Cleveland (continued)

Our painted block gets all of its plugs and fittings. Oil galley plugs are installed first, then deep brass freeze plugs. Don't forget the cam plug at the back of the block in all of this. Speed-O-Motive uses Teflon sealer on the screw-in plugs for security.

Not much clearancing has to be done on the Cleveland block for the stroker kit because Ford has given us a lot of room for stroke and displacement. This block has been mildly notched as shown. Speed-O-Motive dresses up the notch work to ensure there are no burrs.

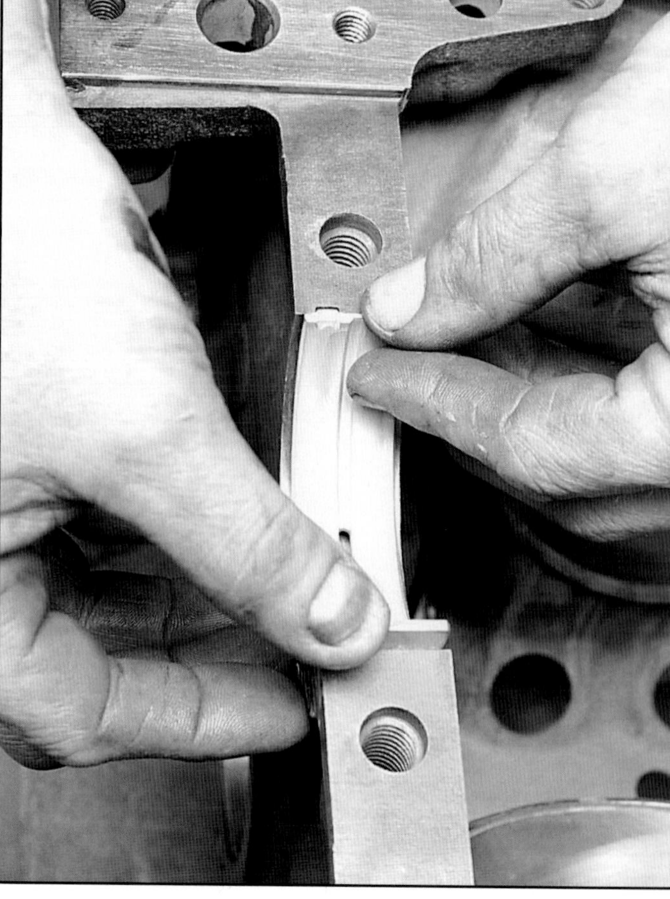

Main bearings are installed first. These are standard size pieces because we're installing a new stroker crankshaft. Note that the main bearing saddles are dry.

Building the Speed-O-Motive 408ci Cleveland (continued)

Above left, left, and above: A word or two about rear-main seals. Originally, small-block Fords in the 1960s and 1970s had rope-type rear-main seals. The rear-main seals were graphite-impregnated rope that worked well as a seal. Both Ford and the aftermarket have gone to two-piece steel and rubber rear-main seals that require a special installation technique to be effective. First, the steel pin in the #5 main cap must be removed when you're installing the two-piece seal. This pin originally retained the rope seal. It isn't necessary with the two-piece replacement seal. If retained, it will damage and distort the two-piece seal. And, yes, it will damage the crankshaft and leak. Use gasket sealer between the main cap and block for added protection. Lubricate the seal with engine oil.

Because Speed-O-Motive has already done the machine work and checked all of the clearances, we're ready to get down to assembly. Speed-O-Motive uses plenty of assembly lube on the main bearings.

The new Speed-O-Motive nodular iron custom crankshaft is laid in the block as shown. It spins easily, indicating a good fit.

Building the Speed-O-Motive 408ci Cleveland (continued)

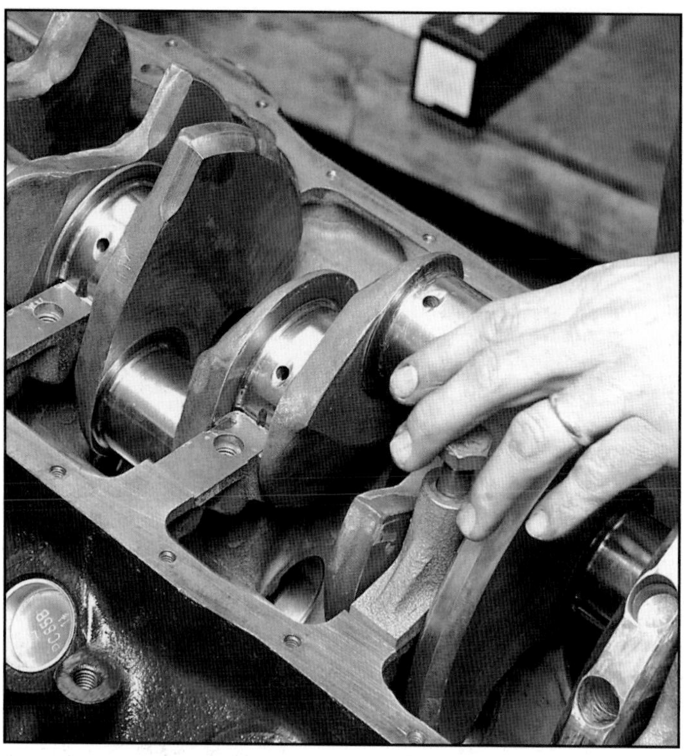

Each main-bearing cap is carefully installed and seated.

Main bearing caps are torqued to 95-105 ft-lbs. Do this in third values, and begin at the #3 main bearing cap. The first torquing should be to 35 ft-lbs. The second to 65 ft-lbs. The final torque should be 95-105 ft-lbs. Check your work – three times.

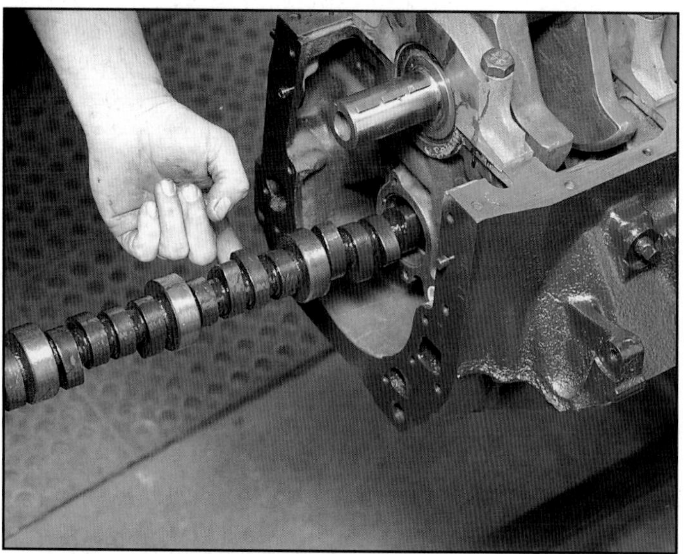

The Comp Cams High Energy hydraulic flat tappet camshaft is next. Note we have lubricated the journals and lobes for protection during start-up. Because this is a flat tappet camshaft, it will have to be broken in during the first engine firing. Break-in will consist of running the engine at 2,500 rpm for 20-30 minutes during the first start-up.

The 351C/351M/400M cam retainer plate is different than those we find on the 289/302/351W small-blocks and should not be interchanged. Install as shown.

Building the Speed-O-Motive 408ci Cleveland (continued)

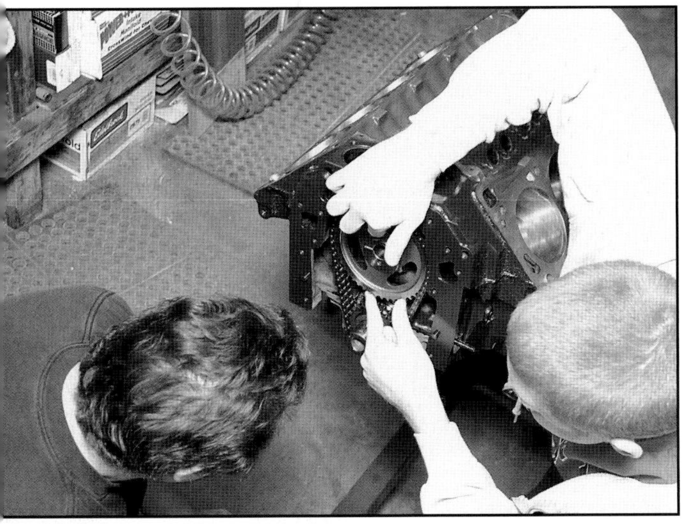

The Comp Cams dual-roller timing set is next. Align the timing marks at 12 and 6 o'clock as shown here. Install the fuel-pump eccentric and run the cam bolt down to 40-45 ft-lbs. Don't forget to install the oil slinger at the crankshaft sprocket. The slinger keeps oil away from the front seal and lubricates the timing set at the same time.

Pistons and rods have already been assembled. Because this is a 408ci stroker, the wrist pin is high in the piston, which calls for a support ring at the oil ring groove.

Compression-ring end gaps are checked next. Although the manufacturer says these rings don't have to be end-gapped, we're checking them anyway.

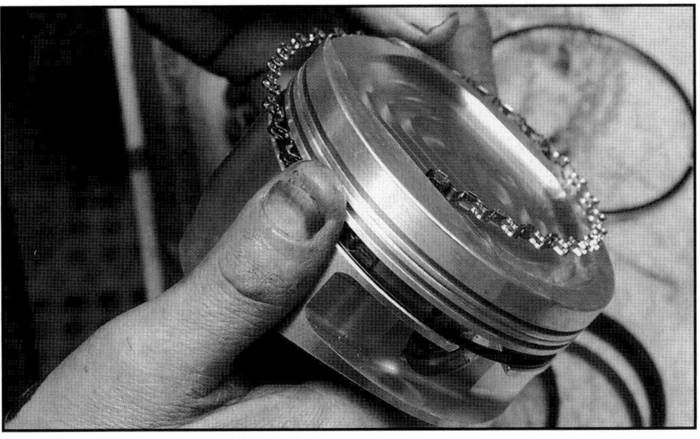

The oil rings and expander are installed next. Make sure the expander interlocks like it should. Otherwise, it can dig into the cylinder wall.

Oil rings are rolled in next. Locate the gaps 180 degrees opposite of each another.

Building the Speed-O-Motive 408ci Cleveland (continued)

Compression rings are installed next. Locate these end gaps 90 degrees around the piston from the oil-ring gaps.

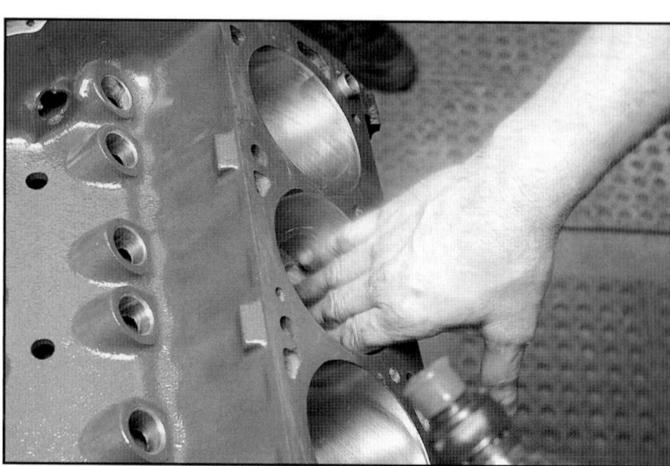

Cylinder walls are wiped clean and lubricated with SAE 30-weight engine oil.

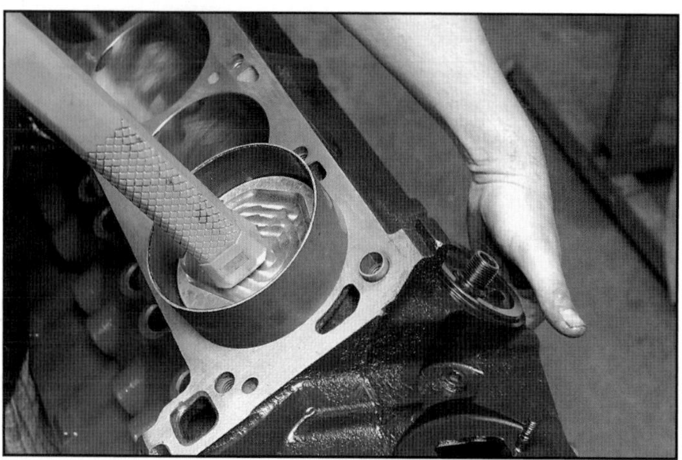

Speed-O-Motive uses billet piston ring compressors for ease of installation. The connecting rod's large end is carefully guided onto the rod journal.

Above: Connecting rod bolts are torqued to 40-45 ft-lbs. Side clearances are checked, along with crankshaft end play. The assembly is hand cranked to check for freedom of movement.

Left: It is easy to get 351C pistons backwards, especially in a stroker. Valve reliefs in the block and piston need to line up as shown. These Ross custom pistons install correctly only one way. Remember that.

Building the Speed-O-Motive 408ci Cleveland (continued)

Comp Cams hydraulic lifters get pre-lubed with assembly lube and installed as shown.

Fel-Pro head gaskets keep the compression, combustion, and coolant contained. Note there is only one right way to install these head gaskets. Lay the end of the gasket labeled "FRONT" toward the front of the block.

Next are the 351C-4V heads to contain 408ci of displacement. Heads are torqued to 95-100 ft-lbs, just like the main bearing caps. Heads must be torqued in three steps. First torque is 55 ft-lbs. Second torque is 75 ft-lbs. The final torque is 95-100 ft-lbs. Begin at the center two head bolts and work your way outward in thirds. Then, check your work again.

Building the Speed-O-Motive 408ci Cleveland (concluded)

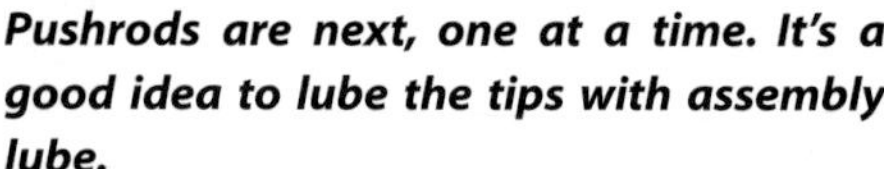

Pushrods are next, one at a time. It's a good idea to lube the tips with assembly lube.

Comp Cams roller rockers, with a 1.6:1 ratio, are installed next. Because these are hydraulics, adjustment is easy. Run the adjustment down until the rocker tip touches the valve stem, then tighten the nut 1/2-turn with the valve closed. Check your adjustment work twice. After the engine has been fired, adjust the valves again.

This 351C stroker gets topped with an Edelbrock Torker single-plane manifold and 750cfm carburetor. For street and strip, this remains a good manifold. For strictly street, the Edelbrock Performer dual plane is a better manifold.

408C Speed-O-Motive Stroker Dyno Test

What Will This Thing Do?

RPM	Horsepower	Torque	VE%
2000	138	363	69.1
2500	181	380	72.4
3000	228	399	76.3
3500	284	427	82.6
4000	338	443	87.7
4500	382	**446**	90.8
5000	412	433	92.4
5500	**414**	395	90.8
6000	396	346	87.0
6500	363	293	82.6

Speed-O-Motive
131 North Lang Ave.
West Covina, CA 91790
626/869-0270
626/869-0278 FAX
www.speed-o-motive.com

BUILDING A STROKER VEHICLE

We added this chapter because we began thinking about what happens whenever we build a powerful engine for a vehicle that isn't up to the job. Building a powerful engine for a vehicle that isn't up to the task is downright dangerous. It can get you killed. Whenever you are building a powerful stroker small block, thought must be given to the vehicle for which it is intended. You know the old saying about power in the hands of a few. Power is only effective when it is handled responsibly, be it a politician or a '66 Fairlane hardtop.

The proper planning of a stroker vehicle begins before the engine is built. How much power do you intend to build? What condition is the vehicle in? Evaluation begins at the foundation – the vehicle's body and chassis. If you have floor pans and frame rails that are rusted out, the vehicle isn't safe for a stock engine, much less one producing 400-500 horsepower. Perhaps your vehicle is a front or rear clip car that has been in an accident and repaired. If this is the case, then it is not a body/chassis combination that is sound enough for serious increases in power. Examine the body and chassis structural integrity before you even plan the engine.Given we have a solid foundation on which to build, we can then look at what the foundation needs to be adequate for the power planned. Even the most solid vehicle needs added support structurally if we're going to throw a lot of power at it. Convertibles, for example, need subframe connectors when power rises above 400 horsepower. Hardtops need the same kind of support. If your Fox-body Mustang has a T-top, it needs subframe connectors and reinforcement plates in order to remain solid during huge bursts of power.

Chassis stiffening kits vary quite a bit. Many of them are available out there for Fox-body (1979-1995) Mustangs. Classic Mustangs and Falcons also enjoy the availability of a good chassis-stiffening kit from Mustangs Plus in Stockton, California. This kit builds strength into your vintage Mustang, Falcon, or Comet. When kits

How prepared is your Ford for the horsepower increases to come? When you start courting 400-500 horsepower, you need strong underpinnings, like subframe connectors, torque boxes, and reinforcement plates.

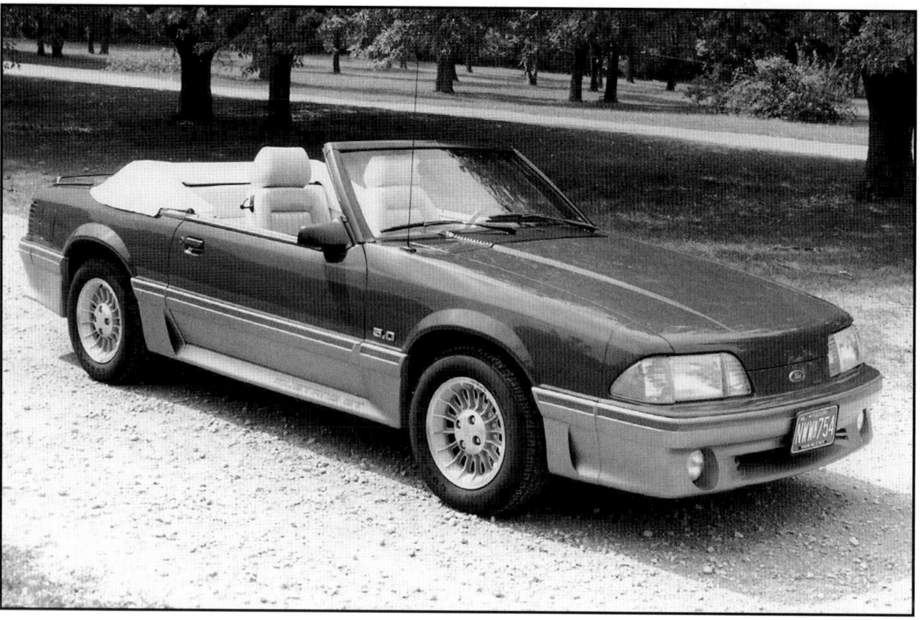

Convertibles need plenty of structural support underneath when power increases. It's a good idea to install a roll bar as well.

aren't available for your type of Ford, you may use raw steel stock that is cut to fit in your application. This requires fabrication experience.

Chassis & Brakes

Horsepower management takes common sense. Building a 400-horse small block is great when you have the chassis (and driving skill) to handle it safely. When we have a solid platform going for us, the next thought should be suspension, brakes, and tires. If you own a vintage Ford with four-wheel drum brakes and a single hydraulic system, your first effort needs to be brakes. At the least, you need front disc brakes with a dual-reservoir braking system. A dual-reservoir braking system covers the bases if we have a hydraulic failure in the front or rear system. If we lose rear brakes, then we still have front brakes to get us stopped, and vice versa. If we lose front brakes, extreme caution must be used to get us stopped safely.

Factory disc brakes do a good job in everyday driving, they just aren't always the solution when power and speed increase. If your driving is going to include road racing, even on weekends only, you're going to need greater than a factory disc brake. You're going to need the kind of stopping power we find in large aftermarket disc brakes with the right pads and rotor size.

With stroker power comes the need for brakes that are just as powerful. If you do opt for larger aftermarket disc brakes, remember to consider wheel size issues before you buy. Not all factory wheels will clear the rotors and calipers of aftermarket disc brakes. Don't forget the master cylinder in your planning. You're going to need a master cylinder that will handle large disc brake calipers. If you install rear disc brakes, keep braking pressure in mind. You don't want the rear brakes applying before the front brakes, which can cause loss of control. This calls for the use of a proportioning valve for the rear brakes, which controls application, and keeps pressure focused more on the front brakes. Having front disc brakes and rear drum brakes without a rear brake proportioning valve is foolish, and certainly dangerous.

If your budget doesn't allow for larger aftermarket disc brakes, then consider slotted brake rotors and racing pads for improved stopping efficiency. Slotted rotors help heat and gas pressure to escape without brake fade. This allows us to improve the stock disc brake, without the expense of an aftermarket brake.

Rear drum brakes need help, too, if disc brakes are beyond your budget. You need to opt for the largest rear drum brake possible, along with semi-metallic brake linings. Drums need to be at like-new specs. The wider the drum and lining, the better. If you're building a Mustang, Falcon, or Fairlane, look for the widest station wagon rear drum brakes, which will stop better than your smaller units.

We are often asked the question – what about silicone brake fluid? What is the right brake fluid for your stroker vehicle? Before we go any further on brake fluid, lets talk about what it does. Brake fluid carries pressure from the master cylinder to each of the brake cylinders at the wheels. When we step on the brake pedal, we are not compressing the fluid, because you cannot compress any fluid. We are simply moving the fluid through lines to wheel cylinders or brake calipers.

Brake fluid gets into trouble whenever it becomes too hot, or absorbs moisture and other contaminates. Whenever brake fluid becomes contaminated, it doesn't perform well. Moisture in brake fluid will boil under hard braking, generating gasses in the fluid, which makes the brake pedal spongy. Mineral-based brake fluids (DOT 3) can withstand high temperatures and still continue to perform normally. Because water has a boiling point of 212 degrees F, moisture in the brake fluid will boil at approximately 212 degrees, adversely affecting braking effectiveness.

Silicone brake fluid (DOT 5) does not absorb moisture, which keeps it stable under some of the most grueling braking conditions. Because it has a boiling point of higher than 700 degrees F, there's little chance of instability in hard braking. One of the nicer aspects of silicone brake fluid, is never having to worry if you spill it on your Ford's paint. It will not harm paint.

The down side to silicone brake fluid is its spongy feel. It gives you the feeling of a spongy brake pedal. Few people care for this aspect of silicone brake fluid. If a spongy pedal isn't to your liking, go with a mineral-based fluid while keeping some important issues in mind.

Take extra care when servicing your brake system with DOT 3 mineral-based fluid. Guard your Ford's paint. Always store DOT 3 brake fluid in a sealed can. Never leave the can open, not even for a minute. Mineral-based brake fluid acts like a sponge. It loves drawing moisture out of the air. The longer you leave the can open, the more moisture it will absorb from the air. If you accidentally leave a can open, properly dispose of it through your local hazardous waste unit or recycler.

Mineral-based brake fluid needs to be changed periodically, just like your engine's oil. It gets contaminated from pressure and heat. It absorbs moisture through your Ford's steel brakes lines, seals, and the like. Every time you do a brake job, bleed your brake system and flush out all of the old fluid. It will keep your braking system safe and serviceable. If your Ford is going to sit a lot, bleed and flush the brake system every year.

Although most of us like to overlook this one, make sure your Ford's parking brake mechanism works. Not enough of them do. The transmission's parking pawl, or your engine's compression, isn't enough to hold the vehicle on a hill. Make sure you have a working parking brake.

When we have a safe and effective braking system, our next effort should be handling. Steering and handling can get us out of trouble when brakes won't. When our stroker Ford won't stop in time to avoid a collision, being able to steer out of harm's way is the next best answer. To effectively and safely steer out of trouble, you need tight, precise steering. You also need handling. To get both, you need a cohesive package of steering and handling working together.

Older Fords, like Fairlanes, Falcons, and Mustangs need a fresh steering gear, with a comfortable mesh between worm and sector. This is an integral part of the system that will steer you out of trouble. And this applies to manual and power steering gears alike. As steering gears are used, they develop excessive wear internally. Most older Fords, if they have never had a steering gear rebuild or replacement, suffer from really sloppy steering. This is where a new steering gear from Flaming River pays off in terms of safety.

With precise steering at our fingertips, we're ready to look at the steering linkage. Inner and outer tie-rod ends, idler arm, and pitman arms must be tight and secure. Any play in these components doesn't bode well for safe handling. If your power steering suffers from leakage and sloppy performance, replacement is in order. Replacement may cost money, but so does a serious accident that happens as a result of you not being able to safely steer out of trouble.

Good handling comes from tight upper and lower control arms, stiffer springs, gas shocks, and properly packaged front and rear sway bars. When we say properly packaged, we mean sway bars that are sized right, with the right complimentary bushings and links. If you desire tight handling and don't mind suspension noise, opt for urethane bushings at the sway bar and strut rods. Polyurethane bushings are quieter, offering you more flexibility, as well as a better ride. Graphite-impregnated urethane bushings provide the stiffness of urethane without the noise.

Good brakes and suspension are pointless if you lack sufficient tire contact patch with the pavement. Powerful engines need good pavement adhesion. They need it to hook up when the accelerator is pressed. They also need adhesion at speed, when it keeps the vehicle safely glued to the pavement. If you have a fully-restored, concours-level show car with those skinny biased-ply tires, there's no point in building a powerful stroker V-8 that will burn the original tires off the rims. If your intent is to make the most of a stroker V-8, fit your Ford with the right kind of tires and wheels for the job.

Tire and wheel selection depends on the kind of driving you will do. Drag racers need minimal drag in front, which calls for skinny tires and narrow wheels. In back, drag racers need wheels offering a wide footprint, with tires that will hook up and make the most of the available power. The key to lower elapsed times at the drag strip is good traction coming out of the hole.

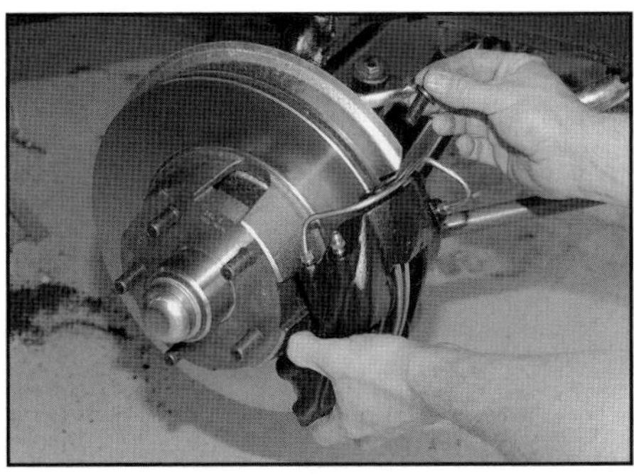

Factory front disc brakes work quite well until horsepower ratings go above 400. This is when you need to step up to larger aftermarket binders like Baer, Ford Racing, or Wilwood.

While you're thinking about tires, you should be thinking of ways to keep the rear axle stable when the throttle is pinned. Traction bars are one choice, but there are others, such as using staggered rear shocks.

If you're going road racing, having a uniform tire size at all four corners is important. Having a wide footprint means having solid adhesion at all four corners. In this area, you have choices. Soft rubber offers good pavement adhesion, but you lose tire service life in the process. Harder rubber compounds offer you longer service life, but they don't hold the road as well. Anyway you slice it, tire selection is a series of compromises. You cannot have it all.

The Team Approach

A good percentage of this chapter has focused on your Ford's foundation – the chassis, body, brakes, suspension,

Better handling comes from the installation of new control arms, springs, shocks, sway bars, and bushings.

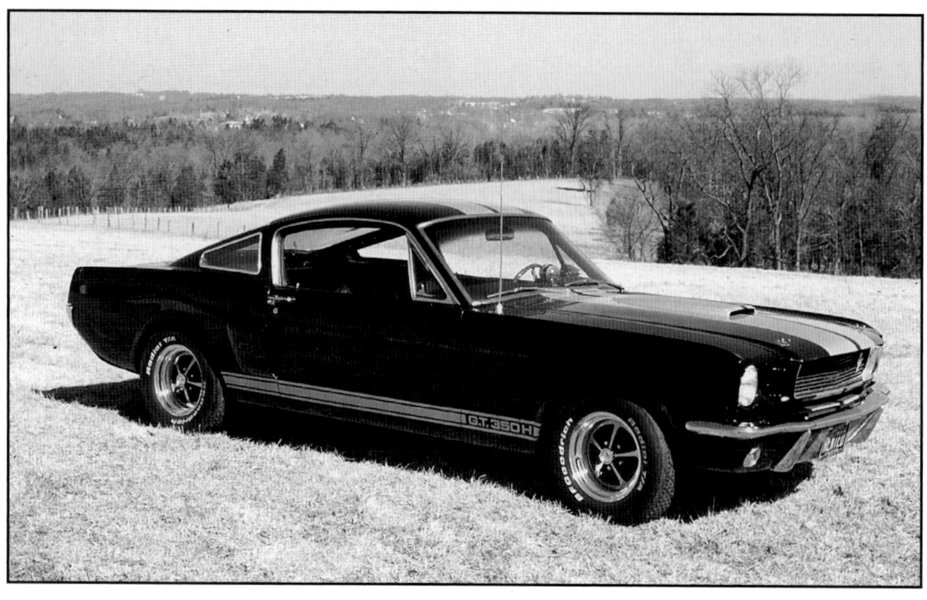

This is a '66 Shelby GT-350H with wide BF Goodrich Radial T/A tires. These tires make an excellent street tire. They offer good handling, coupled with longevity. A softer tire, like the BF Goodrich Comp T/A, holds the road better, but yields less life.

and tires. But there's more. When you spend thousands of dollars on a powerful stroker engine, the last thing you want is failure. Yet, we ask for failure whenever we don't compliment a new engine with the right support system. For example, how many of us build a new engine and drop it into an old engine compartment with a sluggish radiator, dinky header tubes, old water pump, contaminated fuel system, and a host of other adversities?

New engines need clean radiators. They need radiator tubes without restrictions. And they need a high-flow water pump and a new thermostat. Older Fords need a 180-degree thermostat. Newer Fords (1986-up) need a 192-195-degree thermostat. In the interest of safety and security, new hoses need to be installed all around, along with heater hoses and a new radiator. You should also consider new fuel-line hoses (where equipped). Power steering and automatic transmission cooler hoses/lines should be replaced as necessary. If you are asking us what power steering and automatic transmission hoses have to do with your engine, the answer is plenty. When power steering and automatic transmission cooler hoses rupture, they can start a fire, not to mention cause loss of vehicle control.

Today's automotive fuels and additives are hard on fuel systems. This is why we suggest hard-lining your fuel system from the tank to the carburetor. Where fuel is under pressure, like between the pump and carburetor, there should be hard lines, void of rubber hoses. MTBE, a powerful fuel additive, can attack rubber fuel hose and cause them to burst, starting a fire. When it comes to your Ford's fuel system, cut no corners. Use steel lines 100-percent of the way, wherever they are possible. Otherwise, use a heavy-duty, reinforced fuel hose designed for harsh additives.

There are other items included in your engine support system include. Let's begin with the driveline. What condition is your transmission in? All the power in the world is useless if it can't get to the driveshaft and rear axle. A worn out C4 won't help you at all if its clutches and bands are shot. Ditto for a Top Loader with a bad clutch. Your driveline must be up to the job of transmitting power.

If your Ford has a manual transmission, consider the condition of your clutch and flywheel. The transmission must be up to the task mastering a powerful stroker V-8. For example, if you have an early 1980s T-5 transmission, a 347ci stroker will rip it to pieces in short order. Even a World Class T-5 will struggle to take on the power a 347 can deliver. This is where a Tremec five-speed is better suited to the job.

If your Ford needs a clutch and flywheel, we can't think of a better name

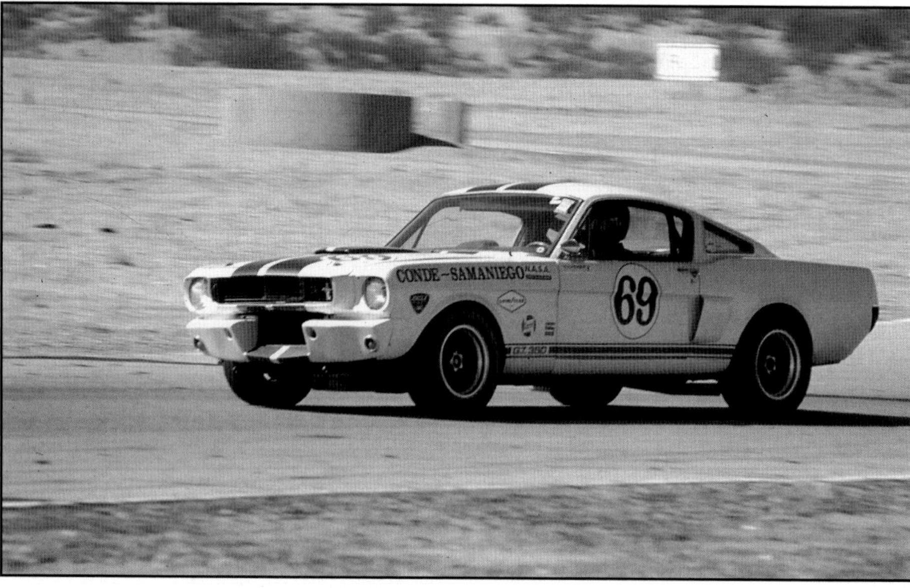

Watching this Shelby Mustang make the rounds on a racetrack, we understand why tire width and contact patch is so important when you're producing 450 horsepower at 6,500 rpm. A stroker V-8 gives us power. Managed carelessly, the stroker doesn't do much for us. This is why we have to think about vehicle packaging when we're building a stroker.

Drag racers need less rubber in front and more rubber in back. We also want a suspension profile that distributes the weight to the rear wheels when the throttle is pressed and the clutch released.

If you are huffing 347ci through your small block, are you going to do it through dinky factory headers? Surely not! Your headers and exhaust system should be up to the job of scavenging spent exhaust gasses effectively. Clogged cats and inadequate pipe sizing can shorten engine life and lead to disappointing performance.

than Centerforce, the most user-friendly clutch on the planet. The folks at Midway Industries, which makes Centerforce clutches, took the diaphragm clutch design and made it better. A typical diaphragm clutch is easy to operate, but they sometimes stick in the disengaged position, leading to abundant frustration. The Centerforce Dual-Friction clutch takes the diaphragm clutch design and gives it flyweights, which are forced outward by centrifugal force as engine speed increases. These flyweights put pressure on the diaphragm, which gives the Centerforce clutch greater holding power at high revs. A meaty dual-friction clutch disc is the other half of this team, also providing greater holding power. When you marry this clutch to a precision-machined Centerforce flywheel, it means never having to worry about the reliable transmission of power.

Older AOD transmissions are not well suited to powerful strokers, which is why you need to consider building one that is. LenTech is a good source for durable AODs, as is Art Carr Transmissions. AOD transmissions need the most current components available, including the Lincoln overdrive drum and band. This comes at a significant cost. Figure on spending at least $1,000 on the parts necessary to make your AOD stronger. These are off-the-shelf parts from Ford. The AOD and AODE need heavy-duty components that can handle the torque a stroker produces. These transmissions can take up to roughly 400 horsepower. After that, you need to seek alternatives.

If the AOD or AODE doesn't work for you, a C4 or small-block C6 may be viable alternatives. If you desire overdrive, with the durability of an older C4 or C6, Gear Vendors in San Diego, California, can help with an overdrive unit that will spline right into your vintage Ford transmission. The Gear Vendors overdrive costs approximately $2,500.00.

While you are evaluating the transmission, don't forget the driveshaft. You need a driveshaft and universal joints sized appropriately for your mission. Chances are, the stock driveshaft isn't sized properly for the amount of power your stroker engine will produce. Inline Empire Driveline can help there with a custom driveshaft, priced under $400,00. Opt for an aluminum shaft and save weight. Always use universal joints designed for an aluminum driveshaft. They're coated to protect the aluminum from dissimilar metal corrosion, which can cause driveshaft failure.

Rear axles tend to be a more complex decision. Should you go with an 8-inch or 9-inch? What about the FOX-body Mustang's 8.8-inch rear axle, which is lighter, and offers less parasitic losses internally? What may surprise you is the 8.8-inch differential's ability

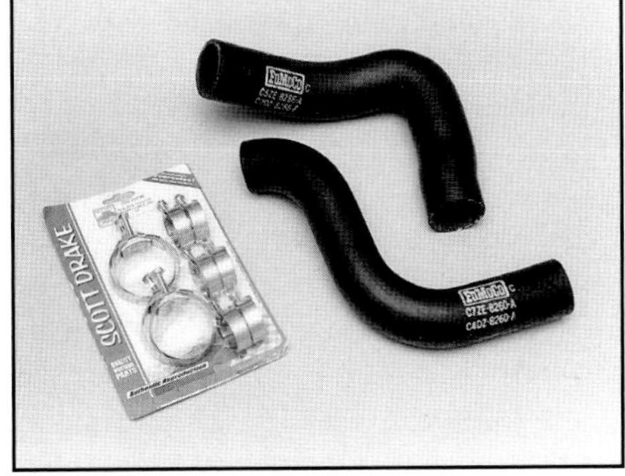

New engines deserve the best in cooling system health. Fit your stroker V-8 with a new radiator, water pump, thermostat, and hoses. Use a 50/50 mix of antifreeze and distilled water. For optimum cooling system health, never use tap water. Never use too much antifreeze either. Opt for a corrosion inhibitor while you are at it.

to withstand the same kind of punishment as the venerable 9-inch. Yet, it does it with less weight and drag.

Axle ratio can be yet another challenging decision, but we can help. If you are running overdrive, opt for 3.55:1 or 3.70:1, which will keep the revs down at freeway speeds. If you are running straight drive and do a lot of driving, opt for 3.00:1 or 3.25:1. If you're building a weekend racer, the field is wide open, with axle ratios ranging from 3.50:1 to 5.30:1. Much depends on the type of racing you will do. The objective with axle ratio is simple. In racing, you need an axle ratio that will put your engine in its peak torque RPM range at speed. You want to blast through the traps in drag racing with engine rpm in the peak horsepower range. If that is 450 horsepower at 6,500 rpm, then you want an axle ratio that will get it there.

Road racers will vary a lot in terms of axle ratio. Much depends on the track. Some shorter tracks will call for a high axle ratio, like 4.11:1 and higher. Longer tracks will call for lower axle ratios. It all depends on the dynamics of the track. You will probably have to experience a track a time or two to get a handle on the best axle ratio. Not all stroker vehicles will need Traction-Lok or Limited-Slip, although we recommend it in all cases for maximum hook-up.

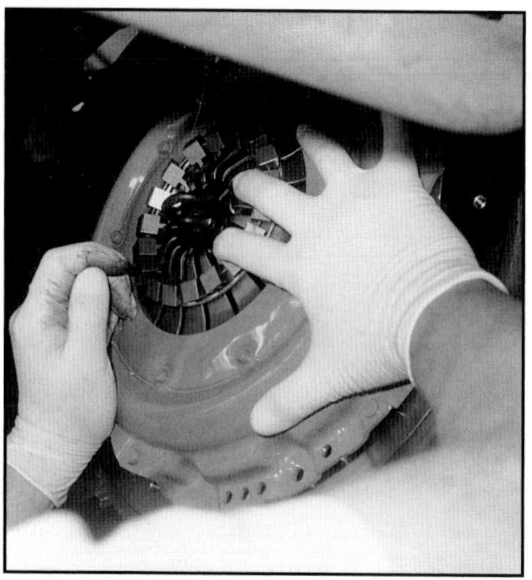

The Centerforce Dual-Friction clutch is one of the best upgrades you can offer your Ford. This clutch is easy to use, once installed. It offers easy pedal effort, while hooking up very well at the same time.

What kind of shape is your rear axle and differential in? Do you have the appropriate axle ratio for your mission? If your Ford has 3.00:1 gears with an engine that makes its peak torque at 5,500 rpm, you're in for a disappointment. Your Ford's gearing should be such that your engine can take mechanical advantage of it. Engines that make peak torque around 4,500 to 5,500 rpm need low gearing. They also need a differential that will stand up to the torque.

Help For Cooling Systems

Just imagine a cooling system without water. Just imagine... Evans Cooling System brings all of us a breakthrough in cooling system protection called a non-aqueous cooling system solution. But it doesn't come cheap. Priced at around $30 a gallon, the Evans non-aqueous coolant is something you run all by itself. No water. No additives. Just Evans coolant. To use Evans, you need to completely drain your cooling system and allow it to dry out, which is what makes it perfect for new engines. Fill your system completely with Evans, allow all air to burp through the upper hoses and ports. Then, let Evans do its work. Because Evans transfers heat better than the water/antifreeze mixture we've long been accustomed to, engines run cooler. On top of that, because Evans works alone, without water, cooling system corrosion will never be an issue again. Look for Evans on-line or at your favorite auto parts store.

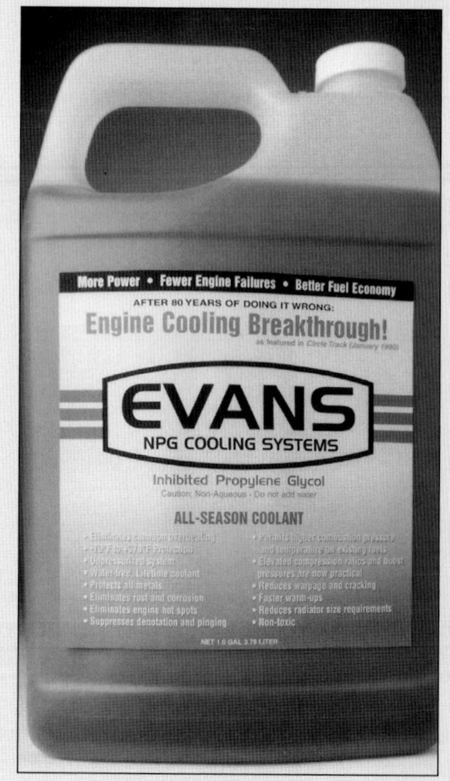

Chapter 8

Engine Math

When you're building an engine, it's nice to be armed with the facts necessary to do it successfully. Much of engine building is about math – machining dimensions, compression and rod ratios, bore sizes, stroke, journal diameters, carburetors, port sizes, dynamic balancing, and all the rest of it. Without math, you cannot successfully build an engine. What follows are quick facts that will help you in your Ford engine building.

Cubic Inch Displacement

Cubic inch displacement is simply the volume displaced by the cylinders of your engine. So, if we calculate the volume of one cylinder, and multiply that figure times the number of cylinders, we have the engine's displacement.

The formula for a cylinder's volume is:

Pi x r^2 x S = Volume of one cylinder

Where Pi is a mathematical constant equal to 3.14159; r is the radius of the cylinder, and S is the stroke. If you think back to your high school geometry, you'll remember that a circle's radius is half the diameter. In this case, the diameter is equal to the bore (B), so *1/2B = r.* Plug that in, and our formula becomes:

Pi x $(1/2B)^2$ x S = Volume of One Cylinder

We can simplify this further by plugging in the numerical value for Pi, then doing some basic algebra that doesn't necessarily need to be covered here – but trust us: the equation before is equal to this equation:

B x B x S x 0.7854 = Volume of One Cylinder

To determine the engine's displacement, factor in the number of cylinders (N):

**B x B x S x 0.7854 x N =
Engine displacement**

So, let's use this to figure out the displacement of a Ford engine that has a 4-inch Bore and a 3-inch Stroke:

**4.000" x 4.000" x 3.00" x 0.7854 x 8 =
301.59 ci**

Ford rounded 301.59 up to 302 ci, or 5.0L. (Note: One liter is equal to about 61 cubic inches.)

Calculating Compression Ratio

An engine's compression ratio is the ratio between two volumes: The volume of the cylinder and combustion chamber when the piston is at BDC, and the volume of the combustion chamber when the piston is at TDC. But there's more to consider than just cylinder volume and head cc's. To get the engine's TRUE compression ratio, you need to know these volumes:

- Combustion Chamber Volume (**C**)
- Compressed Head Gasket Volume (**G**)
- Piston/Deck height (**D**)
- Piston Dish Volume (**P**) or Dome Volume (-**P**)
- Cylinder Volume (**V**)

When the piston is at BDC, the total volume is all of these volumes added together. When the piston is at TDC, the total volume is all of these EXCEPT the Cylinder Volume (V). So ... true compression ratio is this:

$$\frac{V + D + G + C + P}{D + G + C + P}$$

Combustion Chamber Volume

Combustion chamber volumes for stock heads and aftermarket heads are typically available from the manufacturer. If you cant find the info or if you've modified the combustion chambers, you'll have to measure the volumes (using a plastic deck plate, burettes, and a graduated cylinder) or have your local machine shop do it for you.

Converting cc's to ci's

Combustion chamber volume,

dome volume, and dish volume are generally measured in cc's, not cubic inches. To convert cc's to cubic inches, divide the measurement in cc's by 16.4.

Compressed Head Gasket Volume

Compressed head gasket volume is simply the volume of the cylinder hole in the head gasket – think of it as a very shallow cylinder. So, its volume is computed the same way you compute cylinder volume:

B x B x Gasket Thickness x 0.7854 =
Compressed Head Gasket Volume

In this case, the gasket's compressed thickness is .038 inches, so ...

4.000" x 4.000"x .038" x 0.7854 =
0.4775232ci

Piston/Deck Height Volume

Piston/Deck height volume is the small volume at the top of the cylinder that is not swept by the piston. Measure piston/deck height with a dial indicator. Bring the piston to top dead center (TDC) and measure the distance from the top of the piston to the deck of the block. This is normally somewhere between .008 and .025-inch. If the block deck has been machined, say .010-inch, then deck height will be smaller.

Once again, this volume is a shallow cylinder. Compute its volume by plugging the piston/deck height measurement (D) into the cylinder volume formula:

B x B x D x 0.7854 =
Piston/Deck Height Volume

In our example, this measurement was .015 in, so we plug in that value to compute piston/deck height volume in cubic inches.

4.000" x 4.000" x .015" x 0.7854 =
0.188496ci

Piston Dome/Dish Volume

The last bit of information we need is the volume of the piston dome or dish (dish includes valve reliefs, too). Because the dishes or domes are irregularly shaped, it's necessary to either measure the volume using burettes and graduated cylinders, or you can usually get the measurement from the piston manufacturer. If the piston is domed, the dome reduces the amount of volume in the combustion chamber, so its volume is subtracted. If the piston is dished, the dish increases the volume of the combustion chamber, so its volume is added. In this example, our 302 has flat-top pistons with valve reliefs that measure 2cc in volume. That 2cc increases the cylinder volume, so we give it a positive value. If the pistons were domed, the dome would reduce the cylinder volume, so we'd give it a negative value. Either way, the volume has to be converted from cc's to ci's:

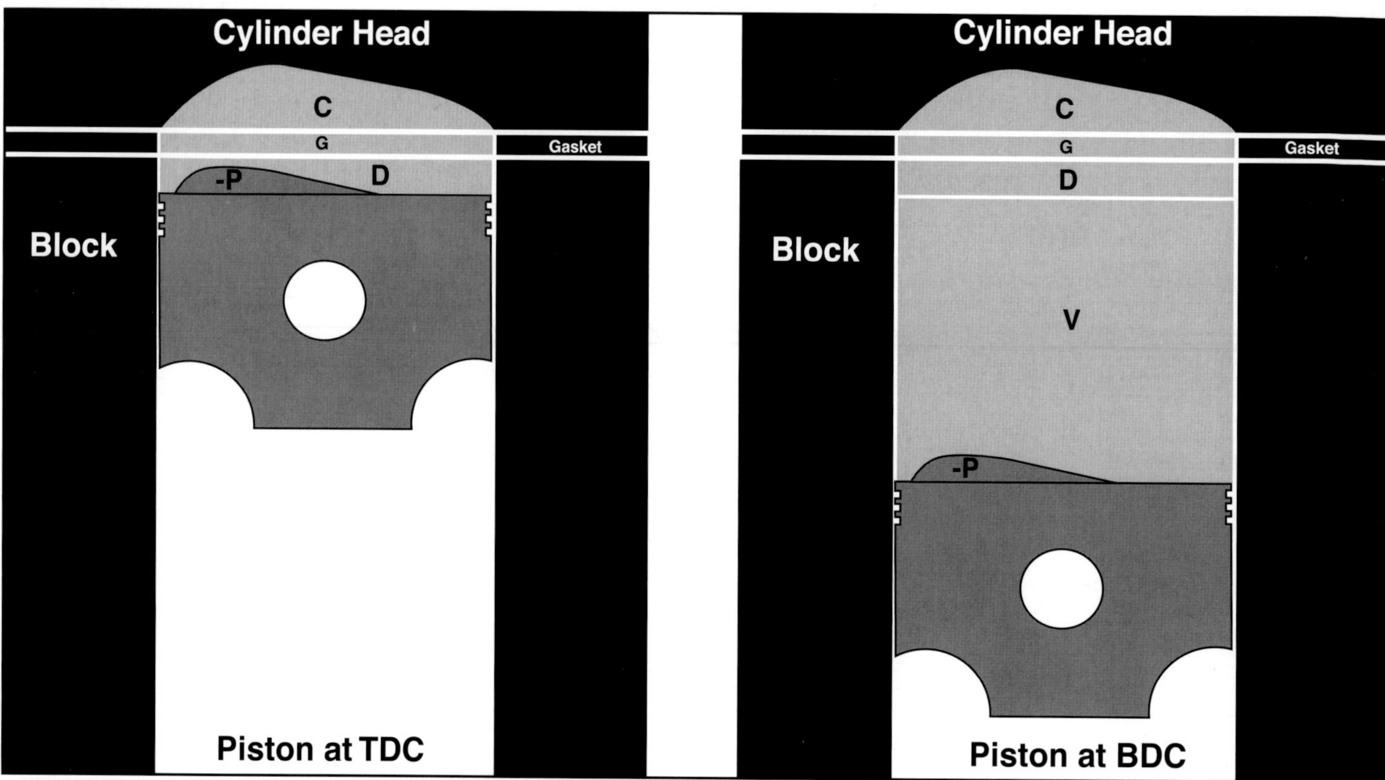

This diagram shows all the volumes you need to know to calculate an engine's true compression ratio: Cylinder volume (V), piston dome (-P) or dish volume (P), piston/deck height (D), compressed gasket volume (G), and the combustion chamber volume (C). The compression ratio is the volume of the piston and combustion chamber (V + P + D + G +C) when the piston is at bottom dead center, compared to the volume of the combustion chamber (P + D + G +C) when the piston as at top dead center.

$$cc / 16.4 = ci$$
$$2cc / 16.4 = 0.121951ci$$

So, let's check the true compression ratio for that 302ci engine, assuming it has a combustion chamber volume of 63cc, a compressed head gasket thickness of .038-inch, and a piston/deck height of .015-inch. Here's what we've figured out so far:

V = *Cylinder Volume: 37.6992ci (calculated)*
C = *Combustion Chamber Volume: 63cc (3.8414634ci) (measured)*
G = *Compressed Head Gasket Volume: 0.4775232ci (calculated)*
P = *Piston Dish Volume: 0.121951ci (measured)*
D = *Piston/Deck Height Volume: 0.188496ci (calculated)*

Now (finally!) we're ready to calculate our true compression ratio, using the formula we developed earlier:

$$\frac{V + D + G + C + P}{D + G + C + P}$$

Plug in the values (all in ci):

$$\frac{37.6992 + 0.188496 + 0.4775232 + 3.8414634 + 0.121951}{0.188496 + 0.4775232 + 3.8414634 + 0.121951}$$

$$\frac{42.328634}{4.629434}$$

That gives us a true compression ratio, for this engine, of 9.1:1.

Choosing The Right Carburetor

Seems a lot of folks specify a larger carburetor than they actually need. Here's an easy formula that will put you on target every time, as long as you're honest with yourself about where your engine's going to operate. We want to look at cubic inches and the best volumetric efficiency (VE). With street engines, volumetric efficiency is typically around 75 to 80%. Boost the performance and VE goes up to 80 to 95%. The best indicator of engine performance is an engine dynamometer. This formula will calculate the required carb size for your engine:

$$\frac{\text{VE (Volumetric Efficiency)} \times \text{CI} \times \text{Max RPMs}}{3456}$$

For example, we've built a 460 that performing strong on the dyno. The dyno figures tell us 85% VE. On the street, we figure the max RPM this engine will see is 5,500 rpm. So, if we plug in the numbers, we get:

$$\frac{0.85 \times 460 \times 5{,}500}{3456}$$

Do the math, and we end up with 622.25115. In this case, we'd opt for a 650cfm carb.

Calculating Horsepower and Torque

Horsepower and torque are words we hear a lot in the automotive realm. Which do you believe is more significant to power output? It may surprise you to learn that torque is the more significant number. Did you know horsepower and torque are the same at 5,252 rpm on any engine? That's because Horsepower is derived from torque. Here's a good formula to remember:

$$\text{Horsepower} = \frac{\text{RPM} \times \text{Torque}}{5{,}252\text{rpm}}$$

If you do a little cross-multiplying, you can also rearrange this equation to compute torque from horsepower:

$$\text{Torque} = \frac{5{,}252\text{rpm} \times \text{Horsepower}}{\text{RPM}}$$

Horsepower at the Drags

Approximate horsepower and torque can be determined with a simple quarter-mile pass at the drag strip. Begin by weighing your vehicle – you can find scales at a farm coop (anyplace that sells grain or feed by the truckload) or truck weigh station along the interstate. Then make several quarter mile passes and calculate an average top mph. Then make the following calculation:

$$\text{Horsepower} = \frac{\text{Weight} \times 0.4 \times 1/4\text{-mile MPH}}{282}$$

Assume your car weighs 3,000 pounds, and your average quarter-mile time was 100mph. Plug in the numbers and we get ...

$$\frac{3{,}000 \text{ lbs} \times 0.4 \times 100 \text{ MPH}}{282} = 425.53191 \text{ HP}$$

If you know what RPM your engine was turning as you went through the traps, you can also figure out the torque your engine generates. If we went through the traps at 6,000 rpm, we can calculate torque is determined by doing the following formula:

$$\frac{5{,}252 \times 425 \text{ HP}}{6000 \text{ RPM}} = 372 \text{ ft-lbs. of torque}$$

Save yourself the cost of a dyno and do the calculations yourself. Remember, these calculations are approximate.

Engine Build Sheet

Photocopy this form and keep it in a file for each engine

Engine Blueprint Record

Engine Blueprint Record	
Engine Type	
Build Date	
Displacement	
Special Notes:	

Block

Block	
Material	
Manuf./PN	
Bore Size	
Cam Location	
Main Bearing Dia.	
Special Mods:	

Piston Diameter and Bore Clearance

Cylinder #	1	3	5	7
Bore Dia.				
Piston Dia.				
Clearance				
Cylinder #	2	4	6	8
Bore Dia.				
Piston Dia.				
Clearance				
Width				

Piston

Piston	
Piston Brand/PN	
Compression Height	
Wrist Pin Brand/PN	
Wrist Pin Dia./Length	
Wrist Pin Clearance	
Wrist Pin Retainer	

Piston Ring

Piston Ring	
Ring Brand/PN	
Top Ring Type	
Width	
Side Clearance	
End Gap	
2nd Ring Type	
Width	
Side Clearance	
End Gap	
Oil Ring Type	
Side Clearance	
Gap	

Piston Deck Height

Cylinder #	1	3	5	7
Deck Height				
Cylinder #	2	4	6	8
Deck Height				

Notes

Rod and Main Bearings

Main Bearing Brand/PN	
Rod Bearing Brand/PN	
Camshaft Bearing Brand/PN	

Crankshaft

Crankshaft Brand/PN					
Stroke					
End Play					
Main	1	2	3	4	5
Main Bore					
Main Bore w/bearing					
Crank Main Journal					
Main Bearing Clearance					

Conn. Rod	1	3	5	7
Big End Dia.				
Big End Dia. w/bearing				
Crank Journal Dia.				
Rod Bearing Clearance				
Conn. Rod	2	4	6	8
Big End Dia.				
Big End Dia. w/bearing				
Crank Journal Dia.				
Rod Bearing Clearance				

Connecting Rods

Rod Brand/PN				
Length (Center to Center)				
Side Clearance	1-2	3-4	5-6	7-8
Wrist Pin/Piston Clearance				
Wrist Pin/Rod Clearance				
Rod Bolt Brand/PN				
Rod Bolt Torque				
Rod Bolt Stretch				

Valvetrain Data

Rocker Arms:	
Make	
PN	
Material	
Offset	
Rocker Arm Ratio:	
Intake	
Exhaust	
Intake Valve Lift	
Exhaust Valve Lift	
Pushrod:	
Length	
Diameter	
Wall Thickness	
Lifter:	
Make/PN	
Diameter	
Offset	
Rev Kit Make	
PN	

Camshaft

Make of Style/Brand	
Cam PN	
Material	
Intake Duration @.050"	
Exhaust Duration @.050"	
Intake installed at Centerline	
Lobe Separation Angle	
Intake Lobe Lift	
Exhaust Lobe Lift	
Intake Valve to Piston Clearance @ 10° ATDC	
Exhaust Valve to Piston Clearance @ 10° BTDC	
Intake Valve Lash	
Exhaust Valve Lash	

Cylinder Head

Cylinder Head	
Brand/PN	
Chamber Volume	
Intake Port Volume (cc)	
Intake Valve Type/PN	
Intake Valve Size	
Exhaust Valve Type/PN	
Exhaust Valve Size	
Valvespring Brand/PN	
Valvespring	
Inside Diameter	
Outside Diameter	
Installed Height	
Intake/Exhaust	
Valvespring Seat Pressure	
Valvespring Open Pressure	
Coil Bind Height	
Retainer Make/PN Keeper Make/PN	
Head Gasket Thickness	

Engine Balancing

Engine Balancing	
Piston Weight (grams)	
Wrist Pin	
Pin Locks	
Ring Set (1 Piston)	
Rod, Small End	
Total Reciprocating Weight	
Rod, Big End	
Rod Bearing (1 Pair)	
Oil	
Total Rotating Weight	
Balance Percent* 0.50 for V-8 90-degree	
Bob Weight = 2 x (Reciprocating Wt. x .50 + Rotating Weight)	

Cylinder Head Flow

Cylinder Head Flow	
Modifications	
Flow Bench	
Test Pressure	
Bore Fixture Dia.	
Intake Valve Dia.	
Exhaust Valve Dia.	

Intake Flow

Lift	CFM
.100	
.200	
.300	
.400	
.500	
.600	
.700	

Exhaust Flow

Lift	CFM	Exh. to Int. %
.100		
.200		
.300		
.400		
.500		
.600		
.700		

Compression Ratio

Compression Ratio	
Swept Volume*	
Dome (-) or Dish (+) Volume	
Ring Land Volume	
Deck Volume	
Head Gasket Volume	
Chamber Volume	
Total Volume	

$$CR = \frac{\text{Total Volume}}{\text{Total - Swept Volume}}$$

CR = ______________ :1

*Swept Volume (cc) = Bore^2 x Stroke x 12.87